AMERICAN SCHOOL OF NEEDLEWORK

PRESENTS

THE GREAT KNITTING BOOK

President: Jean Leinhauser
Editorial Director: Mary Thomas
Art Director: Carol Wilson Mansfield
Art Assistant: Julie Ryan
Operations Vice President: Irmgard Barnes
Book Coordinator/Production Manager: Robert J. Kasbar
Photography by Stemo Photography Inc., Northbrook, IL
Roderick A. Stemo, President
James E. Zorn, Photographer

Published by Columbia House/New York

CONTENTS

Copyright © 1980 by American School of Needlework, Inc.

This volume may not be reproduced in whole or in part in any form
without permission from the publisher.

ISBN 0-930748-15-8
Library of Congress Catalog Card Number: 80-65536
Printed in the United States of America

Published by Columbia House, a Division of CBS Inc.
        1211 Avenue of the Americas, New York, N.Y., 10036

*We have made every effort to ensure the accuracy and completeness
of the instructions in this book. We cannot, however, be responsible for
human error, typographical mistakes or variations in individual work.*

Introduction

Knitting is one of the oldest needlework skills, and one of the most widely practiced throughout the world.

Knitting has played a role in many diverse cultures. On Ireland's Aran isles, wives and mothers knit sweaters for their fishermen made up of unique family patterns — symbols of the rope cables, fields, water, and religion that make up the fabric of their lives.

In Scandinavia, bold geometric representations of snowflakes, reindeer and fir trees decorate heavy winter sweaters. On Scotland's Shetland Islands, the unusually fine wool from native sheep was spun into gossamer shawls treasured around the world.

In Biblical times, it was the man who did the knitting; shepherds knitted while they tended their flocks. And in the 8th and 9th centuries A.D., nomadic Arab chieftains knitted atop their camels while wandering from oasis to oasis.

Perhaps the most famous knitter is Madame Defarge who, in Dickens' *A Tale of Two Cities*, during the French revolution worked the names of all traitors into her long piece of knitting.

Today, knitters range from small girls and boys laboring over a colorful potholder to great-grandmothers creating exquisite layettes. Now, with the fashion trend toward the hand-knit sweater look and our need for warm garments to help in energy conservation, knitting is experiencing a revival.

Whether you're a beginner or an experienced knitter, this book includes projects for you. Even the expert knitter should read the first chapter, *Knitting How-To*, which contains a variety of advanced techniques along with instructions for the beginner.

Our projects let you try your hand at Norwegian knitting, argyles, gloves and socks made on 4 needles, knitting in the round — and much more. Some of the patterns may look complicated, but they're not; each pattern is written with the new knitter in mind, with every technique explained fully and illustrated with large, clear diagrams.

Knitting is easy and fun to do, and is possibly the most satisfying needlework skill. We hope you enjoy making the projects in this book.

Jean Leinhauser

Jean Leinhauser
President
American School of Needlework, Inc.

DEDICATION

We dedicate this book to Lee Leibowitz,
who believes in knitting, and in us.

ACKNOWLEDGEMENTS

Our special thanks go to Thelma Snelten of the Country Yarn Cottage in Long Grove, IL, who shared so much of her knowledge of yarns and techniques with us.

American Thread kindly gave us their permission to include several designs from their publications.

All of the garments and projects in this book were tested to ensure the accuracy and clarity of our instructions. We are grateful to these pattern testers:

Irmgard Barnes, Lake Bluff, IL
Marjorie Bergmann, Waukegan, IL
Nannette M. Berkley, Antioch, IL
Nancy Burnet, Northfield, IL
Virginia Carlson, Deerfield, IL
Judy Demain, Highland Park, IL
Patricia K. Gorsline, Northbrook, IL
Kim Hubal, Evanston, IL
Deanna Kluge, Highland Park, IL
Joan Kokaska, Wildwood, IL
Colette Mazurk, Glenview, IL
Margaret Miller, Chicago, IL
Elizabeth Mitzen, Glenview, IL
Fran Mueller, Libertyville, IL
Wanda Parker, Mundelein, IL
Marion Scoular, Clemson, SC
Beatrice Slattery, Wilmette, IL
Rosemarie Suhr, Island Lake, IL

We also extend thanks and appreciation to these contributing designers:

Nannette M. Berkley, Antioch, IL
Nancy Dent, Des Plaines, IL
Anis Duncan, Northbrook, IL
Doris England, Des Plaines, IL
Jean Leinhauser, Glenview, IL
Carol Wilson Mansfield, Northbrook, IL
Barbara A. Retzke, Libertyville, IL
Evie Rosen, Wausau, WI
Mary Thomas, Libertyville, IL

YARN SOURCES

Whenever we have used a specialty yarn, we have given the brand name. If you are unable to find these yarns locally, write to the following manufacturers or importers who can tell you where to purchase their products:

Chester Farms, R.D. 2, Box 456, Gordonsville, VA 22942
C. J. Bates & Son, Chester, CT 06412
Joseph Galler Inc., 149 Fifth Ave., New York, NY 10010
William Unger & Co., Inc., 230 Fifth Ave., New York, NY 10001

Knitting How-To

Chapter 1

In this chapter, arranged in lesson format, we cover the basic techniques of knitting for the beginner, plus many advanced methods that may be new even to the experienced knitter.

If you're an experienced knitter, you still may want to take needles and yarn in hand and work through the basic lessons. You might pick up some new ways to do old techniques that could greatly improve the look of your knitting.

SPECIAL NOTES

MATERIALS: To work the practice lessons, you'll need one 3½ or 4 oz skein of knitting worsted weight yarn, and a pair of 10″ long, single point size 8 aluminum knitting needles.

DIAGRAMS: In all the diagrams that follow, black is used to identify the yarn coming from the skein.

FOR LEFT HANDERS: Left handers often learn to knit in reverse, by sitting in front of a right-handed knitter. We disagree with this method, as the knitter becomes permanently handicapped by having to reverse instructions for all future knitting patterns used. Because knitting is a two-handed process, in which both hands are used almost equally, we recommend that left handers learn to knit in the normal manner. Although they may feel awkward at first, this is true of all beginning knitters. If a left hander is unable to master this method, we suggest they adopt the Continental style of knitting (instructions are given in Lesson 10) in which the left hand is considerably more active than the right. This method still permits the left-handed knitter to follow ordinary instructions.

LESSON 1
CASTING ON, METHOD 1
Knitting always starts with a row of foundation stitches worked onto one needle. Making a foundation row is called **casting on.** Although there are several ways of casting on, the one which follows—Method 1—is easiest for beginners.

Step 1: Make a slip knot on one needle as follows: Make a yarn loop, leaving about 4″ length of yarn at free end

(Fig 1). Insert knitting needle into loop and draw up yarn from free end to make a loop on needle **(Fig 2).** Pull yarn firmly, but not **tightly,** to form a slip knot on needle **(Fig 3).** This slip knot counts as your first stitch.

Step 2: Place the needle with the knot in your left hand, and hold the empty needle in your right hand.

Step 3: Holding hands as shown in **Fig 4,** insert the point of the right needle—from front to back—into the slip knot and **under** the left needle.

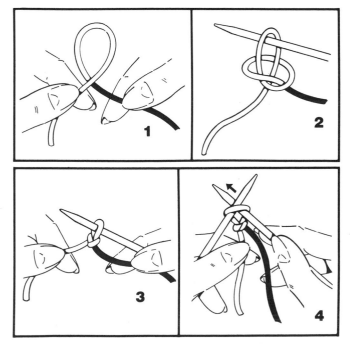

Step 4: Continuing to hold left needle in your left hand, move left fingers over to brace right needle **(Fig 5)**. With right index finger, pick up the yarn from the ball **(Fig 6)** and, releasing right hand's grip on the right needle, bring yarn under and over the point of right needle **(Fig 7)**.

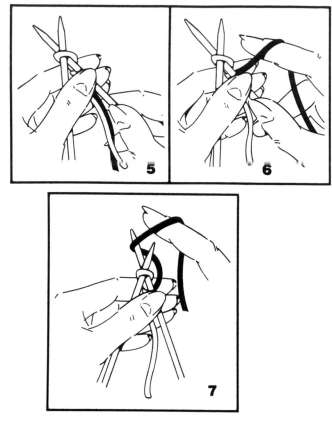

Step 5: Returning right fingers to right needle, draw yarn through stitch with right needle **(Fig 8)**.
Step 6: Slide left needle point into new stitch **(Fig 9)**, then remove right needle.

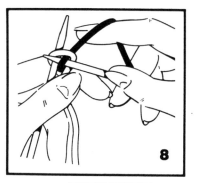

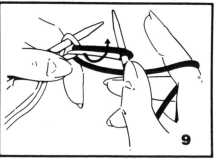

Step 7: Pull ball yarn gently, but **not** tightly **(Fig 10)**, to make stitch snug on needle; you should be able to slip stitch back and forth on the needle easily.

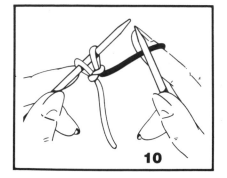

Step 8: Insert point of right needle—from front to back—into stitch you've just made **(Fig 11)** and **under** left needle.

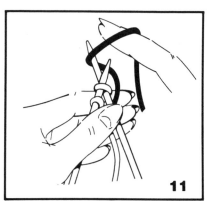

Repeat Steps 4 through 8 for next stitch. Keep on repeating Steps 4 through 8 until you have 24 stitches on the left needle; remember that the starting slip knot **always** counts as a stitch.

Stop and look at your work. It's probably loose and uneven, which is normal for a beginner. As you practice and begin to feel less clumsy, your work will automatically become more even.

Now take all stitches off the needle and start again. To do this, pull the needle out from the stitches, then wind the used yarn back on the skein or ball. Begin again and cast on 24 stitches, trying this time to work more evenly, keeping each stitch snug but **not** tight.

HINT: Beginners usually knit very tightly, making it hard to slide the stitches on the needle. Try to relax; it is better to work too loosely in the beginning, than too tightly. Take care not to make your stitches on the shaped point of the needle; instead, slide the needle well through each stitch as you work. Always be sure to insert needle under full thickness of yarn, to avoid "splitting" the yarn.

LESSON 2
KNIT, PURL and DROPPED STITCHES
All knitting is made up of only two basic stitches, the knit stitch and the purl stitch. These are combined in many ways to create different effects and textures. And now you're half way to being a knitter—for you've already learned the knit stitch as you practiced casting on! That's because the first three steps of the knit stitch are exactly like casting on.

THE KNIT STITCH
Step 1: Hold the needle with the 24 cast-on stitches from Lesson 1 in your left hand. Insert point of right needle in first stitch, from left to right, just as in casting on **(Fig 12)**.
Step 2: With right index finger, bring yarn under and over point of right needle **(Fig 13)**.

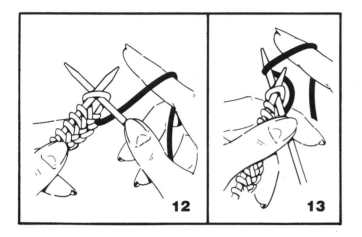

Step 3: Draw yarn through stitch with right needle point **(Fig 14)**.
Step 4: Slip the loop on the left needle off, so the new stitch is entirely on the right needle **(Fig 15)**.

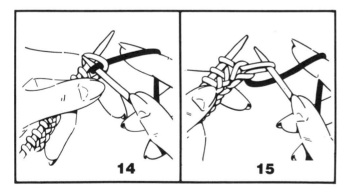

Now you've completed your first knit stitch! Repeat these four steps in each stitch remaining on the left needle. When all stitches are on the right needle and the left needle is free, another row has been completed. Turn right needle, hold it now in your left hand and take free needle in your right hand. Work another row of stitches in same manner as last row, taking care not to work tightly. Work five more rows of knit stitches.
The pattern formed by knitting every row is called **garter stitch (Fig 16)**, and looks the same on both sides. When counting rows in garter stitch, each raised ridge (a ridge is indicated by the arrow in **Fig 16**) indicates you have knitted **two** rows.

THE PURL STITCH
The reverse of the knit stitch is called the purl stitch. Instead of inserting the right needle point from left to right under the left needle (as you did for the knit stitch), you will now insert it from right to left, in front of the left needle. Work as follows on the stitches already on your needle.
Step 1: Insert right needle, from right to left, into first stitch, and in front of left needle **(Fig 17)**.
Step 2: Holding yarn in front of work (side toward you), bring it around right needle counterclockwise **(Fig 18)**.
Step 3: With right needle, pull yarn back through stitch **(Fig 19)**. Slide stitch off left needle, leaving new stitch on right needle **(Fig 20)**.

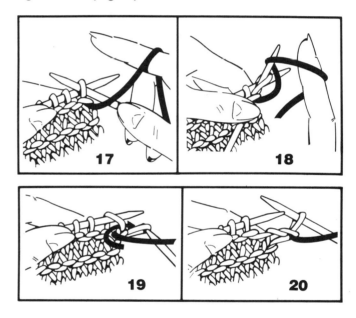

Your first purl stitch is now completed. Continue to repeat these three steps in every stitch across the row. The row you have just purled will be considered the **wrong side** of your work.
Now transfer the needle with stitches from right to left hand; the side of the work now facing you is called the **right side** of your work. Knit every stitch in the row; at end of row, transfer needle with stitches to left hand, then purl every stitch in the row. Knit across another row, purl across another row.
Now stop and look at your work; by alternating knit and purl rows, you are creating one of the most frequently used stitch patterns in knitting, **stockinette stitch.** Turn the work over to the right side; it should look like stitches in **Fig 21**. The wrong side of the work should look like stitches in **Fig 22**.
Continue with your practice piece, alternately knitting and purling rows, until you feel comfortable with the needles and yarn. As you work you'll see that your piece will begin to look more even.

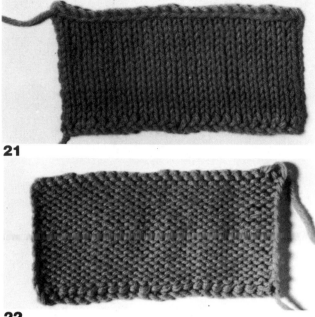

21

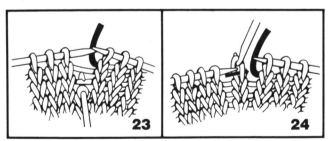

22

DROPPED STITCHES

Each time you knit or purl a stitch, take care to pull the stitch **off** the left needle after completing the new stitch. Otherwise, you will be adding stitches when you don't want to. Don't let a stitch slip off the needle **before** you've knitted or purled it—that's called a dropped stitch. Even expert knitters drop a stitch now and then, but it's easy to pick up when you know how. A dropped stitch can be picked up several rows after it has been dropped by using a crochet hook.

On the knit side (right side of work), insert the crochet hook into the dropped stitch from front to back, under the horizontal strand in the row above **(Fig 23).** Hook the horizontal strand above and pull through the loop on the crochet hook. Continue in this manner until you reach the last row worked, then transfer the loop from the crochet hook to the left needle, being careful not to twist it (see **Fig 24).**

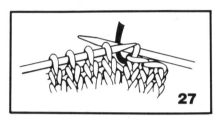

23 **24**

LESSON 3
BINDING OFF

Now you've learned how to cast on, and to knit and purl the stitches; next you need to know how to take the stitches off the needle once you've finished a piece. If you just pull the needle out, the stitches will all "drop," or run down in the exact way you get a run in your hosiery. The process used to secure the stitches is called binding off. Let's bind off your practice piece; be careful to work loosely for this procedure, and begin with the right side (the knit side) of your work facing you.

Step 1: Knit the first 2 stitches. Now insert left needle into the first of the 2 stitches—the one you knitted first **(Fig 25),** and pull it over the second stitch and completely off the needle **(Fig 26).** You have now bound off one stitch.

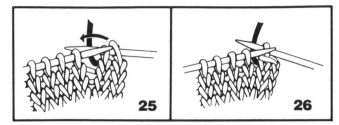

25 **26**

Step 2: Knit one more stitch; insert left needle into first stitch on right needle and pull first stitch over the new stitch and completely off the needle **(Fig 27).** Another stitch is now bound off.

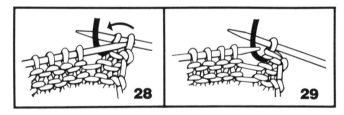

27

Repeat Step 2 ten times more; now knit across the remaining stitches on left needle. You have bound off 12 stitches on the knit side of your work. To bind off on the purl side, turn your practice piece so the wrong side of your work is facing you.

Step 1: Purl the first 2 stitches. Now insert left needle into the first stitch on right needle **(Fig 28),** then pull it over the second stitch and completely off the needle **(Fig 29).** You have now bound off one stitch.

28 **29**

Step 2: Purl one more stitch; insert left needle into first stitch on right needle and pull first stitch over the new stitch and completely off the needle **(Fig 30).** Another stitch is bound off.

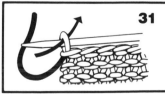

30

Repeat Step 2 until all stitches are bound off, leaving one stitch on right needle. You are now ready to **"finish off"** or **"end off"** the yarn. To do this, cut yarn leaving about a 4″ end. With needle, draw this end up through the final stitch **(Fig 31)** to secure it.

31

You have just learned to bind off knit stitches on the right side of your work and purl stitches on the wrong side of your work. When you wish to bind off in a pattern stitch, where some stitches in a row have been knitted and others purled, knit the knit stitches and purl the purl stitches as you work across the row.

Always bind off loosely to maintain the same amount of stretch or "give" at the edge as in the rest of your work. If bind off is too tight at the neckband ribbing of a pullover sweater, for example, the sweater will not fit over your head!

Hint: You can ensure the binding off being loose enough if you replace the needle in your right hand with a needle one size larger.

LESSON 4
INCREASING and DECREASING
To shape knitted pieces, you will make them wider or narrower by increasing or decreasing a certain number of stitches from time to time.

INCREASING—
Knit (or Purl) 2 Stitches in One
This is the most basic increase which can be used whenever a pattern specifies an increase, without telling you specifically how to do it.

To increase on knit side, insert right needle in **front** of stitch and knit it in the usual manner but don't remove the stitch from the left needle **(Fig 32)**. Then insert right needle in **back** of same stitch and knit it again **(Fig 33)**, this time slipping the stitch off the left needle. You have now increased one stitch.

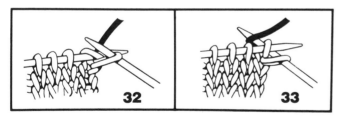

To increase on purl side, insert right needle in **front** of stitch and purl it in the usual manner but don't remove it from the left needle. Then insert right needle in **back** of same stitch **(Fig 34)** and purl it again, this time slipping the stitch off the left needle.

DECREASING, METHOD 1
Knit (or Purl) 2 Stitches Together
This is the method to use when pattern instructions specify a decrease, without telling how to work it. It is done by simply knitting or purling two stitches as one.

To decrease on knit side, insert right needle in front of second stitch on left needle, then in front of first stitch **(Fig 35)**. Now knit the two stitches together **(Fig 36)**, slipping both stitches off left needle. You have now decreased one stitch.

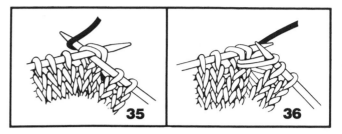

To decrease on purl side, insert right needle in front of first stitch on left needle, then in front of second stitch **(Fig 37)**. Now purl the two stitches together, slipping both stitches off left needle.

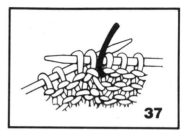

DECREASING, METHOD 2
Pass Slipped Stitch Over
This method is often used in the shaping of raglans or other pieces where a definite decrease line is desired. To use this method you must first know how to "slip" a stitch.

To slip a stitch as to knit, keep yarn at back of work (unless otherwise specified) and insert right needle into stitch on left needle as if you were going to knit it; but instead of knitting, slip the stitch from left needle to right needle **(Fig 38)**.

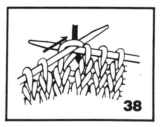

To slip a stitch as to purl, keep yarn at back of work (unless otherwise specified) and insert right needle into stitch on left needle as if you were going to purl it; but instead of purling, slip the stitch from left needle to right needle **(Fig 39)**.

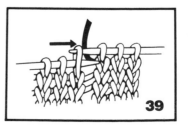

Now you are ready to practice the second method of decreasing. To decrease on knit side, slip the first stitch on left needle as to knit. Knit the next stitch; then pass the slipped stitch over the knitted stitch by using the point of left needle to lift slipped stitch over the next stitch **(Fig 40)** and completely off the needle. You have now decreased one stitch.

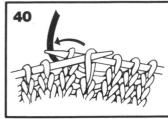

To decrease on purl side, keep yarn to **front** of work and slip the first stitch on left needle as to purl. Purl the next stitch; then pass the slipped stitch over the purled stitch.

Hint: Always slip a stitch as to purl unless decreasing ("pass slipped stitch over") on knit side or if instructions specify otherwise.

LESSON 5
RIBBING
To make garments fit at the waist, sleeve cuffs or neckline, a pattern stitch with some give to it—an elastic effect—is needed. This is called ribbing. It is made by combining knit and purl stitches within the same row.

Knit 2, Purl 2 Ribbing
On a number of stitches divisible by four, for example 24, knit 2 stitches, bring yarn to **front** of work and purl 2 stitches; then bring yarn to **back** of work and knit 2 stitches; bring yarn to **front** again and purl 2 stitches.

Note: You may tend to add stitches accidentally by forgetting to move the yarn to the front before purling, or to the back before knitting. Remembering to move the yarn, repeat this knit 2, purl 2 alternating pattern across the row. Repeat this row as many times as specified in your pattern. Your work should look like **Fig 41.**

41

When binding off ribbing, knit the knit stitches and purl the purl stitches to retain elasticity at edge.

Hint: If you have trouble distinguishing a knit stitch or a purl stitch, remember that the smooth stitches are knit stitches and the bumpy ones are purl stitches (Fig 42).

42

Knit 1, Purl 1 Ribbing
On a number of stitches divisible by two, knit one stitch; yarn to **front,** purl one stitch; yarn to **back,** knit one stitch; yarn to **front,** purl one stitch. Continue across row, alternating one knit stitch with one purl stitch. Repeat this row as many times as specified. Your work should look like **Fig 43.**

43

LESSON 6
READING PATTERNS
Knitting patterns are written in a special language, full of abbreviations, asterisks, parentheses, and other symbols. These short forms are used so that instructions don't take up too much space. They may seem confusing at first, but once you understand what they mean, you'll have no trouble following them.

These are standard abbreviations:

beg	begin(ning)
BO	bind off
CO	cast on
dec	decrease(-ing)
dpn	double pointed needle
EOR	every other row
Fig	figure
inc	increase(-ing)
K	knit
lp(s)	loop(s)
P	purl
patt	pattern
prev	previous
PSSO	pass slipped stitch over
rem	remain(ing)
rnd(s)	round(s)
rep	repeat(ing)
sk	skip
sl	slip
sp(s)	space(s)
st(s)	stitch(es)
stock st	stockinette stitch
tog	together

YB . . . . yarn behind (in back of needle, as to knit)
YF . . . . yarn forward (in front of needle, as to purl)
YO . . . . yarn over the needle

These are standard symbols:

*   An asterisk is used to mark the beg of a portion of instructions which will be worked more than once; thus, "rep from * twice" means after working the instructions once, repeat the instructions following the asterisk twice more (3 times in all).

†   A pair of daggers is used to identify a portion of instructions that will be repeated again later in the pattern.

=   The number after an equal sign at the end of a row indicates the number of stitches you should have when the row has been completed.

( )   Parentheses are used to enclose instructions which should be worked the exact number of times specified immediately following the parentheses, such as: (K1, P1) twice.

[ ]   Brackets (and parentheses) are used to provide additional information to clarify instructions, such as: [rem sts are left unworked] or (abbreviated PC).

These are standard terms:

Work in patt established: Usually used in a pattern stitch, this means to continue following the pattern stitch as it is set up (established) on the needle, working any subsequent increases or decreases in such a way that the established pattern remains the same (usually, working them at the beginning or end of a row, outside the established pattern area).

Work even: Continue to work in the pattern as established, without working any increases or decreases.

LESSON 7
MAKING THINGS FIT
This is the most important lesson of all, for no matter how beautifully you knit, how expert your finishing, if your garments don't fit well, all of your effort has been wasted.

And the key to fit is **gauge.**

GAUGE
Gauge simply means the number of stitches per inch, and the number of rows per inch, that result from a specified yarn worked with needles in a specified size. But since everyone knits differently—some loosely, some tightly, some in between—the measurements of individual work will vary greatly, even when the knitters use the exact same pattern and the exact same size yarn and needles. The photo in **Fig 44** shows the variance clearly. The two mittens were knitted by two different people—but each used the same pattern, the same yarn, and the same needle size.

Needle sizes given in instructions are merely guides, and should never be used without making a 4″ square sample swatch to check your gauge. *It is your responsibility to make sure you achieve the gauge specified in the pattern.* To achieve this gauge, you may

44

need to use a different needle size—either larger or smaller—than that specified in the pattern. **Do not hesitate to change to larger or smaller needles if necessary to achieve gauge.**

Here's how to check your gauge. At the beginning of every knit pattern you'll find a gauge given, like this:

Gauge: In stock st, with size 7 needles, 5 sts = 1″; 7 rows = 1″

This means that you will work your gauge swatch in stockinette stitch, and will try to achieve a gauge of 5 stitches and 7 rows to 1″. You must make a gauge swatch of at least 4″ square to adequately test your work. So, cast on 20 stitches (5 stitches measure 1″; for a 4″ width, multiply 5 times 4 to get 20 stitches). Work in stockinette stitch for 28 rows (7 rows measure 1″; for a 4″ length, multiply 7 by 4 to get 28 rows). Bind off all stitches.

Place the swatch on a flat surface and pin it out, being careful not to stretch it. Measure the outside edges; the swatch should be 4″ square **(Fig 45)**. Now measure the center 2″, and count the actual stitches and rows per inch **(Fig 46)**.

45

11

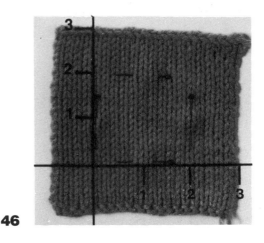

46

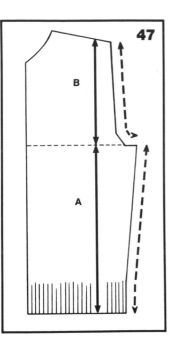

47

If you have **more** stitches or rows per inch than specified, make another swatch with a size **larger** needles.

If you have **less** stitches or rows per inch than specified, make another swatch with a size **smaller** needles.

Making gauge swatches before beginning a garment takes time and is a bother. But if you don't make the effort to do this important step, you'll never be able to create attractive, well-fitting garments.

Hint: Sometimes you'll find that you have the correct stitch gauge, but can't get the row gauge even with a change in needle size. If so, the stitch gauge is more important than the row gauge, with one exception: raglan sweaters. In knitting raglans, the armhole depth is based on row gauge, so you must achieve both stitch and row gauge.

MEASURING WORK IN PROGRESS
Once you've begun a garment, it's a good idea to keep checking your gauge every few inches; if you become relaxed, you'll find yourself knitting more loosely; if you tense up, your knitting will become tighter. To keep your gauge, you may need to change needle sizes in the middle of a garment.

It is advisable when knitting a sweater, for example, to measure the garment's full width when about half way to the armholes. Place the garment out flat, and pin it in place, being careful not to stretch the work. First, compute the width the garment should be at this point by dividing the total number of stitches on the needle by the number of sts per inch of the gauge.

For example, if the gauge is 5 sts per inch, and you have 85 sts on the needle, divide 85 by 5 and the result is 17. Your piece should measure 17″ wide at this point. If it does not, your garment will be either too large or too small. *Now* is the time to rip back and correct the gauge.

You will also need to measure, as you work, distance from bottom of sweater to armhole, and depth from start of armhole to shoulder. The correct, and incorrect, ways to measure these are shown in **Fig 47.**
The solid lines indicate the *correct* way to measure, and the broken lines indicate the *wrong* way to measure. Section A is the area from bottom of garment to armhole; section B is from start of armhole to shoulder.

Fig 48 shows correct and incorrect ways to measure a sleeve from cuff edge to armhole.

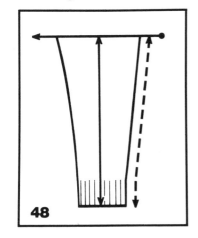

48

Hint: When measuring, use a wooden or metal yardstick or ruler rather than a tape measure, which can stretch and give an inaccurate measurement.

LESSON 8
SPECIAL HELPS

CASTING ON, METHOD 2
This method is used to cast on in the middle of a row, usually when making buttonholes or at thumb base in mittens.
With right hand, make an open loop with yarn **(Fig 49)**, turn loop clockwise and place loop on needle **(Fig 50)**, pull up firmly; repeat for as many stitches as necessary.

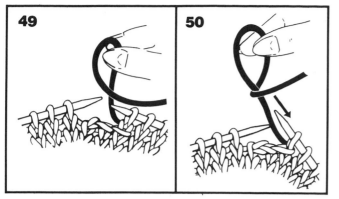

JOINING NEW YARN

A new ball or skein should be added only at the beginning of a row, never in the middle of a row, unless this is required for a color pattern change. To add yarn, tie the new strand around the old strand, making a knot at the edge of work **(Fig 51)**. Leave at least 4″ of yarn end on both old and new strands, to weave in later. Begin to knit again with yarn from new ball.

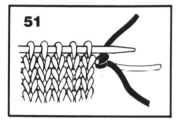

Hint: When you're not sure if remaining yarn is long enough to complete the row, spread the stitches evenly on your needle; take the remaining yarn and fold it back and forth the length of the stitches on the needle four times. If you can do this, you have enough to complete the row; if not, start the new ball of yarn at the beginning of this row.

PICKING UP STITCHES

You will often need to pick up a certain number of stitches around a sweater neckline or armhole, so that ribbing or an edging, can be worked. The pattern instructions will usually state clearly where and how many stitches to pick up. Although this is not difficult, it is often done incorrectly and the results look messy. Picking up is best done with a crochet hook, with the stitches then slipped from it to a knitting needle.

To pick up a stitch, hold the knitting with its right side facing you. Hold yarn from ball or skein in your left hand, behind the work, and crochet hook in your right hand. Insert hook into work from front to back one stitch (at least 2 threads) from the edge **(Fig 52)**; hook yarn and pull a loop through onto hook, making one stitch on hook **(Fig 53)**. Then slip stitch off crochet hook and onto a needle of the correct size for ribbing **(Fig 54)**.

To space your stitches evenly, pick up one loop in each stitch and pick up approximately 3 loops for every 4 rows **(Fig 55)**. If a large number of stitches are to be picked up, it is best to mark off the edge into equal sections, then pick up the same number of stitches in each section.

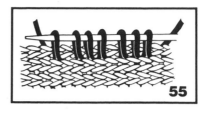

Hint: If the ribbing is to be worked in a different color than the main part of a garment, pick up the stitches with the main color, then switch to the contrast color for the first row of ribbing.

WEAVING ON TWO NEEDLES—
Kitchener Stitch

This method of weaving can be used for garments which have been knitted in stockinette stitch, and which require joining without a seam, such as the toe of a sock or the top of a hood.

To weave the edges together and form an unbroken line of stockinette stitch, divide all stitches evenly onto two knitting needles—one behind the other **(Fig 56)**. Thread yarn into tapestry needle; with wrong sides together, work from right to left as follows:

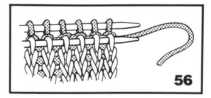

Step 1: Insert tapestry needle into the first st on the front needle as to purl **(Fig 57)**. Draw yarn through st, leaving st on knitting needle.

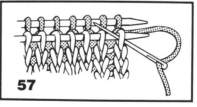

Step 2: Insert tapestry needle into the first st on the back needle (from back to front) as to purl **(Fig 58)**. Draw yarn through st and slip st off knitting needle.

Step 3: Insert tapestry needle into the next st on same (back) needle (from front to back) as to knit **(Fig 59)**, leaving st on needle.

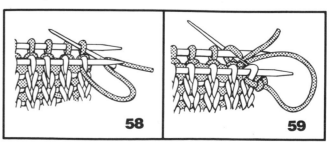

Step 4: Insert tapestry needle into the first st on the front needle as to knit **(Fig 60)**. Draw yarn through st and slip st off knitting needle.

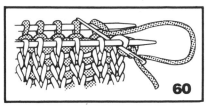

Step 5: Insert tapestry needle into next st on same (front) needle as to purl. Draw yarn through st, leaving st on knitting needle.
Repeat Steps 2 through 5 until one st is left on each needle. Then repeat Steps 2 and 4. Finish off.

Hint: When weaving, do not pull yarn tightly or too loosely; woven sts should be the same size as adjacent knitted sts.

LESSON 9
THE FINISHING TOUCH
Many a well-knitted garment, worked exactly to gauge, ends up looking sloppy and amateurish simply because of bad finishing.

To finish a knitted garment will require no special skill; it does require time, attention, and a knowledge of basic techniques.

WEAVING YARN ENDS
A 4″ yarn end should be left each time you start and finish new yarn. Thread yarn end into a size 16 steel tapestry needle, or a plastic yarn needle. Carefully weave the yarn through the backs of stitches on the wrong side of the garment, if possible close to where a seam will be, just skimming the yarn at the backs of the stitches **(Fig 61)**. First weave about 1½″ in one direction, then weave 1½″ in the reverse direction to secure the yarn. Do not make knots. Cut off excess yarn.

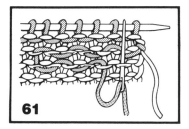

BLOCKING
Next you will block each piece. Blocking simply means "setting" each piece into its final size and shape, with all stitches straight both vertically and horizontally. To block, you'll need a large, flat padded surface (terry toweling provides adequate padding), and a box of rustproof steel straight pins or T-pins.

Decide if you need to launder the pieces before sewing the garment together; if so, wash them by hand. Never wash unassembled garment pieces in a washing machine, even if they are machine washable. Use cool water

and a mild soap, or a special cold water wash. Wash gently, and don't squeeze. Press water out of pieces (don't wring), and roll them up in a terry towel.

Place each piece out on prepared padded surface and pin it into shape, smoothing it out to correct finished measurements as you go—and use a yardstick to be sure of accurate measurements. Place right side of work down, and place pins very close together, no more than ½″ apart **(Fig 62)**.

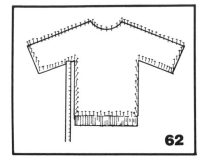

If pieces were washed, let them dry thoroughly before unpinning. If pieces were not washed, you will need to steam them lightly. Use a steam iron or a damp press cloth. Hold the iron just slightly over the garment, never resting on the pieces. Carefully steam edges and bottoms of each piece to eliminate curl. Work slowly so that steam penetrates the garment; never let the iron itself actually touch the yarn. Let the pieces remain pinned out until they are completely dry.

Hint: Ribbing or garter stitch edges on any piece should never be steamed; otherwise, they will lose their elasticity.

ASSEMBLING
Your pattern will usually tell you in what order to assemble pieces. In a garment with set-in sleeves, unless the pattern specifies otherwise, first join both shoulder seams, then both sides seams, then sleeve seams. Last, set in the sleeves.

SEWING METHODS
The choice of sewing method will depend on the type of garment and the type of edge that will be sewn. When you have two straight edges to be joined, especially when the garment is knitted in stock stitch, an "invisible" seam is preferred. When the seam is across the stitches, such as in a shoulder seam, then backstitching is used. The flat seam method is recommended for ribbed edges or bands that are joined to the main part of the garment. Whichever method you use, pin seams first; then as you sew, be sure to match each stitch or each row.

Hint: For a less bulky seam, split the plies of the yarn used to knit the garment and work with one or two of them for sewing.

Invisible Seam: Place pieces side by side, with their right sides facing you. Thread an 18″ length of yarn into a tapestry needle. Anchor yarn securely by weaving in the backs of a few stitches, then bring needle up to right side of work at beginning of seam. Pass needle under the two strands of yarn between the first and 2nd stitches **(Fig 63)** on right-hand piece, and draw the yarn to the right side. Repeat this on the left-hand piece, pass the needle under the two strands of yarn between the first two stitches at the edge.

Continue in this manner, drawing pieces close together as you go **(Fig 64).** Note: For clarity in our diagrams, we've shown the seam loosely drawn together.

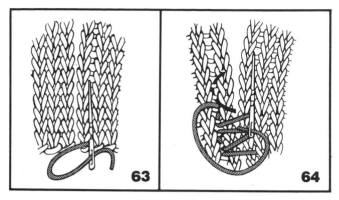

Backstitching: Pin pieces with right sides together; thread 18" length of yarn into tapestry needle. Anchor yarn securely by weaving in backs of a few stitches; bring needle up from back of work through both pieces about ¼" from starting point, and pull yarn through. Bring needle down through both pieces at about midpoint of the first stitch; come up again about ¼" ahead **(Fig 65).** Make stitches firm but not tight; alter the length of the stitch depending on the weight of yarn used and the garment pattern.

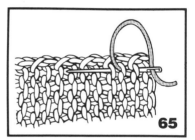

Flat Seam: Place pieces with right sides together; thread 18" length of yarn into tapestry needle. Anchor yarn by weaving in backs of a few stitches. Insert needle through one stitch at edge of back piece and one stitch at edge of front piece; pull yarn through to front. Insert needle through the next stitch at edge of front piece and next stitch at edge of back piece, and pull yarn through to back. Continue working in this manner, making stitches firm but not tight.

Shoulder Seams: Most shoulders on knitted garments are worked in a series of "steps," which should be evened out into a smooth diagonal line when you stitch the shoulder seams.

Hint: To obtain a better shoulder line for sewing seam, complete first shoulder bind off, then begin subsequent bind offs with a slip stitch rather than a knit or purl stitch.

Setting In Sleeves: After sewing and steaming shoulder, side and sleeve seams turn garment wrong side out. Mark center of sleeve cap, and pin sleeve into armhole

with underarm seams matching and center of cap at garment's shoulder seam **(Fig 66).** Working on each side from underarm toward shoulder, pin while you ease sleeve into armhole (use lots of pins) — this means slightly stretching sleeve cap as you go, or scrunching it in a bit. Any extra fullness should be eased in at the armhole sides, not across the top. Then sew sleeve in place and lightly steam seam.

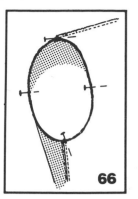

Inserting Zipper: Pin closed zipper into garment opening, being careful not to stretch the knitting. A flexible nylon zipper usually works best in a knitted garment. Teeth of the zipper are usually left exposed, rather than covered by the garment fabric as in a sewn garment. Use matching sewing thread, rather than yarn, to sew zipper in place with a back stitch **(Fig 67).**

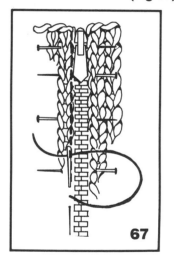

TWISTED CORD
Twisted cords make an attractive trim, and can be used as drawstrings, ties, belts, etc.
Step 1: Cut the desired number of strands of yarn, each 6 times the length of finished cord length.
Step 2: Make a single loop at each end of strands, sufficient in size to slip over a door knob or onto a hook for anchoring.
Step 3: Place one loop on knob or hook.
Step 4: Slip other loop at opposite end on index finger (or several fingers, depending on loop size).
Step 5: Holding strands taut, twist strands to your right until there is a firm even twist along the entire length.
Step 6: Keeping strands taut, fold twisted strands in half lengthwise, slipping loop off index finger and onto knob or hook with other looped end.

Step 7: Form cord by smoothing the twisted strands doubled in a downward direction from knob or hook between the thumb and finger.

Step 8: Cut off looped ends. Knot each end of cord; trim ends.

CROCHETED EDGING

Many knitters have never crocheted, and avoid patterns requiring a crocheted edge to be worked around various knitted pieces. Working such an edge is easy, and is an attractive finishing technique.

To practice this, cast on 20 stitches and work 10 rows in stockinette stitch; bind off loosely. Weave in yarn ends.

Hold knitted swatch in your left hand with cast-on edge at top and with right side facing you.

Take a size F aluminum crochet hook in your right hand, and make a slip loop on hook, leaving a 4" tail of yarn **(Fig 68)**. Hold hook as shown in **Fig 69.**

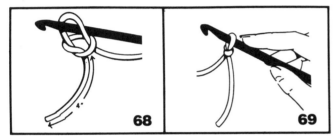

Hold yarn in left hand as shown in **Fig 70,** and with thumb and index finger of left hand hold knitting close to the area where you will be working. Begin in stitch at upper right-hand corner.

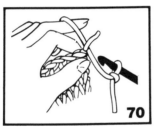

Step 1: Insert hook from front to back under both loops of cast-on stitch **(Fig 71).**

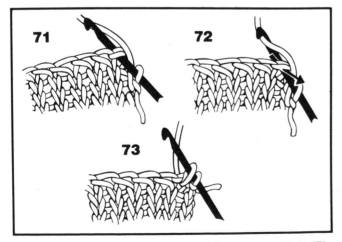

Step 2: Hook yarn and pull through cast-on stitch **(Fig 72).** You will now have 2 loops on hook **(Fig 73).**

Step 3: Hook yarn again and pull through both loops on hook **(Fig 74).** You have now worked one single crochet (abbreviated sc). Repeat Steps 1 through 3 across the 20 cast-on stitches, working fairly loosely and keeping the tension as even as possible. You have now worked across a horizontal edge, and up to a corner. To turn the corner, and still keep work flat, work 2 more scs in the same corner stitch **(Fig 75).**

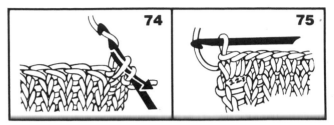

Working across the vertical edge is done in the same manner, except insert the hook at the end of each row *between* the two end knit stitches **(Fig 76)**. Work an sc in each row on your practice piece.

Pattern instructions for working a single crocheted edging on knit pieces will often read: *"Sc around edge, adjusting placement of stitches to keep work flat".*

This means that in order to keep the work from drawing or puckering, you will not always work into *every* row. Sometimes you will need to work into 2 rows, then skip a row; other times, into every other row. You really need to experiment each time to see what works best.

Work 2 scs more in the corner; work scs across bound-off edge, then work corner as before; work scs across last edge. Join to first sc worked by inserting hook under both loops of first sc, hook yarn and pull through both loops on hook (this is called a slip stitch). Finish off.

FRINGING

Fringe adds a special touch to afghans, shawls and other items. Here's how to make single knot, spaghetti and triple knot fringe.

BASIC FRINGE INSTRUCTIONS

Cut a piece of cardboard about 6" wide and half as long as specified in instructions for strands. Wind yarn loosely and evenly lengthwise around cardboard. When card is filled, cut yarn across one end. Do this several times, then begin fringing; you can wind additional strands as you need them.

SINGLE KNOT FRINGE

Hold specified number of strands for one knot of fringe together, then fold in half. Hold garment with wrong side facing you. Use crochet hook to draw folded end through space or st, pull loose ends through folded section **(Fig**

77) and draw knot up firmly **(Fig 78).** Space knots as indicated in pattern instructions. Trim ends of fringe evenly.

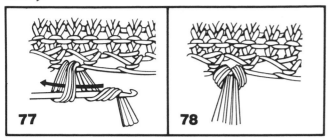

SPAGHETTI FRINGE
Each knot is tied with just one strand of yarn. Use same knotting method as for Single Knot Fringe.

TRIPLE KNOT FRINGE
First work Single Knot Fringe completely across one end. Turn work so right side is facing you. Working from left to right, take half the strands of one knot and half the strands of the knot next to it, and knot them together **(Fig 79).** Repeat across. Do not turn. Again working from left to right, tie third row of knots as in **Fig 80.**

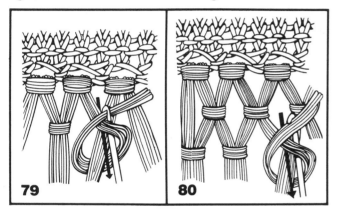

POMPONS AND TASSELS
POMPON —
Cut 2 cardboard circles, each the diameter of finished pompon measurement, plus ½″. Cut a center hole approximately ½″ in diameter in each circle. Thread a tapestry needle with doubled 72″ length of yarn; holding both circles together, pass needle through center hole, over outside edge, through center again **(Fig 81)** until entire circle is covered. Thread more lengths of yarn as needed.

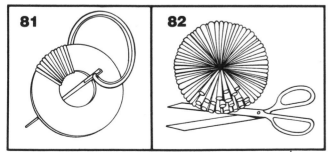

With very sharp scissors, cut yarn between the edges of the two circles **(Fig 82).** Using a 12″ strand of yarn doubled, slip yarn between circles, pull up tightly and tie very firmly. Remove cardboards and fluff out pompon by rolling it between your hands. Trim evenly with scissors.

Hint: To make a very small pompon as for baby clothes, try wrapping the yarn around the tines of a dinner fork; tie wrapped yarn securely between the center of the tines. Fluff and trim as for normal size pompon.

TASSEL
Cut a piece of cardboard about 6″ wide and the desired length of finished tassel. Wind yarn around length of cardboard the number of times specified in pattern instructions. Cut a piece of yarn about 20″ long, and thread into tapestry needle doubled. Insert needle through all strands at top of cardboard, pull up tightly and knot securely, leaving ends for attaching to garment. Cut yarn at opposite end of cardboard **(Fig 83);** remove cardboard.

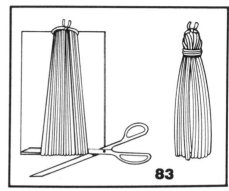

Cut another strand of yarn 12″ long, and wrap it tightly twice around tassel 1½″ (or less on a tiny tassel) below top knot. Knot securely and allow excess ends to fall in as part of tassel.

LESSON 10
ADVANCED TECHNIQUES

CONTINENTAL KNITTING
The method of knitting you have used so far is practiced primarily in the United States and in England. In many other countries what is known as Continental knitting is practiced. In the Continental method, there is less motion of the hands, and the work thus goes faster. Instead of "throwing" the yarn with the right hand, the yarn is held in the left hand and is caught by the point of the right needle and pulled through the stitch.

Although it is faster, the Continental method makes it harder to control gauge. We do recommend this method for left-handed knitters, if they are unable to master comfortably the regular method. To practice Continental knitting, cast on 20 stitches using Method 1.

KNITTING
Hold yarn in left hand, over index finger, as in **Fig 84.**

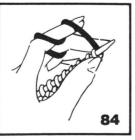

Step 1: Insert point of right needle into front of stitch on left needle as to knit.

Step 2: Catch yarn with point of right needle and draw yarn through **(Fig 85)**, making a new loop.

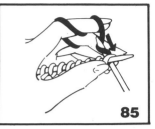

Step 3: Slip stitch off left needle: one knit stitch made. Repeat Steps 1 through 3 across row.

PURLING

Hold yarn in left hand, over index finger, in front of work **(Fig 86)**.

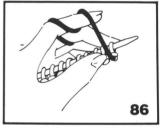

Step 1: Insert point of right needle into front of stitch on left needle as to purl, keeping it behind yarn on left index finger.

Step 2: Catch yarn around point of right needle **(Fig 87)** and draw yarn backward and up through stitch, making a new loop.

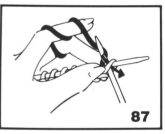

Step 3: Slip stitch off left needle: one purl stitch made. Repeat Steps 1 through 3 across row.

MULTI-COLORED KNITTING FROM CHARTS

Many lovely knitted designs, such as argyles, Norwegian motifs and Fair Isle patterns are worked from charts which show the various color patterns.

These designs are usually worked in stockinette stitch. **Fig 88** shows a typical chart. On the charts, each **square** represents one **stitch** and each horizontal line of squares represents stitches in one row. If the chart isn't printed in color, different symbols are used to indicate the colors (see the **color key** beside the chart).

The chart is usually worked from the bottom to the top. The right-side (knit side) rows are worked from right to left across the squares of the chart; the wrong-side (purl side) rows are worked from left to right across the chart. Arrows on our sample chart indicate the direction the chart is read and worked.

Hint: When working in rounds, work each row of chart from right to left.

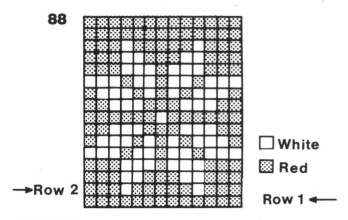

ARGYLES

Argyle patterns, composed of colorful interlocked diamonds, were originally adapted from the tartans of the Scottish Campbell clan whose leaders were the Earls and Dukes of Argyll. Today any colors, ranging from soft pastel pinks, blues and violets (sure to make an ancient Scottish chieftain turn over in his grave!) to bright reds, yellows and oranges, to subdued earth tones, can be used.

When working the design, you will need a yarn bobbin for each color change. Bobbins are small plastic pieces on which you wind several yards of a color; when not in use, the bobbins stay out of your way and help keep the many different colors from tangling.

Whenever a bobbin is used for the first time, it is "tied in" to the yarn color preceding it **(Fig 89)**. Later, when you are finishing the garment, be sure to **untie** these knots before weaving in the yarn ends.

To make a color change, drop the first color, then pick up the new yarn, taking care to bring it from behind the previous color **(Fig 90)**, then up to the needle to form the stitch. This prevents holes from appearing in the work where the colors were changed.

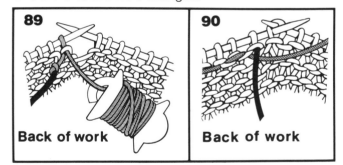

NORWEGIAN and FAIR ISLE KNITTING

The magnificent sweaters of Norway—often used in this country as ski sweaters—and Fair Isle patterns are worked in a different manner, called *stranding*. Though the designs (snowflakes, deer, pine trees, etc.) also appear on a chart, a ball of yarn—rather than a bobbin—is used for each color. These designs traditionally are knitted with only 2 colors in any one row.

When one color is being used, the other color is being **carried** across the back of work and either locked in place with the yarn being used (when carried across more than 2 stitches) or left loose (when carried across 2 stitches or less). Take care to allow plenty of slack in the yarn being carried—probably much more than you think necessary. If enough slack is not used, the color change areas will be tight and puckered when the pieces are blocked and assembled. **Fig 91** shows yarn that has been carried across the back of work. To avoid long loose strands at back of work, a color that will not be used again for several stitches should be carried loosely but locked every couple of stitches by laying it over the yarn being used, then working the next stitch **(Fig 92).**

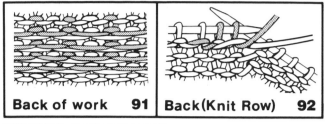

Back of work **91**	**Back (Knit Row)** **92**

KNITTING IN THE ROUND

Knitting in rounds instead of back and forth in rows will form a seamless, tubular piece and requires the use of a circular needle or a set of four double-pointed needles (abbreviated dpn). These needles come in the same sizes as straight knitting needles but have varying lengths—dpns, 7" and 10" lengths; circular needles, 16", 24", 29" and 36" lengths.

Dpns are used when working with a small number of stitches as in knitted mittens, hats, socks, collars or cuffs. To begin on dpns, cast on in the usual manner on **one needle only.** Then divide the stitches on 3 needles **(Fig 93).** Join by inserting the 4th needle into the first stitch **(Fig 94),** being careful not to twist the stitches, and work this stitch. After working all the stitches off a needle, use the free needle to work the stitches off the next needle. Continue in this manner, being sure to pull the yarn tightly across to the first stitch of each needle to avoid loose stitches.

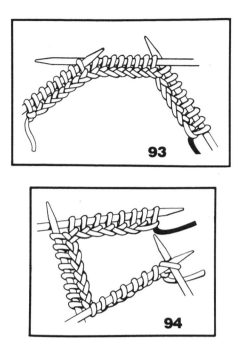

A circular needle is used when working with a large number of stitches as in knitted sweaters, skirts, dresses or afghans. This needle is used much the same way as dpns, except you never reach the point when the needle is free of stitches. Therefore, it is necessary to place a marker (or a knotted loop of yarn in a contrasting color) on the needle to indicate the start of a round, and slip this marker each time you reach it so it will continue up the work with you.

All-Time Favorites

Chapter 2

The sweaters in this chapter are all based on designs that have stood the test of time — styles that will be as wearable in years to come as they are today.

Included are such favorites as a traditional fisherman cardigan, a multi-color Fair Isle pullover, and a classic cardigan for men.

Adding spice to the collection is a comfortable jacket sweater which can be knitted plain or with your choice of three colorful designs worked into the back: a horse, a pheasant or a deer.

FAIR ISLE
PULLOVER AND HAT
designed by Mary Thomas

Once again island folk have given us a traditional style of knitting that has become popular throughout the world. The women of Fair Isle, off the Northern tip of Scotland, designed pullovers and cardigans featuring rounded yokes of geometric patterns in several colors, set into a solid color. Soft, muted tones were generally used.

This garment is constructed in an interesting manner; you will first knit each sleeve, back and front individually to beginning of the yoke; all pieces are then joined and worked as one piece.

SIZES:	Small	Medium	Large
Body Bust:	30-32"	34-36"	38-40"
Garment Measurements:			
bust	34"	38"	42"
length to			
underarm	14"	15"	16"
sleeve length			
to underarm	16½"	17"	17½"

Size Note: Instructions are written for sizes as follows: Small(Medium-Large).

MATERIALS
Worsted weight yarn:
  16(18-20) oz golf green;
  3(3½-4) oz medium blue;
  1 oz navy blue;
  ½ oz white
Size 6, 14" straight and 16" circular knitting needles
Size 8, 14" straight; 16" and 29" circular knitting needles (or size required for gauge)
4 Stitch markers (one in contrasting color)
GAUGE: With larger size needles in stock st,
       9 sts = 2"; 6 rows/rnds = 1"
Gauge Note: It is essential to achieve gauge using both straight and circular needles. A gauge difference may occur with a considerable number of sts on a needle, when working in rnds instead of rows, or when knitting a design with 2 or more colors. Always keep checking for any gauge variation while knitting your sweater. Do not hesitate to change needle size if necessary.

PULLOVER INSTRUCTIONS
Note: Entire sweater, excluding ribbing, is worked in stock st.

LEFT SLEEVE
With smaller size straight needles and green, CO 36(38-40) sts LOOSELY. Work in K1, P1 ribbing for 3", increasing 6(6-8) sts evenly spaced across last row = 42(44-48) sts. Change to larger size straight needles; begin stock st. Work 6 rows even. Inc one st at each end of next row and then EVERY following 8th row, 7(8-8) times = 58(62-66) sts. Work even until sleeve measures 16½(17-17½)" from CO edge or desired length to underarm, ending by working a purl row.
BO 4(5-6) sts (for underarm) at beg of next 2 rows = 50(52-54) sts. **Next Row:** Change to 29" circular needle; knit across. *Do not* cut yarn; set aside.

FRONT
With smaller size straight needles and green, CO 78(86-94) sts *loosely*. Work in K1, P1 ribbing for 2". Change to larger size straight needles; begin stock st. Work even until piece measures 14(15-16)" from CO edge or desired length to underarm, ending by working a purl row.
BO 4(5-6) sts (for underarm) at beg of next 2 rows = 70(76-82) sts. Cut yarn, leaving 6" end for weaving in later. **Next Row:** Change to 29" circular needle (with sts of left sleeve on it). With knit-side facing you, place marker (use markers of one color first) next to sleeve. Continue with yarn of left sleeve and knit across. You should now have 120(128-136) sts on circular needle. *Do not* cut yarn; set aside.

RIGHT SLEEVE
Work same as Left Sleeve until there are 50(52-54) sts on needle after sts are bound-off at underarm. Cut yarn, leaving 6" end for weaving in later. **Next Row:** Change to 29" circular needle (with sts of left sleeve and front on it). With knit-side facing you, place marker (remember to use markers of one color first) next to front. Continue with yarn of front and knit across. You should now have 170(180-190) sts on circular needle. *Do not* cut yarn; set aside.

BACK
Work same as Front until there are 70(76-82) sts on needle after sts are bound-off at underarm. Cut yarn, leaving 6" end for weaving in later. **Next Row:** Change to 29" circular needle (with sts of left sleeve, front and right sleeve on it). With knit-side facing you, place marker next to right sleeve. Continue with yarn of right sleeve and knit across. You should now have 240(256-272) sts on circular needle. Place contrasting marker next to back for end of rnd; continue with green. Join, being careful not to twist pieces; begin working in rnds as follows.

YOKE

Note: Sl markers on each following rnd.

Rnd 1: K2 tog; * knit across to within 2 sts of next marker; sl 1 as to knit, K1, PSSO; K2 tog (dec made on each side of marker); rep from * twice more, knit across to last 2 sts before contrasting marker; sl 1 as to knit, K1, PSSO = 232(248-264) sts [8 sts decreased].

Rnd 2: Knit.

Rep last 2 rnds, 2(3-4) times more = 216(224-232) sts.

Fair Isle Design: Design is worked from charts. On each rnd, * work chart from A to B; rep from * around. To join a new color, tie it to prev color at beg of rnd, leaving approx 4" end for weaving in later. Carry color not in use LOOSELY at back of work so as not to "pucker" or distort the design; or alter the width of your sweater. Avoid carrying color not in use across more than 2 sts (see *Norwegian and Fair Isle Knitting* on page 18). **Note:** Remember to maintain gauge as specified (see Gauge Note).

Next 12 Rnds: [**Note:** On next rnd, remove markers of same color, leaving contrasting marker for end of rnd.] Following Chart in **Fig 1**, work Rnds 1 through 12.

First Dec Rnd: With green, * K 11(8-9), K2 tog; rep from * once more; ** K8(10-12), K2 tog; rep from ** around = 195(205-215) sts.

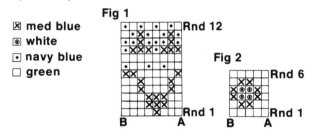

med blue
white
navy blue
green

Fig 1 Rnd 12 — Rnd 1
B A

Fig 2 Rnd 6 — Rnd 1
B A

Next 6 Rnds: Following Chart in **Fig 2**, work Rnds 1 through 6.

2nd Dec Rnd: With green, K 10(10-3), K2 tog; K 11(11-4), K2 tog; * K8(10-10), K2 tog; rep from * around = 176(188-196) sts.

Next 4 Rnds: Following Chart in **Fig 3**, work Rnds 1 through 4.

3rd Dec Rnd: With green, * K9(2-6), K2 tog; rep from * once more; ** K9(8-8), K2 tog; rep from ** around = 160(168-176) sts.

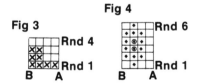

Fig 3 Rnd 4 — Rnd 1
B A

Fig 4 Rnd 6 — Rnd 1
B A

Next 6 Rnds: Following Chart in **Fig 4**, work Rnds 1 through 6.

4th Dec Rnd: With green, * K6(10-5), K2 tog; rep from * once more; ** K6(6-7), K2 tog; rep from ** around = 140(148-156) sts. **Note:** Change to larger size 16" circular needle when sts become too few on needle.

Next 4 Rnds: Following Chart in **Fig 5**, work Rnds 1 through 4.

Fig 5 Rnd 4 — Rnd 1
B A

5th Dec Rnd: With med blue, K2(6-4), K2 tog; K2(6-5), K2 tog; * K4(4-5), K2 tog; K4, K2 tog; rep from * around = 116(124-132) sts.

Next 4 Rnds: Following Chart in **Fig 6**, work Rnds 1 through 4.

6th Dec Rnd: With med blue, K4(2-6), K2 tog; K4(1-5), K2 tog; * K2(3-3), K2 tog; K2, K2 tog; rep from * around = 88(96-104) sts.

Fig 6 Rnd 4 — Rnd 1
B A

Fig 7 Rnd 4 — Rnd 1
B A

Next 4 Rnds: Following Chart in **Fig 7**, work Rnds 1 through 4.

7th Dec Rnd: With med blue, * K2, K2 tog; rep from * around = 66(72-78) sts.

Neck Ribbing: Change to smaller size 16" circular needle. With green, work K1, P1 ribbing in rnds for 2½". With larger size needle, BO all sts LOOSELY. Cut yarn, leaving 30" sewing length.

FINISHING

Fold neck ribbing in half to inside; sew VERY LOOSELY in place. Block sweater to measurements. Sew side and sleeve seams, carefully matching BO sts at underarm of each sleeve with front and back. Weave in all ends.

HAT INSTRUCTIONS

With larger size straight needles and green, CO 92 sts *loosely*. Change to smaller size straight needles. Work in K1, P1 ribbing for 3". **Inc Row:** (K1, P1) 3 times; K1, purl in front and back of next st; * (K1, P1) 5 times; K1, purl in front and back of next st; rep from * across = 100 sts. Change to larger size straight needles and stock st. Work 4 rows even. Then work next 17 rows from chart in **Fig 8.**

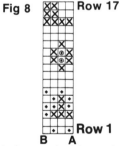

Fig 8 Row 17 — Row 1
B A

On knit rows (odd-numbered rows of chart), rep from A to B across. On purl rows (even-numbered rows of chart), rep from B to A across. When 17 rows of chart are completed, continue with green in stock st (beg with a purl row) until piece measures 9" from CO edge, ending by working a purl row.

Shape Top: Row 1: K1, * K2 tog, K1; rep from * across = 67 sts. **Rows 2 through 4:** Beg with a purl row and work 3 rows even in stock st. **Row 5:** K1, * K2 tog; rep from * across = 34 sts.

FINISHING

Cut yarn, leaving approx 30" sewing length. Thread into tapestry or yarn needle and draw through all sts twice. Draw up tightly and fasten securely. Sew side seam, carefully matching sts of design. Fold up half of ribbing to inside and sew *loosely* in place. Weave in all yarn ends.

Pompon: With med blue, make 2" pompon (see *Pompon* instructions on page 17) and attach securely to top of hat.

V-NECK CABLE

PULLOVER for women and children
designed by Mary Thomas

Sweater has two color versions: Version A, solid color, and Version B, tennis colors, featuring striped ribbing.

SIZES:	Children			Women		
	Small	Medium	Large	Small	Medium	Large
Body Chest/Bust:	24"	28"	31"	31"	35"	39"
Garment Measurements:						
chest/bust	26"	30"	33"	34"	38"	42"
length to underarm	10"	12"	14"	15"	16"	17"
sleeve length to underarm	13"	15"	17"	18"	18½"	19"

Size Note: Instructions are written for children's sizes in parentheses (Small-Medium-Large) and women's sizes in brackets [Small-Medium-Large].

MATERIALS
Worsted weight yarn:
  For Version A: (10-12-14)[16-19-22] oz light blue heather for children *or* beige tweed for women
  For Version B: (10-12-14)[16-19-22] oz white; ½ oz each royal blue and bright red
Sizes 5 and 7, 14" straight knitting needles (or size required for gauge)
2 Small stitch holders
10 Stitch markers
Cable needle

GAUGE: With larger size needles in stock st,
       5 sts = 1"; 7 rows = 1"

CABLE PATTERN STITCH (worked on 9 sts)
Rows 1, 3, 7 and 9 (right side): P2, K5, P2.
Rows 2, 4, 6, 8 and 10: K2, P5, K2.
Row 5 (cable twist row): P2; sl next 3 sts onto cable needle and hold at *front* of work; K2, then K3 from cable needle; P2.
Rep Rows 1 through 10 for patt.

INSTRUCTIONS
Note: For Version A (solid colored sweater), use blue heather for children *or* beige tweed for women throughout instructions. For Version B (tennis sweater), beg with royal blue.

BACK
With smaller size needles, CO (64-76-84)[86-96-106] sts *loosely.* **Version A Ribbing:** Work in K1, P1 ribbing for (2-2½-3)[3-3-3]". **Version B Ribbing:** Work in K1, P1 ribbing in the following stripe sequence: (2-2-3)[3-3-3] rows each of royal blue, white, red, white, royal blue, white and red. When stripe sequence is completed, change to white.
Both versions continue as follows. Change to larger size needles and work even in stock st until piece measures (10-12-14)[15-16-17]" from CO edge or desired length to underarm, ending by working a purl row.

Shape Armholes: Continuing in stock st, BO (3-4-4)[5-6-7] sts at beg of next 2 rows = (58-68-76)[76-84-92] sts. Dec one st at each armhole edge EOR (2-3-4)[4-5-6] times = (54-62-68)[68-74-80] sts. Work even until armhole measures (5-6-7)[7-7½-8]", ending by working a purl row.

Shape Neck and Shoulders: Row 1 (dividing row): BO (5-6-7)[5-6-6] sts, knit *next* [do not count st already on needle] (14-16-17)[19-20-22] sts; sl next (14-16-18)[18-20-22] sts to holder for back of neck; join new yarn of same color and knit rem sts. **Row 2:** BO (5-6-7)[5-6-6] sts, purl across rem sts of left shoulder; BO (3-3-3)[2-2-2] sts at neck edge of right shoulder, purl rem sts. **Row 3:** BO (5-6-6)[5-5-6] sts, knit across rem sts of right shoulder; BO (3-3-3)[2-2-2] sts at neck edge of left shoulder, knit rem sts. **Row 4:** BO (5-6-6)[5-5-6] sts, purl across rem sts of left shoulder, BO (3-3-3)[2-2-2] sts at neck edge of right shoulder, purl rem sts. **Row 5:** BO (4-5-6)[5-5-6] sts; knit (for women sizes only) across rem sts of right shoulder; BO (3-3-3)[2-2-2] sts at neck edge of left shoulder, knit rem sts. **Row 6:** BO (4-5-6)[5-5-6] sts. Children sizes are now completed; continue as follows for women sizes. Purl across rem sts of left shoulder; BO 2 sts at neck edge of right shoulder, purl rem sts. **Row 7:** BO [4-5-5] rem sts of right shoulder; BO 2 sts at neck edge of left shoulder, knit rem sts. BO [4-5-5] sts of left shoulder.

FRONT

Work same as Back until ribbing is completed, ending last row of ribbing by (inc-inc-dec)[inc-inc-dec] one st = (65-77-83)[87-97-105] sts. Change to larger size needles and establish cable patts as follows (remember to change to white for Version B).

Row 1 (right side): K(1-3-4)[6-7-9]; place marker, inc in next st [to inc: purl in front and back of st]; K5, inc in next st, place marker; * K(7-9-10)[10-12-13]; place marker, inc in next st; K5, inc in next st, place marker; rep from * 3 times more, K(1-3-4)[6-7-9] = (75-87-93)[97-107-115] sts. **Note:** Sl markers on each following row.

Row 2: * Purl to marker, work Row 2 of Cable Patt St on next 9 sts; rep from * 4 times more, purl rem sts.

Keeping 9 sts between each set of markers in Cable Patt St and rem sts in stock st, work even until piece measures same as Back to underarm, ending by working a wrong-side row.

Shape Neck and Armholes: Note: Continue to maintain patt as established; when decreasing at edges, keep rem sts of cable patt in knit and purl sts as established.

Row 1 (dividing row): BO (4-5-5)[6-7-8] sts, work across *next* [do not count st already on needle] (32-37-40)[41-45-48] sts; sl next st to holder for center of V-neck; join another ball of yarn (same color) and work across rem (37-43-46)[48-53-57] sts. **Row 2:** BO (4-5-5)[6-7-8] sts, work across rem sts on each side of center neck st = (33-38-41)[42-46-49] sts each side. Continuing to work across each side with a separate ball of yarn, dec one st at each armhole edge EOR (3-4-5)[5-6-6] times AND AT THE SAME TIME dec one st at each neck edge EOR. Then keeping armhole edge even, continue to dec one st at each neck edge EOR until there are a total of (16-12-6)[8-8-8] decreases at each neck edge = (14-22-30)[29-32-35] sts each side. Now continue to dec one st

at each neck edge EVERY 3rd row, (0-5-11)[10-11-12] times = (14-17-19)[19-21-23] sts each side. Work even until armhole measures same as Back, ending by working a wrong-side row.

Shape Shoulders: BO at each armhole edge: (5-6-7)[5-6-6] sts once; (5-6-6)[5-5-6] sts once; (4-5-6)[5-5-6] sts once; (0-0-0)[4-5-5] sts once.

SLEEVE (make 2)

Note: For Version B, beg with royal blue. With smaller size needles, CO (32-36-40)[40-44-48] sts *loosely*. Work ribbing same as Back, ending last row of ribbing by inc one st = (33-37-41)[41-45-49] sts. Change to larger size needles and establish cable patt as follows (remember to change to white for Version B).

Row 1: K(13-15-17)[17-19-21], place marker; inc in next st [to inc: purl in front and back of st]; K5, inc in next st; place marker, knit rem sts = (35-39-43)[43-47-51] sts. **Note:** Sl markers on each following row.

Row 2: Purl to marker, work Row 2 of Cable Patt St on next 9 sts, purl rem sts.

Keeping 9 sts between markers in Cable Patt St and rem sts in stock st, inc one st at each end EVERY (6-6-8)[8-8-8]th row, (8-9-9)[10-10-10] times = (51-57-61)[63-67-71] sts. Maintaining patt as established, work even until sleeve measures (13-15-17)[18-18½-19]" from CO edge or desired length, ending by working a wrong-side row.

Shape Cap: Maintaining patt as established, BO (3-4-4)[5-6-7] sts at beg of next 2 rows = (45-49-53)[53-55-57] sts. Dec one st at each end EOR until (29-29-27)[27-25-21] sts rem. Then dec one st each end EVERY row until (13-13-15)[15-17-17] sts rem. BO rem sts.

FINISHING

Block pieces to measurements, being careful not to flatten cable patterns. Sew right shoulder seam.

Neckband: Note: For Version B, beg with white. With right side facing, beg at left front neck edge. Using smaller size needles, pick up (30-36-42)[42-46-50] sts along left neck edge; knit st from holder and mark this st with a piece of contrasting yarn or small safety pin; pick up (30-36-42)[42-46-50] sts along right neck edge to shoulder seam; pick up (8-8-8)[10-10-10-] sts along right back neck edge; knit (14-16-18)[18-20-22] sts from back neck holder; pick up (8-8-8)[10-10-10] sts along left back neck edge = (91-105-119)[123-133-143] sts. **Note:** Continue to mark center st of front V-neck on each following row.

Row 1 (wrong side): P1, * K1, P1; rep from * across. For Version B, change to red.

Row 2: * K1, P1 rep from * to within 2 sts of marked st, sl 1, K1, PSSO; knit marked st, K2 tog; ** P1, K1; rep from ** across.

Row 3: P1, * K1, P1; rep from * to within 2 sts of marked st; K2 tog, purl marked st, K2 tog; P1, ** K1, P1; rep from ** across. For Version B, change to white.

Rows 4 and 5: Rep Rows 2 and 3. For Version B, change to royal blue.

Rows 6 and 7: Rep Rows 2 and 3. BO *loosely* in ribbing. Sew left shoulder seam and weave ends of neckband tog. Sew side and sleeve seams; sew sleeves in armholes. Weave in all ends.

NORWEGIAN PULLOVER

and SKI HAT

designed by Mary Thomas

Norwegian sweaters have a distinctive look all their own, and usually feature bright colors and bold motifs. Our version, shown in black, white and gray, would be equally attractive in the more traditional colors.

SIZES:	Small	Medium	Large
Body Bust:	31″	35″	39″
Garment Measurements:			
bust	35″	39″	43″
length to underarm	16″	16½″	17″
sleeve length	21″	22″	22½″

Size Note: Instructions are written for sizes as follows: Small(Medium-Large).

MATERIALS
Worsted weight yarn:
11(13-15) oz white;
12(14-16) oz gray;
1½(2-2½) oz black
Sizes 4 and 7, 14″ straight knitting needles (or sizes required for gauge)
2 Small stitch holders
Materials Note: Yarn requirements include 4 oz gray for hat.
GAUGE: For Pullover:
With smaller size needles in ribbing,
7½ sts = 1″; 8 rows = 1″
With larger size needles in stock st,
5 sts = 1″; 7 rows = 1″
For Ski Hat:
With smaller size needles in stock st,
6 sts = 1″; 8 rows = 1″

PULLOVER INSTRUCTIONS

Note: Entire sweater, excluding ribbing, is worked in stock st.

BACK

With white and smaller size needles, CO 104(116-128) sts. Work in K1, P1 ribbing for 1½″. **Dec Row:** * (K1, P1) twice, P 2 tog; rep from * to last 2 sts; K1, P1 = 87(97-107) sts. Change to larger size needles; begin stock st. Work even until piece measures 12¼(12¾-13¼)″ from CO edge, or 3¾″ less than desired length to underarm, ending by working a purl row.

Knit-in Design: Design is worked from charts. On each knit row (odd-numbered row of chart), * work chart from A to B; rep from * across, ending by working from A to C. On each purl row (even-numbered row of chart), work chart from C to A once, then * work from B to A; rep from * across. To join a new color, tie it to prev color at beg of row, leaving approx 4″ end for weaving later. When changing colors, always bring the color you have just used over and to the left of the color you are going to use, bringing the new color up from underneath. This twists the two colors and prevents a hole in your work. Carry color not in use LOOSELY at back of work so as not to pucker or distort the design; or alter the width of your knitted piece. Avoid carrying color not in use across more than 2 sts (see *Norwegian and Fair Isle Knitting* on page 18).

Next 14 Rows: Following Chart 1(2-3) in **Fig 1,** work Rows 1 through 14.

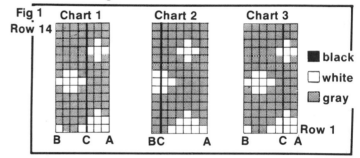

Next 12 Rows: Following Chart 1(2-3) in **Fig 2,** work Rows 1 through 12.

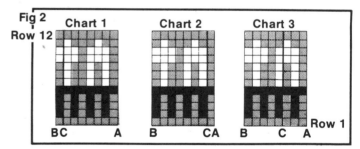

Shape Armholes: Continuing with gray, BO 5(6-8) sts at beg of next 2 rows = 77(85-91) sts.

Next 18 Rows: Following Chart 1(2-1) in **Fig 3,** work Rows 1 through 18.

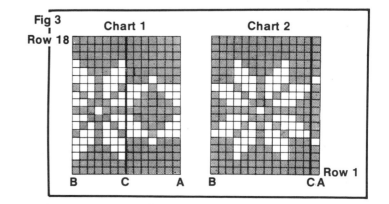

Next 12 Rows: Following Chart 1(1-2) in **Fig 4,** work Rows 1 through 12.

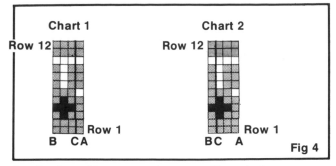

Continuing with gray, work even until armhole measures 7(7½-8¼)″, ending by working a purl row.

Shape Neck and Shoulders: Row 1. BO 6(7-7) sts, knit *next* [do not count st already on needle] 22(24-26) sts; K 19(21-23) and sl these sts to holder for back of neck; knit rem 29(32-34) sts. **Row 2:** BO 6(7-7) sts, purl to neck edge, drop yarn. Join a new ball of gray yarn at right neck edge, BO 2 sts, purl rem sts. **Row 3:** BO 6(7-7) sts, knit to neck edge; BO 2 sts at left neck edge, knit rem sts. **Row 4:** BO 6(7-7) sts, purl to neck edge; BO 2 sts at right neck edge, purl rem sts. **Row 5:** BO 6(6-7) sts, knit to neck edge; BO 2 sts at left neck edge, knit rem sts. **Row 6:** BO 6(6-7) sts, purl to neck edge; BO 2 sts at right neck edge, purl rem sts. **Row 7:** BO rem 5(6-7) sts of right shoulder; BO 2 sts at left neck edge, knit rem sts. BO rem 5(6-7) sts of left shoulder.

FRONT

Follow instructions for Back until armhole measures 6 (6½-7¼)″, or 1″ less than armhole of Back, ending by working a purl row.

Shape Neck and Shoulders: Row 1: K 31(34-36) for left front; K 15(17-19) and sl these sts to holder for front of neck; knit rem sts for right front. **Row 2:** Purl to within 2 sts of neck edge, P2 tog, drop yarn; with another ball of gray yarn, P2 tog at left neck edge, purl rem sts. **Row 3:** Knit to within 2 sts of neck edge, K2 tog at each neck edge, knit rem sts. **Row 4:** Purl to within 2 sts of neck edge, P2 tog at each neck edge, purl rem sts. **Rows 5 and 6:** Rep Rows 3 and 4. You should now have 26(29-31) sts each side. **Row 7:** BO 6(7-7) sts, knit to within 2 sts of neck edge, K2 tog at each neck edge, knit rem sts. **Row 8:** BO 6(7-7) sts, purl across both sides. **Rows 9 and 10:** Rep Rows 7 and 8. **Row 11:** BO 6(6-7) sts, knit to within 2 sts of neck edge, K2 tog at each neck edge, knit rem sts. **Row 12:** BO 6(6-7) sts, purl across both sides. **Row 13:** BO rem 5(6-7) sts of left front; knit sts of right front. BO rem 5(6-7) sts.

SLEEVE (make 2)

With white and smaller size needles, CO 48 (52-56) sts. Work in K1, P1 ribbing for 2″. **Inc Row:** (K1, P1) 3(5-0) times; *inc in next st, P1; (K1, P1) 2(2-3) times; rep from * across = 55(59-63) sts. Change to larger size needles; begin stock st. Inc one st at each end EVERY 8th row, 8(8-10) times = 71(75-83) sts. Work even until sleeve measures 15½(16½-17)″ from CO edge, or 5½″ less than desired length, ending by working a purl row.

Knit-in Design: Next 14 Rows: Following Chart 1(2-3) in **Fig 5,** work Rows 1 through 14.

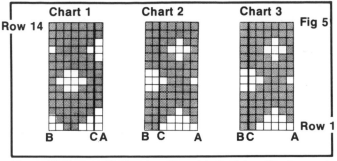

Next 12 Rows: Following Chart 1 (3-3) in **Fig 2,** work Rows 1 through 12.

Next 12 Rows: Following Chart 2 in **Fig 4,** work Rows 1 through 12. Then BO all sts *loosely.*

FINISHING

Block pieces to measurements. Sew right shoulder seam.

Neckband: With right side facing, beg at left front neck edge. Using smaller size needles and gray, pick up 20 sts along left front neck shaping; K 15(17-19) from front neck holder; pick up 20 sts along right front neck shaping to shoulder seam; pick up 10 sts along right back neck shaping; K 19(21-23) from back neck holder; pick up 10 sts along left back neck shaping = 94(98-102) sts. Work in K1, P1 ribbing for 3″. Change to larger size needles and work one more row in ribbing. BO all sts LOOSELY in ribbing.

Sew left shoulder seam and weave ends of neckband tog. Fold neckband in half to inside and sew VERY LOOSELY in place. Sew each sleeve in armhole **(Fig 6).** Sew side and sleeve seams. Weave in all ends.

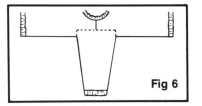

Fig 6

SKI HAT INSTRUCTIONS

Beg at hem with smaller size needles and gray, CO 114 sts loosely. Work in stock st for 3½″, ending by working a knit row. **Next Row (wrong side):** Knit across for turning ridge. Beg with a knit row and work even in stock st for 1″. Continuing in stock st, work stripe sequence as follows: 2 rows black, 6 rows white and 2 rows black. When 10 rows of stripe sequence are completed, continue with gray in stock st until piece measures 10½″ from CO edge, ending by working a purl row.

Shape Top

First Half: Row 1: K2 tog, K 53, K2 tog; sl rem 57 sts to holder for second half to be worked later. **Row 2:** P2 tog, purl to within 2 sts of end, P2 tog = 53 sts. Dec one st each end EVERY row until 9 sts rem. BO all sts.

Second Half: With smaller size needles, sl sts from holder to needle. With knit-side facing you, join gray and work in same manner as First Half.

FINISHING

Weave top and back seam tog, carefully matching stripes. Turn hem to inside and sew LOOSELY in place. Weave in all ends.

26

JACKET SWEATER
for men and women
designed by Mary Thomas
knit-in designs by Carol Wilson Mansfield

This comfortable, zippered jacket sweater can be worked plain, or can be made into a real conversation piece by working in one of our three designs: a horse, a pheasant or a deer.

The designs are worked from a chart, using bobbins. Or, if you prefer, you can work the sweater plain, then embroider the designs in duplicate stitch (see Fig 1).

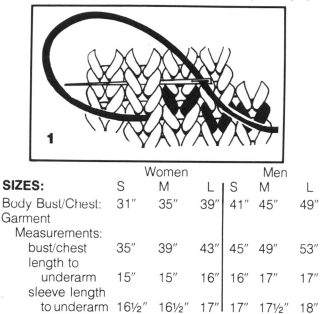

SIZES:	Women			Men		
	S	M	L	S	M	L
Body Bust/Chest:	31"	35"	39"	41"	45"	49"
Garment Measurements:						
bust/chest	35"	39"	43"	45"	49"	53"
length to underarm	15"	15"	16"	16"	17"	17"
sleeve length to underarm	16½"	16½"	17"	17"	17½"	18"

Size Note: Instructions are written for women's sizes in parentheses (Small-Medium-Large) and men's sizes in brackets [Small-Medium-Large].

MATERIALS
Worsted weight yarn: (17-19-21) [22-24-26] oz ecru;

Horse Design	Pheasant Design	Deer Design
½ oz pale yellow	1 oz camel	¼ oz light beige
1 oz medium gold	½ oz rust	1 oz tan
½ oz dark gold	½ oz brown	1 oz medium brown
¼ oz brown	½ oz medium gray	½ oz dark brown
¼ oz medium sage	¼ oz forest green	¼ oz charcoal gray
¼ oz medium blue	¼ oz cardinal	½ oz medium sage
¼ oz light gray		½ oz forest green

Sizes 7 and 8, 14″ straight knitting needles (or size required for gauge)
Size F aluminum crochet hook (for front edging only)
Stitch holders: 2 small and 1 medium
2 Stitch markers
Yarn bobbins (for working knit-in design)
Separating zipper (medium weight): (20-20-22) [22-24-24]″ length

GAUGE: With larger size needles in stock st,
9 sts = 2″; 6 rows = 1″

TWISTED RIBBING PATTERN STITCH
Row 1 (right side): Knit in back lp **(Fig 2)** of first st; * P1, knit in back lp of next st; rep from * across.

Row 2: Purl in back lp **(Fig 3)** of first st; * K1, purl in back lp of next st; rep from * across.

Rep Rows 1 and 2 for patt.

INSTRUCTIONS
Note: Entire sweater, excluding ribbing, is worked in stock st.

Back
With ecru and smaller size needles, CO (79-87-97) [101-111-119] sts. Work in Twisted Ribbing Patt St for 2½", ending by working Row 2. Change to larger size needles; begin stock st. Work even until piece measures (5½-5½-6½) [6½-7½-7½]″ from CO edge, ending by working a knit row. **Next Row:** P (12-16-21) [23-28-32]; place marker for working knit-in design (beg on next row), P 55, place marker; purl rem sts. **Note:** Sl markers on each following row until design is completed.

27

Knit-in Design: Select charted design — deer **(Fig 4** on page 29), horse **(Fig 5** on page 30) or pheasant **(Fig 6** on page 31). Refer to *Multi-Colored Knitting from Charts* on page 18 for instructions on working from charts and techniques on changing or carrying colors. Keeping (12-16-21) [23-28-32] sts at each end in ecru, work selected charted design on center 55 sts (between markers) AND AT THE SAME TIME (while working the design) when piece measures (15-15-16) [16-17-17]″ from CO edge, begin raglan shaping.

Raglan Shaping: BO (5-6-7) [7-8-10] sts at beg of next 2 rows = (69-75-83) [87-95-99] sts. Dec one st at each armhole edge EOR until (23-25-29) [29-31-33] sts rem. Sl rem sts to med holder for back of neck.

POCKET LINING (make 2)
With ecru and larger size needles, CO (29-29-31) [31-33-33] sts. Work in stock st until piece measures (8-8-8½) [8½-9-9]″ from CO edge. BO all sts; set aside.

LEFT FRONT
With ecru and smaller size needles, CO (41-45-49) [51-57-61] sts. Work in Twisted Ribbing Patt St for 2½″, ending by working Row 2. Change to larger size needles.

Row 1 (right side): Knit to last 6 sts; place marker to separate sts of center band and front; * P1, knit in back 1p of next st; rep from * twice more. **Note:** Sl marker on each following row. **Row 2:** * Purl in back 1p of next st, K1; rep from * twice more; purl rem sts. Rep last 2 rows until piece measures 4″ from CO edge, ending by working a wrong-side row.

Next Row (right side): BO 5 sts for beg of side pocket opening; knit to last 6 sts, work in established ribbing across rem sts = (36-40-44) [46-52-56] sts. Work even [keep 6 sts of center band in Twisted Ribbing Patt St and rem sts in stock st] until piece measures (10-10-10½) [10½-11-11]″ from CO edge, ending by working a wrong-side row.

Next Row (right side): CO 5 sts (see *Casting On, Method 2* on page 12) for end of side pocket opening; knit across to last 6 sts, work in established ribbing across rem sts = (41-45-49) [51-57-61] sts. Work even until piece measures same as Back to underarm, ending by working a wrong-side row.

Raglan Shaping: Note: Continue to keep 6 sts of center band in Twisted Ribbing Patt St and rem sts in stock st. BO (5-6-7) [7-8-10] sts at beg of next row for underarm = (36-39-42) [44-49-51] sts. Dec one st at armhole edge EOR until (20-22-24) [24-28-29] sts rem on needle, ending by working a right-side row.

Shape Neck: Continuing to dec one st at armhole edge EOR until 2 sts rem, shape neck as follows. At beg of next row, work across first (6-6-6) [6-8-9] sts and sl these sts to holder for front of neck; then dec one st at neck edge EOR (5-7-8) [7-8-8] times. When 2 sts rem on needle, BO.

Pocket Ribbing: With right side facing and ecru, use smaller size needles and pick up (31-31-33) [33-35-35] sts along pocket opening (between BO and CO sts at side edge). Work in Twisted Ribbing Patt St (beg and end with Row 2) for 1″. BO in ribbing patt. Sew ends of ribbing to front (BO and CO sts of pocket opening). Position pocket lining on front as follows. With knit-side of lining facing purl-side of front and side edge of each piece tog, align top edge ½″ above CO sts of pocket opening and bottom edge along top of bottom ribbing. Sew lining in place, leaving side edge open between BO and CO sts of pocket opening.

RIGHT FRONT
Work same as Left Front until 2½″ of ribbing are completed, ending by working Row 2. Change to larger size needles. **Row 1 (right side):** * Knit in back 1p of next st, P1; rep from * twice more; place marker to separate sts of center band and front; knit rem sts. **Note:** Sl marker on each following row. **Row 2:** Purl to last 6 sts; * K1, purl in back 1p of next st; rep from * twice more. Rep last 2 rows until piece measures 4″ from CO edge, ending by working a right-side row.

Next Row (wrong side): BO 5 sts for beg of side pocket opening; purl to last 6 sts, work in established ribbing across rem sts = (36-40-44) [46-52-56] sts. Work even [keep 6 sts of center band in Twisted Ribbing Patt St and rem sts in stock st] until piece measures (10-10-10½) [10½-11-11]″ from CO edge, ending by working a right-side row.

Next Row (wrong side): CO 5 sts for end of side pocket opening; purl across to last 6 sts, work in established ribbing across rem sts = (41-45-49) [51-57-61] sts. Work even until piece measures same as Left Front to underarm, ending by working a right-side row.

Raglan Shaping: Note: Continue to keep 6 sts of center band in Twisted Ribbing Patt St and rem sts in stock st. BO (5-6-7) [7-8-10] sts at beg of next row for underarm = (36-39-42) [44-49-51] sts. Dec one st at armhole edge EOR until (20-22-24) [24-28-29] sts rem on needle, ending by working a wrong-side row. Complete front in same manner as Left Front (beg with *Shape Neck* instructions).

SLEEVE (make 2)
With ecru and smaller size needles, CO (37-41-43) [45-47-49] sts. Work in Twisted Ribbing Patt St for 3″, increasing across last row [Row 2 of ribbing] (8-8-10) [12-12-14] sts evenly spaced = (45-49-53) [57-59-63] sts. Change to larger size needles; begin stock st. Work (8-8-8) [8-6-6] rows even. Inc one st at each end of *next* row and then each following (8-8-8) [8-6-6]th row, (6-7-8) [8-10-12] times more = (59-65-71) [75-81-89] sts. Work even until sleeve measures (16½-16½-17) [17-17½-18]″ from CO edge or desired length to underarm, ending by working a purl row.

Raglan Shaping: BO (5-6-7) [7-8-10] sts at beg of next 2 rows = (49-53-57) [61-65-69] sts. Dec one st at each end EOR until 3 sts rem. BO rem sts.

continued on Page 32

28

Fig 4

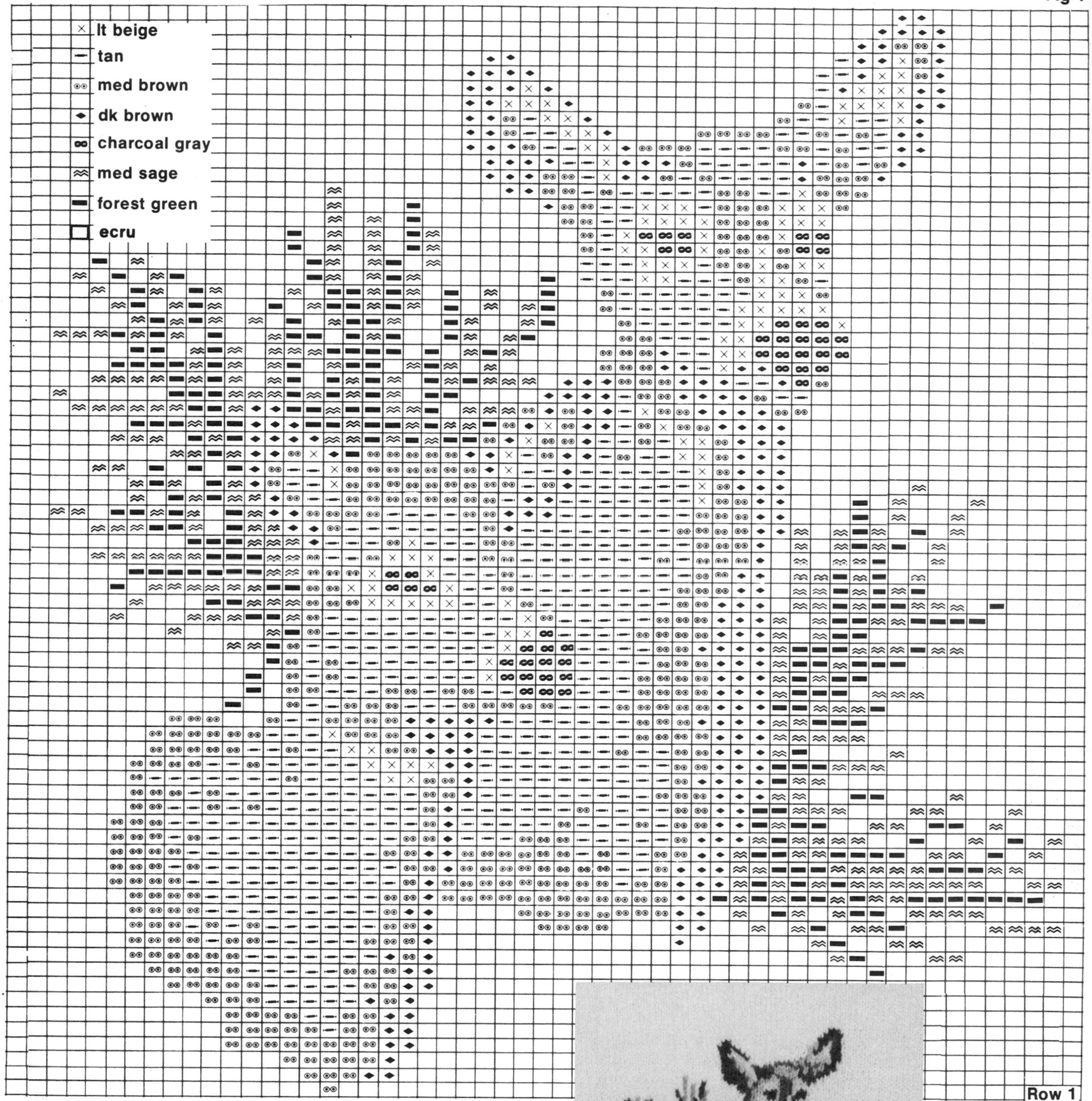

	lt beige
×	lt beige
−	tan
∞	med brown
◆	dk brown
∞	charcoal gray
≋	med sage
▬	forest green
□	ecru

center stitch ●

Row 1

Fig 5

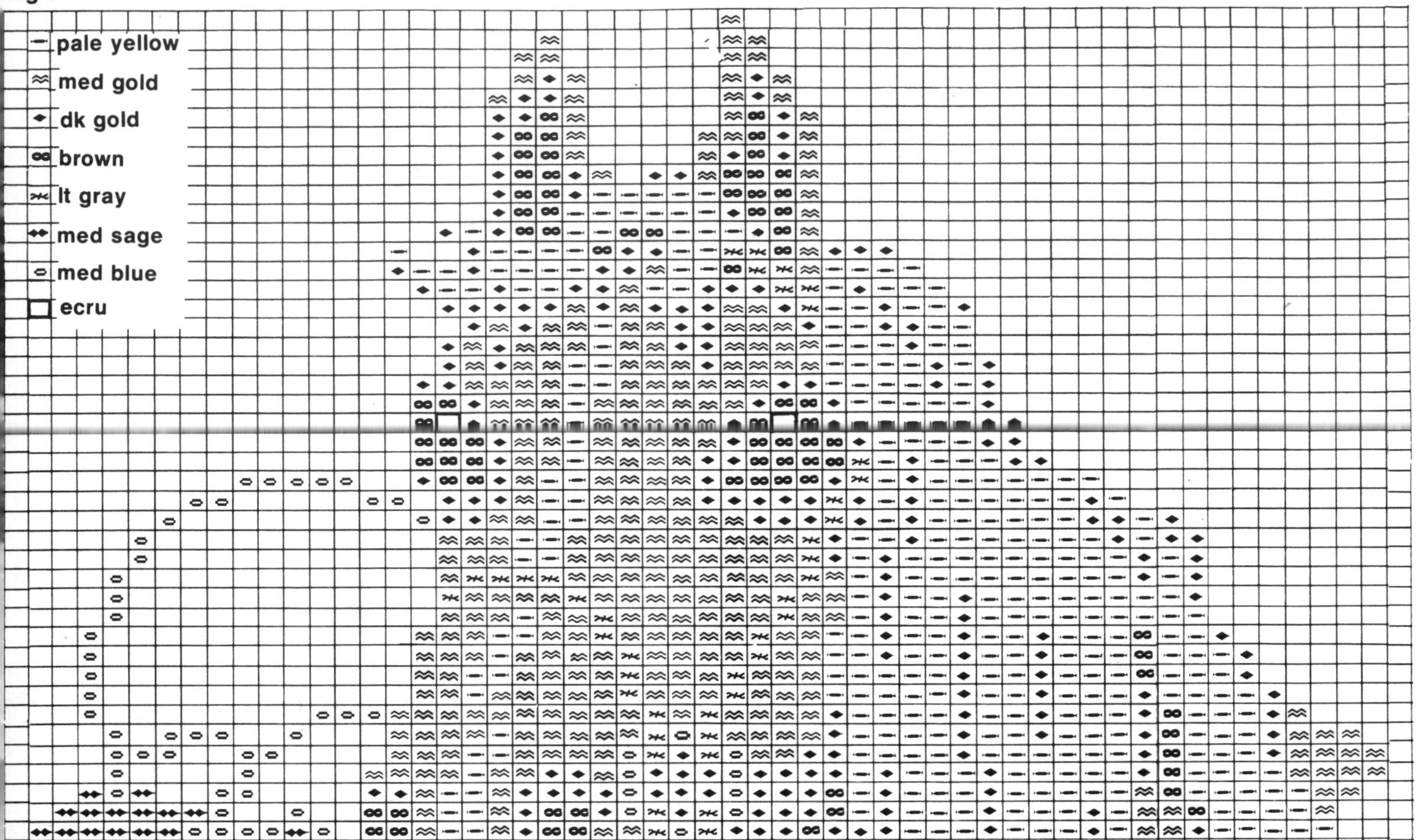

Legend:
- − pale yellow
- ≈ med gold
- ◆ dk gold
- ∞ brown
- ✂ lt gray
- ◆◆ med sage
- ⊘ med blue
- ☐ ecru

Row 1

● center stitch

30

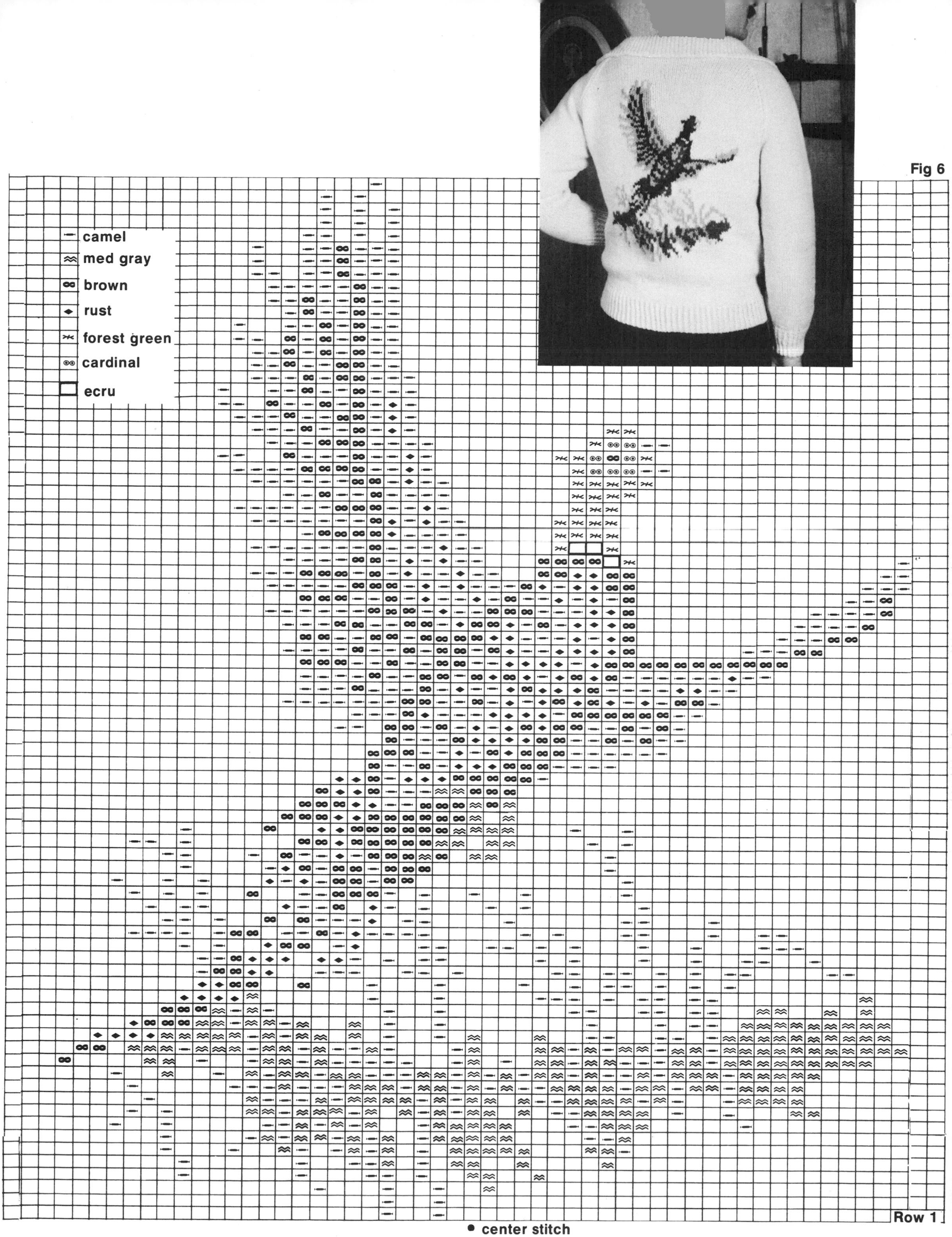

Fig 6

Legend:
- — camel
- ≋ med gray
- ∞ brown
- ◆ rust
- ⋈ forest green
- ⊚⊚ cardinal
- ☐ ecru

● center stitch

Row 1

31

FINISHING

On padded ironing board, place back right side down. Using a press cloth, steam area of knit-in design to help stitches lie flat. Leave on board until completely dry. Sew sleeves to front and back at armholes, carefully matching decreases of raglan shaping. Sew sleeve and side seams, completing pocket by sewing rem side edge of pocket lining (between BO and CO sts of pocket opening) to back.

Collar: With right side facing, beg at right front center neck edge. With ecru and smaller size needles, sl (6-6-6) [6-8-9] sts from holder to needle, work in established ribbing across these sts; pick up (22-24-26) [26-28-28] sts along right front neck shaping and top edge of right sleeve; sl (23-25-29) [29-31-33] sts from back holder to free needle and knit across these sts; pick up (22-24-26) [26-28-28] sts along top edge of left sleeve and left front neck shaping; sl (6-6-6) [6-8-9] sts from holder to free needle and work in established ribbing across these sts = (79-85-93) [93-103-107] sts. **Note:** On next row, 6 sts of each center band will reverse in Twisted Ribbing Patt St. Work in Twisted Ribbing Patt St (beg with Row 1) for 4 rows. Change to larger size needles; continue in ribbing for 5 more rows. **Inc Row:** (**Note:** Wrong side of collar; right side of sweater.) Maintaining Twisted Ribbing Patt St, work across first (20-22-24) [24-26-28] sts; * purl in BACK and then in front of next st (inc made); knit in FRONT and then in back of next st (inc made); rep from * (19-20-22) [22-25-25] times more; work across rem sts = (119-127-139) [139-155-159] sts. Continuing in Twisted Ribbing Patt St (beg with Row 1), work until collar measures 4½" from neck edge, ending by working Row 2. BO all sts in ribbing patt. Weave in all ends.

With crochet hook and ecru, work single crochets evenly spaced (approx one st EOR) along each center front edge to collar (see *Crocheted Edging* on page 16). Then sew zipper in place using sewing thread (see *Inserting Zipper* on page 15).

SKI SWEATER
and HAT
designed by Mary Thomas

SIZES:

	Small	Medium	Large
Body Bust:	31"	35"	39"
Garment Measurements:			
bust	35"	39"	43"
length to underarm	15½"	16"	16½"
sleeve length	21"	22"	22½"

Size Note: Instructions are written for sizes as follows: Small(Medium-Large).

MATERIALS
Worsted weight yarn:
   20(23-26) oz burnt orange;
   2 oz yellow-orange;
   1 oz white
Sizes 4 and 7, 14" straight knitting needles (or sizes required for gauge)
2 Small stitch holders
Materials Note: Yarn requirements include 3 oz burnt orange for hat.
GAUGE: With smaller size needles in ribbing,
7½ sts = 1"; 8 rows = 1"
With larger size needles in stock st,
5 sts = 1"; 7 rows = 1"

PULLOVER INSTRUCTIONS
Note: Entire sweater, excluding ribbing, is worked in stock st.

BACK
With yellow-orange and smaller size needles, CO 104(116-128) sts. **Ribbing Stripes:** Work in K1, P1 ribbing with color sequence of 2 rows each yellow-orange, burnt orange and yellow-orange. When 6 rows of ribbing stripes have been completed, continue with burnt orange in K1, P1 ribbing until piece measures 2" from CO edge.
Dec Row: *(K1, P1) twice, P2 tog; rep from * across to last 2 sts; K1, P1 = 87(97-107) sts. Change to larger size needles; begin stock st.

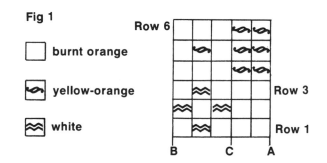

Fig 1

	burnt orange
	yellow-orange
	white

Knit-in Design: Work the next 21 rows from chart in **Fig 1** as follows. Work Rows 1 through 6, 3 times; then work Rows 1 through 3 once more. On knit rows (odd-numbered rows of chart), * work chart from A to B; rep from * across, ending by working from A to C. On purl rows (even-numbered rows of chart), work chart from C to A once, then * work from B to A; rep from * across. To join a new color, change colors and carry color not in use, see *Multi-Colored Knitting From Charts on page* 18 .

When 21 rows of design are completed, continue with burnt orange and work until piece measures 15½(16-16½)" from CO edge or desired length to underarm, ending by working a purl row.

Shape Armholes: BO 5(6-8) sts at beg of next 2 rows = 77(85-91) sts. Work even until armhole measures 7½(8¼-8¾)", ending by working a purl row.

Shape Neck and Shoulders: Row 1: BO 6(7-7) sts, knit *next* [do not count st already on needle] 22(24-26) sts; K 19(21-23) and sl these sts to holder for back of neck; knit rem 29(32-34) sts. **Row 2:** BO 6(7-7) sts; purl to neck edge, drop yarn; join new ball of burnt orange at right neck edge, BO 2 sts, purl rem sts. **Row 3:** BO 6(7-7) sts, knit to neck edge; BO 2 sts at left neck edge, knit rem sts. Working across both sides of neck opening, continue to dec 2 sts EOR at each neck edge twice more AND AT THE SAME TIME BO 6(7-7) sts at beg of next row; BO 6(6-7) sts at beg of next 2 rows; BO 5(6-7) sts at beg of next 2 rows.

FRONT
Follow instructions for Back until armhole measures 6½(7¼-7¾)", or 1" less than armhole of Back, ending by working a purl row.

Shape Neck and Shoulders: Row 1: K 31(34-36); K 15(17-19) and sl these sts to holder for front of neck; knit rem sts. **Row 2:** Purl to within 2 sts of neck edge, P2 tog, drop yarn; join another ball of burnt orange at left neck edge, P2 tog, purl rem sts. Continue working across both sides of neck opening as follows. Dec one st at each neck edge: EVERY row 5 times; then EOR twice AND AT THE SAME TIME when armhole measures same as Back to shoulder, BO from each armhole edge: 6(7-7) sts twice; 6(6-7) sts once; 5(6-7) sts once.

SLEEVE (MAKE 2)

With yellow-orange and smaller size needles, CO 46(46-50) sts. Work Ribbing Stripes same as Back. When 6 rows of ribbing stripes have been completed, continue with burnt orange in K1, P1 ribbing until piece measures 2½″ from CO edge. **Inc Row:** K1, P1; * inc in next st, P1; K1, P1; rep from * across = 57(57-62) sts. Change to larger size needles; begin stock st.

Knit-in Design: Work design same as Back. When 21 rows of design are completed, continue with burnt orange and work as follows. Inc one st at each end of next row and then EVERY following 8(6-6)th row, 8(12-12) times = 75(83-88) sts. Work even until sleeve measures 21(22-22½)″ from CO edge or desired length. BO all sts *loosely*.

FINISHING

Block pieces to measurements. Sew right shoulder seam.

Neckband: With right side facing, beg at left front neck edge. Using smaller size needles and burnt orange, pick up 20 sts along left front neck shaping; K 15(17-19) from front neck holder; pick up 20 sts along right front neck shaping to shoulder seam; pick up 10 sts along right back neck shaping; K 19(21-23) from back neck holder; pick up 10 sts along left back neck shaping = 94(98-102) sts. Work in K1, P1 ribbing for 1″. Then work Ribbing Stripes same as Back. When 6 rows of ribbing stripes have been completed, continue with burnt orange in K1, P1 ribbing until ribbing measures 3″ from neck edge. Change to larger size needles, work one more row in ribbing. BO *loosely* in ribbing.

Sew left shoulder seam and weave ends of neckband tog. Fold neckband in half to inside and sew VERY LOOSELY in place. Sew each sleeve in armhole **(Fig 2)**. Sew side and sleeve seams. Weave in all ends.

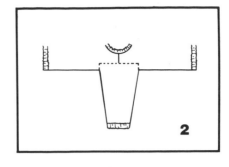

HAT INSTRUCTIONS

With burnt orange and larger size needles, CO 92 sts *loosely*. Work in K1, P1 ribbing in the following stripe sequence: 8 rows burnt orange; 2 rows yellow-orange; 2 rows burnt orange; 2 rows yellow-orange and 6 rows burnt orange. When 20 rows of stripe sequence are completed, continue with burnt orange; begin stock st.

Knit-in Design: Work same as Back. When 21 rows of design are completed, continue with burnt orange and work until piece measures 8″ from CO edge, ending by working a purl row.

Shape Top: Row 1: K2; * K2 tog, K1; rep from * across = 62 sts. **Rows 2 through 6:** Beg with a purl row and work 5 rows even in stock st. **Row 7:** * K2 tog; rep from * across = 31 sts. Cut yarn, leaving 24″ sewing length.

FINISHING

Thread sewing length into tapestry or yarn needle; draw through rem sts twice. Draw up tightly and fasten securely. Then sew side seam, carefully matching rows of design. Weave in all ends. **Pompon:** With each color used in hat, make 3″ diameter pompon (see *Pompon* instructions on page 17). Attach securely to top of hat.

FISHERMAN
CARDIGAN for women
designed by Evie Rosen, Knitting Nook, Wausau, WI

This beautiful sweater, which we recommend only for the experienced knitter, is an authentic adaptation of those worn by fishermen from the villages of the Aran Islands off the west coast of Ireland.

Their wives and mothers knit these sweaters, of thick natural sheep's wool, with traditional stitches which relate to the daily lives of the fishing villages.

Cables represent the ropes used at seas; diamonds, the mesh of fishing nets; ribbed stitches depict rows of grain, and seed stitch, the seed itself. There are also textured "berry' stitches, stitches relating to waves and anchors, and most sweaters included at least one stitch representing faith (such as Trinity stitch).

SIZES:	Petite	Small	Medium	Large
Body Bust:	31"	34"	37"	40"
Garment Measurements:				
bust	33"	36"	39"	42"
length to underarm	16"	16"	16½"	17"
sleeve length to underarm	17"	17"	17½"	18"

Size Note: Instructions are written for sizes as follows: Petite (Small-Medium-Large).

MATERIALS
Worsted weight yarn: 20(24-28-32) oz ecru
Sizes 5 and 7, 14" straight knitting needles (or size required for gauge).
Cable needle
Stitch holders: 2 small
7 Buttons (5/8" diameter)
GAUGE: With larger size needles in stock st,
        5 sts = 1"; 7 rows = 1"

PATTERN STITCHES
Moss Stitch (worked on even number of sts)
Rows 1 and 2: * K1, P1; rep from * across.
Rows 3 and 4: * P1, K1; rep from * across.
Rep Rows 1 through 4 for patt.

Mock Cable (worked on 3 sts)
Row 1: K2; with yarn in *back* of work, sl 1 as to purl.
Row 2: With yarn in *front* of work, sl 1 as to purl; P2.
Row 3 (cable twist row): With yarn in **back** of work, sl next 2 sts as to purl to right-hand needle; drop next st (sl st) off left-hand needle to **front** of work; sl the 2 sts from right-hand needle back onto left-hand needle; pick up dropped st and place back onto left-hand needle; now knit these 3 sts.
Row 4: Purl.
Rep Rows 1 through 4 for patt.

Basket Cable (worked on 16 or 32 sts)
Rows 1 and 3: Knit.
Rows 2 and 4: Purl.

Row 5 (cable twist row): * Sl next 4 sts onto cable needle and hold at **front** of work; knit next 4 sts, then K4 from cable needle; rep from * across.
Rows 6, 8 and 10; Purl.
Rows 7 and 9: Knit.
Row 11 (cable twist row): K4; * sl next 4 sts onto cable needle and hold at **back** of work; knit next 4 sts, then K4 from cable needle; rep from * to last 4 sts, K4.
Row 12: Purl.
Rep Rows 1 through 12 for patt.

Little Plait Cable (worked on 6 sts)
Row 1 (cable twist row): Sl next 2 sts onto cable needle and hold at **front** of work; knit next 2 sts, then K2 from cable needle; K2.
Row 2: Purl.
Row 3 (cable twist row): K2, sl next 2 sts onto cable needle and hold at **back** of work; knit next 2 sts, then K2 from cable needle.
Row 4: Purl.
Rep Rows 1 through 4 for patt.

Plaid Lattice (worked on 14 sts)

Row 1: KI through back lp *(hereafter abbreviated K1-b)*, P4; sl next 2 sts onto cable needle and hold at **front** of work; knit next 2 sts, then K2 from cable needle; P4, KI-b.
Row 2: P1, K4; P4, K4, P1.
Row 3: SINGLE FRONT CROSS (abbreviated SFC) [*to work SFC: sl next st onto cable needle and hold at **front** of work; purl next st, then KI-b from cable needle = SFC made*]; P2; BACK CROSS (abbreviated BC) [*to work BC: sl next st onto cable needle and hold at **back** of work; knit next 2 sts, then P1 from cable needle = BC made*]; FRONT CROSS (abbreviated FC) [*to work FC: sl next 2 sts onto cable needle and hold at **front** of work; purl next st, then K2 from cable needle = FC made*]; P2; SINGLE BACK CROSS (abbreviated SBC) [*to work SBC: sl next st onto cable needle and hold at **back** of work; KI-b, then P1 from cable needle = SBC made*].
Row 4: K1, P1; (K2, P2) twice; K2, P1, K1.
Row 5: P1, SFC; BC, P2, FC, SBC, P1.
Row 6: K2, P3, K4, P3, K2.
Row 7: P2; BACK KNIT CROSS (abbreviated BKC) [*to work BKC: sl next st onto cable needle and hold at **back** of work; knit next 2 sts, then KI-b from cable needle = BKC made*]; P4; FRONT KNIT CROSS (abbreviated FKC) [*to work FKC: sl next 2 sts onto cable needle and hold at **front** of work; KI-b, then K2 from cable needle = FKC made*]; P2.
Row 8: Rep Row 6.
Row 9: P1, BC; SFC, P2, SBC; FC, P1.
Row 10: K1, P2, (K2, P1) twice; K2, P2, K1.
Row 11: BC, P2; SFC, SBC; P2, FC.
Row 12: P2, (K4, P2) twice.
Row 13: K2, P4, sl next st onto cable needle and hold at **front** of work; KI-b, then KI-b from cable needle; P4, K2.
Row 14: Rep Row 12.
Row 15: FC, P2; SBC, SFC; P2, BC.
Row 16: Rep Row 10.
Row 17: P1, FC; SBC, P2, SFC; BC, P1.
Row 18: Rep Row 6.
Row 19: P2, FKC; P4, BKC; P2.
Row 20: Rep Row 6.
Row 21: P1, SBC; FC, P2, BC; SFC, P1.
Row 22: Rep Row 4.
Row 23: SBC, P2; FC, BC; P2, SFC.
Row 24: Rep Row 2.
Rep Rows 1 through 24 for patt.

INSTRUCTIONS

BACK
With smaller size needles, CO 102(110-118-126) sts *loosely*. Work 14 rows in K1, P1, ribbing; increasing 10 sts evenly spaced across last row of ribbing = 112(120-128-136) sts. Change to larger size needles and establish patterns as follows.

Row 1 (right side): [*Note: Work Row 1 of each Patt St.*] **Moss St: 4(6-6-8) sts;** P2(2-3-3); **Little Plait Cable: 6 sts;** P2(3-3-3); **Mock Cable: 3 sts;** P2(2-3-4); **Plaid Lattice: 14 sts;** P2(2-3-4); **Mock Cable: 3 sts;** P2(3-4-4); **Basket Cable: 32 sts;** P2(3-4-4); **Mock Cable: 3 sts;** P2(2-3-4); **Plaid Lattice: 14 sts;** P2(2-3-4); **Mock Cable: 3 sts;** P2(3-3-3); **Little Plait Cable: 6 sts;** P2(3-3-3); **Moss St: 4(6-6-8) sts.**

Row 2: [*Note: Work Row 2 of each Patt St.*] **Moss St: 4(6-6-8) sts;** K2(3-3-3); **Little Plait Cable: 6 sts;** K2(3-3-3); **Mock Cable: 3 sts;** K2(2-3-4); **Plaid Lattice: 14 sts;** K2(2-3-4); **Mock Cable: 3 sts;** K2(3-4-4); **Basket Cable: 32 sts;** K2(3-4-4); **Mock Cable: 3 sts;** K2(2-3-4); **Plaid Lattice: 14 sts;** K2(2-3-4); **Mock Cable: 3 sts;** K2(3-3-3); **Little Plait Cable: 6 sts;** K2(3-3-3); **Moss St: 4(6-6-8) sts.**

Work even in patterns as established until piece measures 16(16-16½-17)" from CO edge, ending by working a wrong-side row.

Shape Armholes: Keeping continuity of patterns, BO 6(8-9-11) sts at beg of next 2 rows = 100(104-110-114) sts. Dec one st at each armhole edge EOR 6 times = 88(92-98-102) sts. Work even until armhole measures 8(8½-9-9½)", ending by working a wrong-side row.

Shape Shoulders: Keeping continuity of patterns, BO 10(10-11-11) sts at beg of next 4 rows; BO 9(10-10-11) sts at beg of next 2 rows; BO rem 30(32-34-36) sts for back of neck.

LEFT FRONT
With smaller size needles, CO 59(63-67-71) sts *loosely*.

Ribbing Row 1 (right side): * K1, P1; rep from * to last st, K1. **Ribbing Row 2:** P1; * K1, P1; rep from * across. Rep last 2 rows until 14 rows of ribbing have been completed, increasing 5 sts evenly spaced over *rem* 51(55-59-63) sts on last row of ribbing = 64(68-72-76) sts. Change to larger size needles and establish patterns as follows.

Row 1 (right side): [*Note: Work Row 1 of each Patt St.*] **Moss St: 4(6-6-8) sts;** P2(2-3-3); **Little Plait Cable: 6 sts;** P2(3-3-3); **Mock Cable: 3 sts;** P2(2-3-4); **Plaid Lattice: 14 sts;** P2(2-3-4); **Mock Cable: 3 sts;** P2(3-4-4); **Basket Cable: 16 sts;** (P1, K1) 4 times for front band.

Row 2: [*Note: Work Row 2 of each Patt St.*] (P1, K1) 4 times; **Basket Cable: 16 sts;** K2(3-4-4); **Mock Cable: 3 sts;** K2(2-3-4); **Plaid Lattice: 14 sts;** K2(2-3-4); **Mock Cable: 3 sts;** K2(3-3-3); **Little Plait Cable: 6 sts;** K2(2-3-3); **Moss St: 4(6-6-8) sts.**

Keeping 8 sts of front band in ribbing and rem sts in patterns as established, work even until piece measures same as Back to underarm, ending by working a wrong-side row.

Shape Neck, Armhole and Shoulder: [*Note: Keep continuity of patterns and 8 sts of front band in ribbing.*]

Next Row: BO 6(8-9-11) sts for underarm; work across to last 10 sts; K2 tog *(neck decrease);* work across rem 8 sts of band = 57(59-62-64) sts.
Dec one st at armhole edge EOR 6 times AND AT THE SAME TIME continue to dec one st EVERY 4th row at inside edge of band (as before) for neck shaping. Continue to dec one st EVERY 4th row for neck shaping until there are a total of 15(16-17-18) neck decreases AND AT THE SAME TIME when armhole measures same as Back to shoulder, BO from armhole edge as follows: 10(10-11-11) sts twice; 9(10-10-11) sts once. Continuing on rem 8 sts of band, work in ribbing as established for 2¼(2¼-2½-2½)" more. SI sts to holder.
Measure and mark positions on band for 7 buttons evenly spaced, with first button 4 rows above bottom edge and last button at first neck decrease.

RIGHT FRONT

Work same as Left Front until 4 rows of ribbing have been completed. **Buttonhole Row 1:** K1, P1, BO next 3 sts; work in ribbing as established across rem sts. **Buttonhole Row 2:** Work in ribbing as established to BO sts; CO 3 sts (see *Casting On, Method 2* on page 12); K1, P1. Continue in ribbing as established until 14 rows have been completed, increasing 5 sts evenly spaced over *first* 51(55-59-63) sts on last row of ribbing = 64(68-72-76) sts. Change to larger size needles and establish patterns as follows.

Row 1 (right side): [*Note: Work Row 1 of each Patt St.*] (K1, P1) 4 times for front band; **Basket Cable: 16 sts;** P2(3-4-4); **Mock Cable: 3 sts;** P2(2-3-4); **Plaid Lattice: 14 sts;** P2(2-3-4); **Mock Cable: 3 sts;** P2(3-3-3); **Little Plait Cable: 6 sts;** P2(2-3-3); **Moss St: 4(6-6-8) sts.**

Row 2: [*Note: Work Row 2 of each Patt St.*] **Moss St: 4(6-6-8) sts;** K2(2-3-3); **Little Plait Cable: 6 sts;** K2(3-3-3); **Mock Cable: 3 sts;** K2(2-3-4); **Plaid Lattice: 14 sts;** K2(2-3-4); **Mock Cable: 3 sts;** K2(3-4-4); **Basket Cable: 16 sts;** (K1, P1) 4 times.

Keeping 8 sts of front band in ribbing and rem sts in patterns as established, work even until piece measures same as Back to underarm, ending by working a wrong-side row AND AT THE SAME TIME work buttonholes at marked intervals in same manner as first buttonhole.

Shape Neck, Armhole and Shoulder: [*Note: Keep continuity of patterns and 8 sts of front band in ribbing.*]

Row 1: Work across 8 sts of front band; sl 1 as to knit, K1, PSSO *(neck decrease);* work across rem sts. **Row 2:** BO 6(8-9-11) sts for underarm; work across rem sts = 57(59-62-64) sts. Complete in same manner as Left Front.

SLEEVE (make 2)

With smaller size needles, CO 46(50-54-54) sts *loosely.* Work in K1, P1 ribbing for 2½", increasing 16 sts evenly spaced across last row of ribbing = 62(66-70-70) sts. Change to larger size needles and establish patterns as follows.

Row 1 (right side): [*Note: Work Row 1 of each Patt St.*] P2; **Plaid Lattice: 14 sts;** P2(3-4-4); **Mock Cable: 3 sts;** P2(3-4-4); **Basket Cable: 16 sts;** P2(3-4-4); **Mock Cable: 3 sts;** P2(3-4-4); **Plaid Lattice: 14 sts;** P2.

Row 2: [*Note: Work Row 2 of each Patt St.*] K2; **Plaid Lattice: 14 sts;** K2(3-4-4); **Mock Cable: 3 sts;** K2(3-4-4); **Basket Cable: 16 sts;** K2(3-4-4); **Mock Cable: 3 sts;** K2(3-4-4); **Plaid Lattice: 14 sts;** K2.

Keeping patterns as established and working increased sts in Moss St, inc one st at each end EVERY 6th row, 10(12-13-15) times = 82(90-96-100) sts. Work even until sleeve measures 17(17-17½-18)", ending by working a wrong-side row.

Shape Cap: [*Note: Keep continuity of patterns.*] BO 6(8-9-11) sts at beg of next 2 rows = 70(74-78-78) sts. Dec one st at each end EOR until 40(42-44-42) sts rem. Then BO 4 sts at beg of next 6 rows; BO rem 16(18-20-18) sts.

FINISHING

Sew shoulder seams. Sew sleeve caps into armholes, placing center of cap at shoulder seam. Sew side and sleeve seams. Weave sts on front band holders tog; then sew band to back neck edge. Sew on buttons. Weave in all ends.

U-NECK PULLOVER
VEST
designed by Mary Thomas and Barbara Retzke
Pattern is written in two versions—solid color vest and
vest with an argyle design on the front.

SIZES
Body Bust: 32″ 34″ 36″ 38″ 40″ 42″
Garment Measurements:
   bust   34″ 36″ 38″ 40″ 42″ 44″
   length to underarm 15″ 15″ 15″ 15″ 15″ 15″
Size Note: Instructions are written for bust sizes as fol-
lows: 32(34-36-38-40-42)″.
MATERIALS
Worsted weight yarn:
   For Solid Color Vest: 10(11-12-13-14-15) oz camel
   For Argyle Vest:
      7(8-9-10-11-12) oz light beige heather;
      1 oz camel;
      2 oz brown;
      2 oz green
**Sizes 4 and 7, 14″ straight knitting needles (or sizes
   required for gauge)**
**Size 4, 24″ circular knitting needle (or size required
   for gauge)**
2 Small stitch holders
For Argyle Vest Only: 13(13-17-17-17-17) yarn bobbins

GAUGE: With smaller size needles in ribbing,
              7½ sts = 1″; 8 rows = 1″
       With larger size needles in stock st,
              5 sts = 1″; 7 rows = 1″

SOLID COLOR VEST INSTRUCTIONS
Note: Entire vest, excluding ribbing, is worked in stock
st.

FRONT
With smaller size straight needles, CO 92(98-102-108-
112-118) sts. Work in K1, P1 ribbing for 1½″. **Dec Row:**
* (K1, P1) 5(5-6-6-6-7) times, P2 tog; rep from * 6 times
more, ending (K1, P1) 4(7-2-5-7-3) times = 85(91-95-101-
105-111) sts. Change to larger size straight needles;
begin stock st. Work even until piece measures 14″ from
CO edge, or 1″ less than desired length to underarm
[armhole band allowance], ending by working a purl row.

Shape Neck and Armholes: Row 1: BO 5(7-7-8-8-9) sts,
knit *next* [do not count st already on needle] 29(30-31-
33-34-36) sts; K 15(15-17-17-19-19) and sl these sts to
holder for front of neck; knit rem 35(38-39-42-43-46) sts.

Row 2: BO 5(7-7-8-8-9) sts, purl to within 2 sts of neck
edge, P2 tog, drop yarn; join new ball of yarn at left neck
edge, P2 tog, purl rem sts. Continue to work across both
sides as follows. Dec one st at each armhole edge *and* at
each neck edge EVERY row 6 times = 17(18-19-21-22-24)
sts each side. Then dec one st at each armhole edge
EOR 2(2-3-4-4-5) times AND AT THE SAME TIME dec one
st at each neck edge EOR 4 times = 11(12-12-13-14-15)
sts each side. Work even until armhole measures 9(9¼-
9½-9¾-10¼-10¾)″, ending by working a purl row.

Shape Shoulders: BO at each armhole edge as follows:
6(6-6-6-7-8) sts once; 5(6-6-7-7-7) sts once.

BACK
With smaller size straight needles, CO 92(96-102-106-
112-116) sts. Work in K1, P1 ribbing for 1½″. **Dec Row:**
* (K1, P1) 5(5-6-6-6-7) times, P2 tog; rep from * 6 times
more, ending (K1, P1) 4(6-2-4-7-2) times = 85(89-95-99-
105-109) sts. Change to larger size straight needles;
begin stock st. Work even until piece measures same as
Front to underarm, ending by working a purl row.

Shape Armholes: BO 5(6-7-7-8-8) sts at beg of next 2
rows = 75(77-81-85-89-93) sts. Dec one st at each armhole edge EVERY row 6 times = 63(65-69-73-77-81) sts.
Then dec one st at each armhole edge EOR 2(2-3-4-4-5)
times more = 59(61-63-65-69-71) sts. Work even until
armhole measures 8(8¼-8½-8¾-9¼-9¾)″, or 1″ less than
armhole of Front, ending by working a purl row.

Shape Neck and Shoulders: K 17(18-18-19-20-21); knit
next 25(25-27-27-29-29) sts and sl these sts to holder for
back of neck; knit rem sts. Working across both sides
(join new ball of yarn to work right shoulder), BO 2 sts at
each neck edge EOR 3 times = 11(12-12-13-14-15) sts
each side. Beg with a knit row, BO at each armhole edge
for shoulder as follows: 6(6-6-6-7-8) sts once; 5(6-6-7-7-7)
sts once.

FINISHING
Block pieces to measurements. Sew shoulder seams.

Neckband: With right side facing, beg at left shoulder
seam. Using circular needle, pick up 63(65-67-69-72-75)
sts along left front neck shaping; K 15(15-17-17-19-19) sts
from front neck holder; pick up 63(65-67-69-72-75) sts
along right front neck shaping to shoulder seam; pick up
12 sts along right back neck shaping; K 25(25-27-27-
29-29) sts from back neck holder; pick up 12 sts along left
back neck shaping = 190(194-202-206-216-222) sts. Join
and work K1, P1 ribbing in rnds for 1½″. BO *loosely* in
ribbing. Sew side seams.

Armhole Band (make 2): With right side facing, beg at
side seam. Using circular needle, pick up 126(130-134-
138-144-150) sts around armhole edge. Join and work K1,
P1 ribbing in rnds for 1″. BO *loosely* in ribbing. Weave in
all ends.

38

ARGYLE VEST INSTRUCTIONS

Note: Any adjustment in length to underarm, must be made in bottom ribbing only.

FRONT

With beige, follow instructions for Front of Solid Color Vest until ribbing and Dec Row have been completed = 85(91-95-101-105-111) sts. Change to larger size straight needles and stock st; begin argyle design.

Argyle Design: Design is worked from chart in **Fig 1** (see *Multi-Colored Knitting from Charts* on page 18). Separate bobbins are used for each color change; wind bobbins of yarn as follows: 6(6-8-8-8-8) camel; 1(1-3-3-3-3) brown; 4 beige and 2 green. To join a new color, tie it to the prev color with a knot right up against the needle, leaving approx 4″ end for weaving later. When changing colors, always bring the color you have just used over and to the left of the color you are going to use, bringing the new color up from underneath. This twists the two colors and prevents a hole in your work (see page 18).

Work **Row 1 of Chart** as follows:

SIZE 32 ONLY: With first beige bobbin, K 13; join first green bobbin, K1; join 2nd beige bobbin, K 13; join first camel bobbin, K1; join 2nd camel bobbin, K1; continue with 2nd beige bobbin, K 13; join brown bobbin, K1; join 3rd beige bobbin, K 13; join 3rd camel bobbin, K1; join 4th camel bobbin, K1; continue with 3rd beige bobbin, K 13; join 2nd green bobbin, K1; join 4th beige bobbin, K 13. **Note:** On next row, join 5th camel bobbin at beg of row and 6th camel bobbin at end of row.

SIZE 34 ONLY: With first beige bobbin, K1; join first camel bobbin, K2; continue with first beige bobbin, K 13; join first green bobbin, K1; join 2nd beige bobbin, K 13; join 2nd camel bobbin, K1; join 3rd camel bobbin, K1; continue with 2nd beige bobbin, K 13; join brown bobbin, K1; join 3rd beige bobbin, K 13; join 4th camel bobbin, K1; join 5th camel bobbin, K1; continue with 3rd beige bobbin, K 13; join 2nd green bobbin, K1; join 4th beige bobbin, K 13; join 6th camel bobbin, K2; continue with 4th beige bobbin, K1. **Note:** On Rows 14, 15 and 16, additional bobbins are not required, use a 12″ length of brown yarn to work sts at each end of these rows.

SIZES 36(38-40-42): With first beige bobbin, K3(6-8-11); join first camel bobbin, K1; join 2nd camel bobbin, K1; continue with first beige bobbin, K 13; join first green bobbin, K1; join 2nd beige bobbin, K 13; join 3rd camel bobbin, K1; join 4th camel bobbin, K1; continue with 2nd beige bobbin, K 13; join first brown bobbin, K1; join 3rd beige bobbin, K 13; join 5th camel bobbin, K1; join 6th camel bobbin, K1; continue with 3rd beige bobbin, K 13; join 2nd green bobbin, K1; join 4th beige bobbin, K 13; join 7th camel bobbin, K1; join 8th camel bobbin, K1; continue with 4th beige bobbin, K3(6-8-11). **Note:** On Row 12 (9-7-4), join 2nd and 3rd brown bobbins at beg and end of row.

ALL SIZES: Beg with Row 2 of chart and work through Row 58; then work Rows 1 through 29 of chart once more. When 87 rows of argyle design have been completed, finish off all bobbins and continue with beige only. Purl next row. Then complete front by following instructions for Front of Solid Color Vest (beg with Shape Neck and Armholes). Weave in all ends, being careful to weave each end into back of sts of matching color. Examine sts of argyle design to be sure they are uniform and in correct position.

BACK AND FINISHING

With beige, work same as Solid Color Vest.

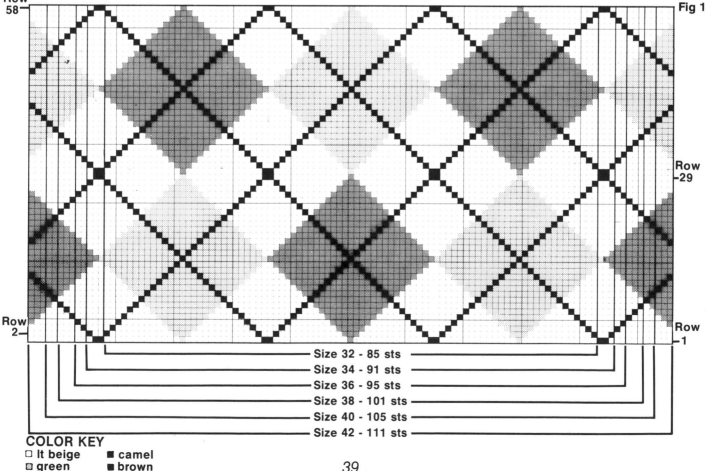

Row 58 ... **Fig 1**
Row 29
Row 2 ... **Row 1**

Size 32 - 85 sts
Size 34 - 91 sts
Size 36 - 95 sts
Size 38 - 101 sts
Size 40 - 105 sts
Size 42 - 111 sts

COLOR KEY
□ lt beige   ■ camel
▨ green   ■ brown

Men's CARDIGAN
designed by Mary Thomas

SIZES:

	Small	Medium	Large	X-Large
Body Chest:	34-36"	38-40"	42-44"	46-48"
Garment Measurements:				
chest	38"	42"	46"	50"
length to underarm	16"	17"	18"	18"
sleeve length to underarm	18"	18½"	19"	19"

Size Note: Instructions are written for sizes as follows: Small(Medium-Large-Extra Large).

MATERIALS
Worsted weight yarn: 19(21-24-26) oz light gray heather

Sizes 6 and 8, 14" straight knitting needles (or size required for gauge)

Stitch holders: 2 small and 3 medium

6 Buttons (3/4" diameter)

GAUGE: With larger size needles in stock st,
9 sts = 2"; 6 rows = 1"

INSTRUCTIONS
Note: Entire sweater, excluding ribbing, is worked in stock st.

BACK
With smaller size needles, CO 87(97-105-113) sts.

Ribbing Row 1: * K1, P1; rep from * across to last st, K1.
Ribbing Row 2: P1, * K1, P1; rep from * across. Rep last 2 rows until ribbing measures 1½" from CO edge, ending by working Ribbing Row 2. Change to larger size needles and stock st. Work even until piece measures 16(17-18-18)" from CO edge or desired length to underarm, ending by working a purl row.

Shape Armholes: BO 4 (5-6-8) sts at beg of next 2 rows = 79(87-93-97) sts. Dec one st at each armhole edge EOR 3(4-5-5) times = 73(79-83-87) sts. Work even until armhole measures 8½(9-9½-10)", ending by working a purl row.

Shape Shoulders: BO 5(5-6-6) sts at beg of next 4 rows; BO 4(5-5-6) sts at beg of next 4 rows; BO rem 37(39-39-39) sts for back of neck.

Pocket Lining (make 2)
With larger size needles, CO 23 sts. Work even in stock st for 4½". Sl all sts to med holder; set aside.

RIGHT FRONT
With smaller size needles, CO 51(55-59-63) sts. Work ribbing same as Back, ending by working Ribbing Row 2. **Next Row:** (K1, P1) 4 times; sl these first 8 sts just worked to sm holder to be worked later for front band; change to larger size needles and knit rem sts = 43(47-51-55) sts. Continuing in stock st (beg with a purl row), work even until piece measures 6" from CO edge, ending by working a purl row.

Pocket Opening: K 10(12-14-16); sl next 23 sts to med holder; then sl sts of one pocket lining with knit-side facing you to left-hand needle behind sts on holder; knit across 23 sts of lining and rem sts = 43(47-51-55) sts. Continuing in stock st (beg with a purl row), work even until piece measures same as Back to underarm, ending by working a purl row.

Shape Armhole, Neck and Shoulder: Row 1: K2 tog (neck decrease); knit rem sts = 42(46-50-54) sts. **Row 2:** BO 4(5-6-8) sts; purl rem sts = 38(41-44-46) sts. Dec one st at armhole edge EOR 3(4-5-5) times AND AT THE SAME TIME continue to dec one st at neck edge EVERY 4th row. Then keeping armhole edge even, continue to dec one st at neck edge EVERY 4th row until there are a total of 3(6-9-12) neck decreases = 33(32-31-30) sts. Now continue to dec one st at neck edge EVERY 3rd row, 15(12-9-6) times AND AT THE SAME TIME when armhole measures same as Back to shoulder, BO from armhole edge as follows: 5(5-6-6) sts twice; 4(5-5-6) sts twice.

LEFT FRONT

Work same as Right Front until ribbing measures ¾", ending by working Ribbing Row 2. **Buttonhole Row 1:** Work Ribbing Row 1 to last 5 sts, BO 3 sts; [one st now left on left-hand needle] K1. **Buttonhole Row 2:** P1, K1; CO 3 sts (see *Casting On, Method 2* on page 12); * K1, P1; rep from * across. Rep Ribbing Rows 1 and 2 until ribbing measures same as Right Front, ending by working Ribbing Row 2. **Next Row:** Change to larger size needles; knit across to last 8 sts, sl rem 8 sts to sm holder to be worked later for front band = 43(47-51-55) sts. Work same as Right Front (including pocket) to underarm, ending by working a purl row.

Shape Armhole, Neck and Shoulder: Row 1: BO 4(5-6-8) sts; knit across to last 2 sts, K2 tog (neck decrease) = 38(41-44-46) sts. Complete shaping by working in same manner as Right Front.

SLEEVE (MAKE 2)

With smaller size needles, CO 43(45-47-49) sts LOOSELY. Work ribbing same as Back until ribbing measures 2", increasing 10 sts evenly spaced across last row (Ribbing Row 2) = 53(55-57-59) sts. Change to larger size needles and stock st. Work 6 rows even. Then inc one st at each end of *next* row and then each following 8(8-8-6)th row, 6(7-8-9) times = 67(71-75-79) sts. Work even until sleeve measures 18(18½-19-19)" from CO edge or desired length to underarm, ending by working a purl row.

Shape Cap: BO 4(5-6-8) sts at beg of next 2 rows = 59(61-63-63) sts. Dec one st at each end EOR until 29(29-29-25) sts rem on needle. Then dec one st at each end EVERY row until 13 sts rem. BO all sts.

FINISHING

Block pieces to measurements. Sew shoulder, side and sleeve seams. Sew sleeves into armholes.

Right Front Band: With wrong side facing you, join yarn at inside edge of front band, leaving sufficient length for sewing band to front and back of neck later. Using smaller size needles, sl sts from holder to needle; continue in K1, P1 ribbing until band, slightly stretched, reaches the center of back neck edge. Place sts on holder; do not cut yarn. Sew band to front first; then adjust band to fit exactly to center of back neck edge. If too short, work more rows of ribbing as needed. If too long, rip out as many rows as needed. When length is determined, BO sts and complete seam. Measure and mark positions on band for 6 buttons evenly spaced, with first button opposite buttonhole already worked on left front and last button ½" below first neck decrease.

Left Front Band: With right side facing you, join yarn at inside edge of band, leaving sufficient sewing length. Using smaller size needles, sl sts from holder to needle; continue in K1, P1 ribbing in same manner as Right Front Band AND AT THE SAME TIME work buttonholes at marked intervals same as buttonhole already worked. Sew band to front and back neck edge; weave ends of bands tog at center back neck edge.

Pocket Ribbing (make 2): With right side facing and smaller size needles, sl sts from holder to needle; work Ribbing Rows 1 and 2 of Back for 1". BO all sts in ribbing. Sew each end of ribbing to sweater; sew lining in place. Weave in all ends. Sew on buttons.

Men's CABLE
CARDIGAN VEST

designed by Evie Rosen, Knitting Nook, Wausau, WI

SIZES:

	Small	Medium	Large	X-Large
Chest:	34-36"	38-40"	42-44"	46-48"
Garment Measurements:				
chest	37"	41"	45"	49"
length to underarm	16"	17"	18"	18"

Size Note: Instructions are written for sizes as follows: Small(Medium-Large-Extra Large).

MATERIALS

Worsted weight yarn: 14(16-18-20) oz red

Sizes 5 and 7, 14" straight knitting needles (or size required for gauge)

Cable needle

4 Small stitch holders

3 Stitch markers

5 Buttons (3/4" diameter)

GAUGE: With larger size needles in stock st, 5 sts = 1"; 7 rows = 1"

CABLE PATTERN STITCH (worked on 11 sts)

Row 1 (wrong side): K3, P2, K1; P2, K3.

Row 2 (cable twist row): P3, sl next 3 sts [2 knit sts and 1 purl st] onto cable needle and hold at *back* of work; knit next 2 sts, then sl *only* the purl st from cable needle back onto left-hand needle and purl this st; K2 from cable needle, P3.

Row 3: Rep Row 1.

Row 4: P2, work **Back Cross** as follows: sl next st (purl st) onto cable needle and hold at *back* of work, knit next 2 sts, then P1 from cable needle [Back Cross completed]; P1, work **Front Cross** as follows: sl next 2 sts (knit sts) onto cable needle and hold at *front* of work, purl next st, then K2 from cable needle [Front Cross completed]; P2.

Note: The knit sts are now separated by 3 center purl sts.

Row 5: K2, P2, K3; P2, K2.

Row 6: P1, Back Cross; P3, Front Cross; P1.

Note: The knit sts are now separated by 5 center purl sts.

Row 7: K1, P2, K5; P2, K1.

Row 8: P1, K2, P5; K2, P1.

Row 9: Rep Row 7.

Row 10: P1, Front Cross; P3, Back Cross; P1.

Note: The knit sts are now separated by 3 center purl sts.

Row 11: Rep Row 5.

Row 12: P2, Front Cross; P1, Back Cross; P2.

Note: The knit sts are now separated by 1 center purl st.

Rep Rows 1 through 12 for cable patt.

INSTRUCTIONS

BACK

With smaller size needles, CO 93(103-113-123) sts. **Ribbing Row 1:** * K1, P1; rep from * to last st, K1. **Ribbing Row 2:** P1; * K1, P1; rep from * across. Rep last 2 rows, 5 times more. Change to larger size needles and stock st. Work even until piece measures 15(16-17-17)" from CO edge or 1" less than desired length to underarm [armhole ribbing allowance], ending by working a purl row.

Shape Armholes: BO 6(7-9-11) sts at beg of next 2 rows = 81(89-95-101) sts. Dec one st at each armhole edge EOR 5(6-7-7) times = 71(77-81-87) sts. Work even until armhole measures 9½(10-10½-11)", ending by working a purl row.

Shape Neck and Shoulders: Row 1 (dividing row): K 24(27-29-32); BO next 23 sts for neck opening, knit rem sts. **Note:** Continue by working across each shoulder with a separate ball of yarn; join new yarn at neck edge for working right shoulder. **Row 2:** Purl sts of left shoulder; BO 3 sts at right neck edge, purl rem sts of right shoulder. **Row 3:** Knit sts of right shoulder; BO 3 sts at neck edge of left shoulder, knit rem sts. **Row 4:** Rep Row 2. **Row 5:** BO 5(6-7-8) sts; knit rem sts of right shoulder; BO 3 sts at neck edge of left shoulder, knit rem sts. **Row 6:** BO 5(6-7-8) sts; purl rem sts of left shoulder; BO 3 sts at neck edge of right shoulder; purl rem sts. **Row 7:** Rep Row 5. **Row 8:** BO 5(6-7-8) sts; purl rem sts of left shoulder; purl sts of right shoulder. **Row 9:** BO rem 5(6-6-7) sts of right shoulder; knit sts of left shoulder. BO rem 5(6-6-7) sts.

Pocket Lining (make 2)

With larger size needles, CO 27 sts. Work even in stock st for 4". Cut yarn, leaving 30" sewing length. Sl all sts to holder; set aside.

RIGHT FRONT

With smaller size needles, CO 57(63-67-73) sts. **Row 1 (right side):** K6 for facing; with yarn at back of work, sl 1 as to purl for turning ridge; K6, P1 for front band; place marker to separate sts of band and front; * K1, P1; rep from * to last st, K1. **Row 2:** P1, * K1, P1; rep from * to marker; sl marker, K1, P 13. Rep last 2 rows, 5 times more.

Change to larger size needles and establish patt as follows. **Row 1 (right side):** K6, sl 1 as to purl, K6, P1; sl marker, K 19(21-21-24); place marker for cable panel, work Row 2 of Cable Patt St over next 11 sts, place marker; knit rem 13(17-21-24) sts. **Note:** Sl markers on each following row. **Row 2:** Purl to marker; work Row 3 of Cable Patt St over next 11 sts, purl to next marker; K1, P 13. Continue in patt as established [keep 14 sts of facing and front band as established, 11 sts of cable panel in Cable Patt St, and rem sts in stock st] and work until piece measures approx 4" above ribbing, ending by working a wrong-side row.

Pocket Opening: Work across 14 sts of facing and front band; K 11(13-13-16), †sl next 27 sts to holder (removing markers); then sl sts of one pocket lining with knit-side facing you to left-hand needle behind sts on holder; work across sts of lining as follows: K8, place marker for cable panel, continue in established Cable Patt St over next 11 sts, place marker, K8†; then knit rem sts = 57(63-67-73) sts. Continuing in patt as established (now and throughout front), work until piece measures same as Back to underarm, ending by working a wrong-side row.

Shape Armhole, Neck and Shoulder: Row 1: Work across 14 sts of facing and front band; sl 1 as to knit, K1, PSSO [neck decrease made]; work in patt as established across rem sts = 56(62-66-72) sts. **Row 2:** BO 6(7-9-11) sts for underarm, work in patt as established across rem sts = 50(55-57-61) sts.
Dec one st at armhole edge EOR 5(6-7-7) times AND AT THE SAME TIME continue to dec one st at inside edge of front band for neck shaping [same as in Row 1] EVERY 4th row. Keeping armhole edge even, continue to dec one st at inside edge of front band: EVERY 4th row until there are 29(32-37-40) sts rem on needle; then EVERY 6th row, 0(0-3-3) times more = 29(32-34-37) sts. Work even until armhole measures same as Back to shoulder. Then BO from armhole edge for shoulder as follows: 5(6-7-8) sts twice; 5(6-6-7) sts once. Continuing on rem 14 sts of facing and front band, work 4" more. Sl sts to holder; cut yarn, leaving 12" sewing length.
Measure and mark positions on front band for 5 buttons evenly spaced, with first button ½" above bottom edge and 5th button ½" below first neck decrease.

LEFT FRONT
With smaller size needles, CO 57(63-67-73) sts. **Row 1 (right side):** K1; * P1, K1; rep from * to last 14 sts; place marker to separate sts of front band and facing; P1, K6 for front band; with yarn at back of work, sl 1 as to purl for turning ridge; K6 for facing. **Row 2:** P 13, K1, sl marker; P1, * K1, P1; rep from * across. Rep last 2 rows once more. Now work double buttonhole as follows:

Buttonhole Row 1: Work in established ribbing patt to marker; P1, K2, BO next 2 sts for buttonhole on front band; K1, sl 1 as to purl, K2; BO next 2 sts for buttonhole on facing, K1.

Buttonhole Row 2: P2, CO 2 sts (see *Casting On, Method 2* on page 12); P5, CO 2 sts; P2, K1; sl marker, work in established ribbing patt across rem sts. Now rep beginning Rows 1 and 2, 3 times more.
Change to larger size needles and establish patt as follows. **Row 1 (right side):** K 13(17-21-24); place marker for cable panel, work Row 2 of Cable Patt St over next 11 sts, place marker; K 19(21-21-24), sl marker; P1, K6, sl 1 as to purl, K6. **Note:** Sl markers on each following row.
Row 2: P 13, K1; purl to marker, work Row 3 of Cable Patt St over next 11 sts; purl rem sts. Work in patt as established until piece measures approx 4" above ribbing (same as Right Front), ending by working a wrong-side row AND AT THE SAME TIME work double buttonhole at marked interval in same manner as one already worked.

Pocket Opening: K5(9-13-16); rep from † to † in Pocket Opening of Right Front; K 11(13-13-16); work across sts of front band and facing = 57(63-67-73) sts. Continuing in patt as established (now and throughout front), work until piece measures same as Back to underarm, ending by working a wrong-side row AND AT THE SAME TIME work double buttonholes at marked intervals.

Shape Armhole, Neck and Shoulder: Row 1: BO 6(7-9-11) sts for underarm, work in patt as established to within 2 sts of front band marker; K2 tog [neck decrease], work across sts of front band and facing = 50(55-57-61) sts. Complete in same manner as Right Front.

FINISHING
Sew shoulder seams. Weave ends of neckband tog (see *Weaving on Needles* on page 13). Fold front facings at turning ridge to inside; sew in place. Sew neckband to back neck edge.

Armhole Ribbing (make 2): With right side facing you, beg at underarm. Use smaller size needles and pick up 117(123-129-135) sts around armhole edge. Rep Ribbing Rows 1 and 2 of Back until ribbing measures 1". BO loosely in ribbing. Sew side seams.

Pocket Ribbing (make 2): With right side facing and smaller size needles, sl sts from holder to needle. Rep Ribbing Rows 1 and 2 of Back until ribbing measures 1". BO loosely in ribbing. Sew ends of ribbing to front; sew lining in place. Overcast double buttonholes; sew on buttons.

RAGLAN PULLOVER and HAT
knitted from the top down

designed by Mary Thomas

Here's a garment for the whole family, sized for men, women and children. We've shown you a variety of ways to stripe it, and of course it can be made in a solid color too. Use your own imagination to devise new color combinations and striping patterns.

SIZES:

	Children			Women			Men		
	Small (4-6)	Medium (8-10)	Large (10-12)	Small	Medium	Large	Small	Medium	Large
Chest/Bust:	24"	28"	31"	32"	36"	40"	38"	42"	46"
Garment Measurements:									
chest/bust	26"	30"	33"	34"	38"	42"	40"	44"	48"
length to underarm	9"	11"	13"	14"	15"	16"	15"	16"	17"
sleeve length to underarm	12"	14"	15½"	16½"	16½"	17"	18"	18½"	18½"

MATERIALS
Worsted weight yarn:

	Children			Women			Men		
	Small	Medium	Large	Small	Medium	Large	Small	Medium	Large
Main Color (MC): ___ oz	9	11	13	14	16	18	17	19	21
Color A: ___ oz	2	2 (red)	2	2	2½ (brick heather)	3	3	4 (brown heather)	4
Color B: ___ oz		2 (blue)	2		light beige heather		3	3 (olive green heather)	3
Color C: ___ oz		1 (yellow)	white		1½ (light beige heather)		1½	1½ (brick heather)	

Sizes 6 and 8, 14" straight knitting needles (or size required for gauge) Size 8, 16" and 29" (for child's small only) circular knitting needles (or size required for gauge)
4 Stitch markers (one in contrasting color)
3 Large stitch holders

GAUGE: With larger size needles in stock. st, 9 sts = 2", 6 rows = 1"
Gauge Note: For correct fit, it is essential to achieve both stitch and row gauge. If stitch gauge is incorrect, the sweater will be either too wide or too narrow. If row gauge is incorrect, the sweater will be too long or too short, or the armhole of the sweater will be too loose or too tight.

Children			Women			Men		
sm 64	**med** 68	**lge** 72	**sm** 72	**med** 76	**lge** 80	**sm** 84	**med** 88	**lge** 88
26	28	30	30	32	34	34	36	38
6	6	6	6	6	6	8	8	6
25	27	29	29	31	33	33	35	37
4	4	4	4	4	4	6	6	4
67	71	75	75	79	83	87	91	91

PULLOVER INSTRUCTIONS
Neck Ribbing
With MC and larger size straight needles, CO ___ sts LOOSELY. Work one row in K1, P1 ribbing. Change to smaller size straight needles; continue in ribbing until piece measures 2½" from CO edge.
Yoke
Change to 16" circular needle. **Marking Rnd:** For back: K ___; place marker [use markers of one-color first]; for right sleeve: K ___; place marker; for front: K ___ inc in next st [*to inc: knit in front and back of st = inc made*]; place marker; K ___ inc in next st, K ___ inc in last st; place contrasting marker for left sleeve: inc in next st, K ___ inc in last st; place contrasting marker [*identifies end of rnd*] = ___ sts. **Note:** Sl markers on each following row/rnd.

Front Neck Shaping: Note: Shaping is worked in short rows; when instructions say "TURN", leave rem sts on needle unworked, turn work and beg next row.

Row 1: Join; work across sts of back and right sleeve as follows: *inc in next st, knit to within one st of next marker, inc in next st; rep from * once more. Now work across first 2 sts of right front as follows: inc in next st, K1, TURN.

Row 2: Work back across sts of prev row as follows: sl first st as to purl [be sure to keep even tension so this st will not be too loose or too tight], purl to contrasting marker. Now purl across first 3 sts of left front, TURN.

Row 3: Sl first st as to purl [remember to keep even tension]; *knit to within one st of next marker, inc in each of next 2 sts [st on each side of marker]; rep from * 3 times more; K1, knit sl st (first st of prev row); knit next 2 sts, TURN.

Row 4: Sl first st as to purl; purl back across sts of right front, right sleeve, back, left sleeve and left front, ending with sl st (first st of prev row); purl next 2 sts, TURN.

Row 5: Sl first st as to purl, *knit to within one st of next marker, inc in each of next 2 sts [st on each side of marker]; rep from *3 times more; knit across sts of right front, ending with sl st (first st of prev row); knit next 2 sts, TURN.

Rep Rows 4 and 5, _____ time(s) more; then rep Row 4 once. ....

Joining Rnd: Rep Row 5. At end of row, DO NOT TURN; continue knitting across sts of front and left sleeve, ending at contrasting marker. Note: Small "hole" at left front neckline will be adjusted later when finishing. Short rows are now completed; you should have _____ sts ....

[_____ sts each for back and front .... and _____ sts for each sleeve].

Change to Color A for children and men only; continue with MC for women. Join and continue working in rnds as follows.

Rnd 1: Knit around to within one st of 3rd marker (st before left sleeve); inc in each of next 2 sts [st on each side of marker]; knit to within one st of contrasting marker, inc in last st. **Rnd 2:** Inc in first st; *knit to within one st of next marker, inc in each of next 2 sts [st on each side of marker]; rep from * once more; knit across sts of front and left sleeve, ending at contrasting marker.

Work stripe sequence which follows AND AT THE SAME TIME rep last 2 rnds, _____ times [change to 29" circular needle when sts become too crowded on needle] = _____ sts ....

[_____ sts each for back and front .... and _____ sts for each sleeve].

Stripe Sequence (for children and men):
Color A: _____ rnd(s); ....
Color B: _____ rnds; ....
Color C: _____ rnd(s); ....
Color A: _____ rnds; ....
Color C: _____ rnd(s); ....
MC: _____ rnds; ....
Color B: _____ rnds ....

Stripe Sequence (for women):
MC: _____ rnds; ....
Color A: 2 rnds; ....
MC: 4 rnds; ....
Color A: 2 rnds; ....
MC: 6 rnds; ....
Color A: _____ rnds ....

	1	1	2	2	2	2	3	3	3
should have _____ sts	104	108	120	120	124	128	140	144	144
_____ sts each for back and front	36	38	42	42	44	46	48	50	52
and _____ sts for each sleeve	16	16	18	18	18	18	22	22	20
rep last 2 rnds, _____ times	9	12	14	14	16	18	17	19	21
= _____ sts	184	212	240	240	260	280	284	304	320
_____ sts each for back and front	56	64	72	72	78	84	84	90	96
and _____ sts for each sleeve	36	42	48	48	52	56	58	62	64
Stripe (children/men) Color A	1	2					2	2	2
Color B	5	6				8	8	8	8
Color C	1	2					2	2	2
Color A	6	8					12	12	16
Color C	1	2					2	2	2
MC	2	3					4	6	6
Color B	2	3					4	6	6
Stripe (women) MC			4	6	8				
Color A			10	12	14				

When striping sequence and increases are completed, continue with MC and work even until armhole measures ___" (measure as shown in **Fig 1**).

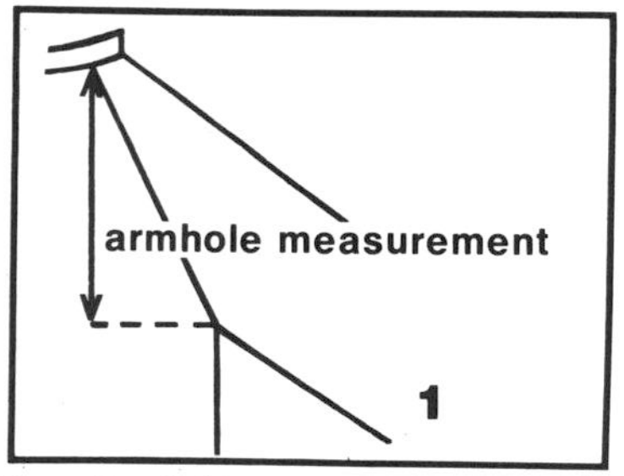

armhole measurement

1

Dividing Rnd: K ___ and sl these sts of back to holder; drop marker; K ___ then CO ___ sts (see *Casting On, Method 2* on page 12) for underarm, now sl these ___ sts to holder for right sleeve; drop marker; K ___ and sl these sts of front to holder; drop marker; knit rem ___ sts of left sleeve; CO ___ sts for underarm; drop contrasting marker.

LEFT SLEEVE
Change to larger size straight needles; begin working in rows. **Row 1 (wrong side):** Purl across; CO ___ sts for underarm = ___ sts. Continuing in stock st, work even for 2" and then EVERY 8th row until there are ___ sts left on needle. Work even until sleeve measures ___" from underarm or ___" less than desired length. **Next Row:** Dec ___ sts evenly spaced across row = ___ sts.

Change to smaller size needles and work in K1, P1 ribbing for ___". BO LOOSELY in ribbing, leaving sufficient sewing length for seam. Thread into tapestry or yarn needle; sew sleeve seam to underarm.

RIGHT SLEEVE
With larger size straight needles, sl ___ sts from right sleeve holder to free needle. Join MC and work same as Left Sleeve.

With MC and 29" circular needle. **Joining Rnd:** With knit side facing you, pick up ___ sts over CO sts at underarm of right sleeve; knit sts from back holder; pick up ___ sts over rem CO sts at underarm of left sleeve; knit sts from front holder; pick up ___ sts over rem CO sts at underarm of left sleeve; place marker for end of rnd (remember to sl marker on each following rnd) = ___ sts. Join and knit even in rnds until work measures ___" from underarm or ___" less than desired length.

Instruction	Children sm 6	Children med 7	Children lge 8	Women sm 8	Women med 8½	Women lge 9	Men sm 9½	Men med 10	Men lge 10½
work even until armhole measures ___"	6	7	8	8	8½	9	9½	10	10½
Dividing Rnd: K ___ and sl these sts of back	56	64	72	72	78	84	84	90	96
K ___ then	36	42	48	48	52	56	58	62	64
CO ___ sts for underarm	2	2	3	3	4	5	4	5	6
sl these ___ sts to holder for right sleeve	38	44	51	51	56	61	62	67	70
K ___ and sl these sts of front	56	64	72	72	78	84	84	90	96
knit rem ___ sts of left sleeve	36	42	48	48	52	56	58	62	64
CO ___ sts for underarm	2	2	3	3	4	5	4	5	6
LEFT SLEEVE — CO ___ sts for underarm	2	2	3	3	4	5	4	5	6
= ___ sts	40	46	54	54	60	66	66	72	76
until there are ___ sts left on needle	30	32	38	38	42	48	48	52	56
measures ___" from underarm	9	11	12	13	13	13½	14½	15	15
or ___" less than desired length	3	3	3½	3½	3½	3½	3½	3½	3½
Next Row: Dec ___ sts evenly spaced	0	0	2	2	4	8	6	8	10
across row = ___ sts	30	32	36	36	38	40	42	44	46
K1, P1 ribbing for ___"	3	3	3½	3½	3½	3½	3½	3½	3½
RIGHT SLEEVE — sl ___ sts from right sleeve holder	38	44	51	51	56	61	62	67	70
pick up ___ sts over CO sts at underarm of right	2	2	3	3	4	5	4	5	6
pick up ___ sts over rem CO sts (left)	4	4	6	6	8	8	10	10	12
pick up ___ sts over rem CO sts at underarm of left	2	2	3	3	4	5	4	5	6
= ___ sts	120	136	156	156	172	188	184	200	216
work measures ___" from underarm	7½	9½	11	12	13	14	13	14	15
or ___" less than desired length	1½	1½	2	2	2	2	2	2	2

Note: Bottom ribbing is worked in two sections and then seamed.
Dividing Rnd: K ____ and sl these sts to holder; _____ knit rem ____ sts. Change to smaller size straight needles; work K1, P1 ribbing in rows for ____". BO LOOSELY in ribbing. With smaller size straight needles and MC, sl sts from holder to needle; work ribbing same as other section. Weave ends of bottom ribbing tog.

FINISHING
Weave ends of neck ribbing tog. Fold neck ribbing in half to inside and sew VERY LOOSELY in place. Adjust "hole" or any loose st on front neck shaping by drawing yarn of loose st on wrong side until st is same size as adjacent sts or until "hole" is gone; then secure by tacking in place. Weave in all ends.

HAT INSTRUCTIONS
With MC and larger size straight needles, CO ____ sts. Change to smaller size straight needles and work in K1, P1 ribbing for ____". Change to larger size straight needles. Work even in stock st until piece measures ____" from CO edge. Continuing in stock st, work the following stripe sequence.

Stripe Sequence (for children and men):
Color A: ____ rows;
Color B: 2 rows;
Color C: ____ rows;
Color B: 2 rows

Stripe Sequence (for women):
Color A: 6 rows;
MC: 3 rows;
Color A: 1 row;
MC: 2 rows;
Color A: 1 row

When striping sequence is completed, continue with MC in stock st until piece measures ____" from CO edge, ending by working a wrong-side row. _____

Shape Top: First Dec Row: K ____ : *K2 tog, K1; rep from * _____ across = ____ sts. Beg with a purl row and _____ work ____ rows even in stock st. **2nd Dec Row:** K ____ : *K2 tog; rep from * _____ across = ____ sts. Cut yarn, leaving 24" sewing length.

Finishing: Thread sewing length into tapestry or yarn needle; draw through rem sts twice. Draw up tightly and fasten securely. Then sew side seam, carefully matching stripes. Weave in all ends. **Pompon:** With each color used in hat, make ____ diameter pompon (see *Pompon* instructions on page 17). Attach securely to top of hat.

	Children			Women			Men		
	sm	med	lge	sm	med	lge	sm	med	lge
Dividing Rnd: K ____	60	68	78	78	86	94	92	100	108
knit rem ____ sts	60	68	78	78	86	94	92	100	108
rows for ____"	1½	1½	2	2	2	2	2	2	2
CO ____ sts	84	88	90	92	92	92	96	96	96
ribbing for ____"	2	2½	3	3	3	3	3	3	3
measures ____"	2½	3	3½	4	4	4	4	4	4
Color A: ____ rows	4	4	6				6	6	6
Color C: ____ rows	6	6	8				8	8	8
measures ____"	7	8	8	8	8	8	8	8	8
across = ____ sts	0	1	0	2	2	2	0	0	0
work ____ rows	56	59	60	62	62	62	64	64	64
rows even	3	3	5	5	5	5	5	5	5
2nd Dec Row: K ____	0	1	0	0	0	0	0	0	0
across = ____ sts	28	30	30	31	31	31	32	32	32
make ____ diameter pompon	3	3	3	3	3	3	1½	1½	1½

48

Big Needle Knits

Chapter 3

Want to make something in a hurry? Then choose from this selection of fashion garments, all made on large needles from easy patterns.

VEST
designed by Doris England

This lovely vest is made with the butterfly stitch, using two strands of yarn. Although not difficult to make, we suggest working a sample swatch of the pattern stitch before starting your garment.

SIZES:	Small	Medium	Large
Body Bust:	32-34"	36-38"	40-42"
Garment Measurements:			
back width (at shoulders)	14½"	16"	17½"
length (bottom edge to shoulder)	22"	22"	22"

Size Note: Instructions are written for sizes as follows: Small(Medium-Large)

MATERIALS
Worsted weight yarn: 12(14-16) oz light blue tweed
Size 11, 14" straight knitting needles (or size required for gauge)
Materials Note: Yarn is used doubled throughout patt.

GAUGE: With 2 strands of yarn:
   in garter st, 11 sts = 4"; 6 rows = 1"
   in Butterfly Patt St, 12 sts = 5"; 5 rows = 1"

BUTTERFLY PATTERN STITCH
To make a practice swatch, use 2 strands of yarn and CO 17 sts; knit 2 rows and then work as follows.
Rows 1 and 3: Purl.
Rows 2 and 4: Knit.
Row 5: * K3, work **butterfly st** as follows: *insert right-hand needle in next st 6 rows below as to knit* **(Fig 1)** *[you will be skipping 5 rows]; keeping needle in this position, sl st above off left-hand needle and unravel this st down 5 rows; then insert left-hand needle in st with right-hand needle and knit this st, pulling up approx 1¼" lp in front of unraveled strands* **(Fig 2)** *[butterfly st made]*; rep from * *[Note: Keep yarn slack at back of work when working next st so strands will form a "V" as shown in Fig 3.]* to last st, K1.
Rep Rows 1 through 5 for patt.

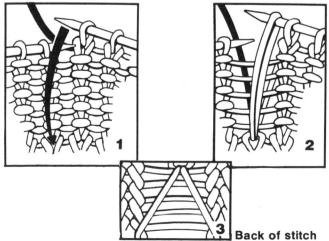

Back of stitch

INSTRUCTIONS

Note: Use 2 strands of yarn throughout patt.

BACK

CO 45(51-55) sts *loosely*. Knit 3 rows. **Dec Row:** Knit across, decreasing 6 sts evenly spaced = 39(45-49) sts. Knit one more row. Garter st border is now completed; continue by working in patt as follows.

Row 1 (right side): K2(3-3) for garter st edge, purl to last 2(3-3) sts; knit rem sts for garter st edge.

Row 2: Knit.

Row 3: Rep Row 1.

Row 4: Knit.

Row 5 (butterfly st row): K3(4-4), butterfly st; * K3, butterfly st; rep from * to last 3(4-4) sts; knit rem sts.

Rows 6 through 9: Rep Rows 1 through 4.

Row 10 (butterfly st row): K5(6-6), butterfly st; * K3, butterfly st; rep from * to last 5(6-6) sts; knit rem sts. Rep last 10 rows, 8 times more = 18 butterfly st rows.

Yoke: Knit 7 rows. **Dividing Row:** K 12(14-15), BO next 15(17-19) sts for neck opening; knit rem sts. Continuing to work across each side of neck opening (join new yarn at neck edge), knit 6 more rows. Yoke should now have a total of 14 rows (7 ridges). BO all sts *loosely*.

LEFT FRONT

CO 23(24-28) sts *loosely* (remember to use 2 strands of yarn). Knit 3 rows. **Dec Row:** Knit across, decreasing 3 sts evenly spaced = 20(21-25) sts. Knit one more row. Garter st border is now completed; continue by working in patt as follows.

Row 1: K2(3-3) for garter st side edge, purl to last 3 sts; knit rem sts for garter st center edge.

Row 2: Knit.

Row 3: Rep Row 1.

Row 4: Knit.

Row 5 (butterfly st row): K3(4-4), butterfly st; * K3, butterfly st; rep from * to last 4 sts, K4.

Rows 6 through 9: Rep Rows 1 through 4.

Row 10 (butterfly st row): K6, butterfly st; * K3, butterfly st; rep from * to last 5(6-6) sts; knit rem sts. Rep Rows 1 through 10, 6 times more; then rep Rows 1 through 5 once = 15 butterfly st rows.

Yoke: Knit 4 rows. **Next Row (wrong side):** BO 8(7-10) sts for neck opening, knit rem sts = 12(14-15) sts. Knit 23 more rows. Yoke should now have a total of 28 rows (14 ridges). BO all sts *loosely*.

RIGHT FRONT

Work same as Left Front until garter st border is completed. Then work in patt as follows.

Row 1: K3 for garter st center edge, purl to last 2(3-3) sts; knit rem sts for garter st side edge.

Row 2: Knit.

Row 3: Rep Row 1.

Row 4: Knit.

Row 5 (butterfly st row): K4, butterfly st; * K3, butterfly st; rep from * to last 3(4-4) sts; knit rem sts.

Rows 6 through 9: Rep Rows 1 through 4.

Row 10 (butterfly st row): K5(6-6), butterfly st; * K3, butterfly st; rep from * to last 6 sts, K6. Rep Rows 1 through 10, 6 times more; then rep Rows 1 through 5 once = 15 butterfly st rows.

Yoke: Knit 4 rows. **Next Row (wrong side):** K 12(14-15), BO rem 8(7-10) sts. Cut yarn, leaving 4" end for weaving in later. Turn work; join yarn (2 strands) at neck edge and knit 23 more rows. Yoke should now have a total of 28 rows (14 ridges). BO all sts *loosely*.

FINISHING

Sew shoulder seams. Sew side seams, leaving approx 10(10-11)" open for armhole. **Ties:** Using 3 strands of yarn, make two twisted cords (see *Twisted Cord* instructions on page 15) each 18" long; or using crochet hook (size J) and 2 strands of yarn, make two chains each 18" long. Attach one end of tie to each side of center front neck opening. Knot and fringe opposite end of ties.

QUICK KNIT TOP

designed by Mary Thomas

This versatile wardrobe addition can be made in just a couple of evenings, with very little yarn. Wear it to top off slacks, jeans or skirts.

SIZES:	Small	Medium	Large
Body Bust:	32"	35"	38"
Garment Measurements:			
bust	35"	38"	41"
length (bottom edge			
to shoulder)	18"	18½"	19"

Size Note: Instructions are written for sizes as follows: Small (Medium-Large).

MATERIALS
Mohair-blend yarn: 7(9-11) oz blue
Size 17, 14" straight knitting needles (or size required for gauge)
Materials Note: Yarn is used doubled throughout patt, excluding bottom hem.

**GAUGE: With 2 strands of yarn in stock st,
5 sts = 2"; 8 rows = 3"**

INSTRUCTIONS

BACK
With single strand of yarn, CO 43(47-51) sts. **Row 1:** Purl.

Row 2: Knit. **Row 3 (turning ridge):** Join another strand of yarn; knit across. Continuing with 2 strands of yarn, beg with a knit row and work in stock st until piece measures 10" from turning ridge, ending by working a purl row.

Yoke: Row 1 (right side): * K1, YF (yarn to front of work); sl l as to purl, YB (yarn to back of work); rep from * to last st, K1.

Row 2: Purl.

Row 3: K2; * YF, sl l as to purl; YB, K1; rep from * to last st, K1.

Row 4: Purl.
Rep last 4 rows until yoke measures 8(8½-9)" or piece measures 18(18½-19)" from turning ridge or desired length to shoulder, ending by working Row 1 or Row 3. BO *loosely* as follows: P1, * P2 tog; pass first st over 2nd st on right-hand needle; rep from * to last 2 sts, BO rem sts in purl. Cut yarn, leaving approx 12" sewing length.

FRONT
Work same as Back until Row 3 (turning ridge) is completed. **Next Row:** Continuing with 2 strands of yarn, K 19(21-23); YO, K2 tog; K1, YO, K2 tog; K 19(21-23). **Note:** Each YO counts as one st; the openings created by the YO sts will be used later for inserting drawstring. Beg with a purl row and complete in same manner as Back.

FINISHING
Using single strand of yarn, sew approx 1" shoulder seams; then sew side seams, leaving approx 10(10½-11)" open for armholes. Fold hem at turning ridge to inside and sew *very loosely* in place. Weave in all ends.

Drawstring: Using 4 strands of yarn, make a twisted cord (see *Twisted Cord* instructions on page 15) 50(54-58)" long or desired length; *or* using crochet hook (size H) and 3 strands of yarn, make a chain to same measurement. Knot and trim each end of drawstring. Insert drawstring through one YO opening at center front and pass through hem, ending at other YO opening.

SHOULDERETTE BED JACKET

designed by Jean Leinhauser

A perfect gift, this light, airy bed jacket works up quickly and is comfortable to wear.

SIZE: Pattern is written in one size, which will fit through size 16.

MATERIALS
Sweater and afghan weight yarn: 8 oz light blue
100% Acrylic mohair type yarn: 6 oz light blue
Size 9, 10″ straight knitting needles
Size 15, 14″ straight knitting needles(or size required for gauge)
Cable needle
Stitch marker
Materials Note: One strand of each yarn is used throughout patt, excluding cuffs.

GAUGE: With larger size needles and one strand of each yarn in garter st, 10 sts = 3″

INSTRUCTIONS

Beg at right cuff, with 2 strands of sweater and afghan weight yarn and smaller size needles, CO 44 sts. Work in K1, P1 ribbing for 6″, increasing 5 sts evenly spaced across last row = 49 sts. Cut off one strand; join one strand of mohair-type yarn. Continuing with one strand of each yarn, work in patt as follows.

Rows 1, 3, 5 and 7 (wrong side): K 10 for garter st border; P 29; K9, YF (yarn to front of work), sl 1 as to purl [last 10 sts = garter st border].

Row 2: K 10 (border); K1, * † YO; sl 1 as to knit, K1, PSSO; K1, K2 tog; YO †, K6; rep from * once more; then rep from † to † once, K1; now work border as follows: K9, YF, sl 1 as to purl. **Note:** Each YO counts as one st throughout patt.

Row 4 (cable twist row): K 10, (border); K2, * † YO; sl 1 as to knit, K2 tog, PSSO; YO †, K1; sl next 3 sts to cable needle and hold at *back* of work; knit next 3 sts, then K3 from cable needle, K1; rep from * once more; then rep from † to † once, K2; now work border as follows: K9, YF, sl 1 as to purl.

Row 6: Rep Row 2.

Row 8: K 10 (border); K2, * † YO; sl 1 as to knit, K2 tog, PSSO; YO †, K8; rep from * once more; then rep from † to † once, K2; now work border as follows: K9, YF, sl 1 as to purl.

Work in patt (rep Rows 1 through 8) until work measures 14″ from ribbing, ending by working a wrong-side row and placing a marker before last 10 border sts for collar shaping. **Note:** S l marker on each row of collar shaping.

Collar Shaping: Row 1 (inc row): Knit to within 2 sts of marker, knit in front and back of next st [inc made], K1 work in patt as established across rem 39 sts. **Row 2:** Work in patt as established to marker; knit to last st, YF, sl 1 as to purl. Rep last 2 rows, 7 times more = 57 sts (18 border/collar sts).

Dec Row (right side): Knit to within 3 sts of marker, K2 tog, K1; work in patt as established across rem sts. **Next Row:** Work in patt as established to marker; knit to last st, YF, sl 1 as to purl. Rep last 2 rows, 7 times more = 49 sts. Collar shaping is now completed; you should again have 10 border sts.

Continuing in patt as established, work even until work measures 14″ from last dec row, ending by working Row 8 of patt. Cut off strand of mohair-type yarn; join another strand of sweater and afghan weight yarn. Change to smaller size needles and work left cuff as follows. **Dec Row:** * (K1, P1) 3 times; K2 tog, P1; rep from * 4 times more; (K1, P1) twice = 44 sts. Continue in K1, P1 ribbing for 6″. BO *loosely* in ribbing.

FINISHING
Weave in all loose ends. Beg at cuff edge and sew (use single strand of sweater and afghan weight yarn) approx 12″ seam at each end of garment.

HAT, SCARF and MITTENS *for women*

designed by Mary Thomas

SIZE: Hat and mittens are written in one size; scarf measures approx 7½″ wide x 72″ long.

MATERIALS
Worsted weight yarn: 20 oz wine heather
Needle Sizes:
   For Hat and Scarf: Size 13, 14″ straight knitting needles (or size required for gauge)
   For Mittens: Size 10½, 10″ straight knitting needles (or size required for gauge)
Materials Note: Yarn is used doubled throughout patt.

GAUGE: With 2 strands of yarn in patt st,
      with smaller size needles, 3 sts = 1″
      with larger size needles, 8 sts = 3″

HAT INSTRUCTIONS

With 2 strands of yarn and larger size needles, CO 53 sts. Work in pattern stitch as follows.

Row 1 (right side): K1; * P2, K2; rep from * across.

Row 2: P1; * K2, P2; rep from * across.
Rep last 2 rows until piece measures 10″ from CO edge, ending by working Row 2.

Shape Top: Row 1: S l first st as to knit; * K2 tog; rep from * across = 27 sts. **Row 2:** * P2 tog; rep from * to last st, P1 = 14 sts. Cut yarn, leaving approx 24″ sewing length.

FINISHING

Thread sewing length into tapestry or yarn needle and draw through all sts. Draw up tightly and fasten securely; then sew side seam. Weave in all ends.

SCARF INSTRUCTIONS

With 2 strands of yarn and larger size needles, CO 23 sts. Work in pattern stitch as follows.

Row 1: * K2, P2; rep from * to last 3 sts, K2, P1.

Row 2: P2; * K2, P2; rep from * to last st, K1.
Rep last 2 rows until scarf measures approx 72″ from CO edge. BO all sts; weave in all ends.

MITTEN INSTRUCTIONS *(make 2)*

With 2 strands of yarn and smaller size needles, CO 21 sts. **Row 1:** * K1, P1; rep from * to last st, K1. **Row 2:** P1; * K1, P1; rep from * across. Rep last 2 rows until ribbing measures 2″, ending by working Row 2. Work in pattern stitch as follows.

Row 1 (right side): K1; * P2, K2; rep from * across.

Row 2: P1; * K2, P2; rep from * across.
Rep last 2 rows, 3 times more.

Thumb: Dividing Row (right side): K1, (P2, K2) twice; K4, CO 2 sts (see *Casting On, Method 2* on page 12); leave rem 8 sts on left-hand needle unworked. **Next Row:** Purl across both CO sts, P5, CO one st = 8 sts.

Continuing on these 8 sts *only* [leave 8 sts on each needle unworked], work 8 rows in stock st, ending by working a purl row. **Dec Row:** (K2 tog) 4 times = 4 sts. Cut yarn leaving 12″ sewing length. Thread into tapestry or yarn needle and draw through rem sts. Draw up tightly and fasten securely; then sew thumb seam.

Hand: Joining Row: With right side facing, hold thumb down next to work (toward ribbing). Join 2 strands of yarn next to sts on right-hand needle; pick up 5 sts across open edge at base of thumb; continue across sts on left-hand needle as follows: (P2, K2) twice. You should now have 21 sts. Continue in pattern stitch as follows.

Row 1 (wrong side): P1; * K2, P2; rep from * across.

Row 2: K1; * P2, K2; rep from * across.
Rep last 2 rows until mitten measures 7″ from ribbing, ending by working Row 1.

Shape Top: Row 1: S l first st as to knit; * K2 tog; rep from * across = 11 sts. **Row 2:** * P2 tog: rep from * to last st, P1 = 6 sts. Cut yarn, leaving approx 24″ sewing length.

FINISHING

Thread sewing length into tapestry or yarn needle and draw through all sts. Draw up tightly and fasten securely; then sew side seam. Weave in all ends.

T-SWEATER
designed by Carol Wilson Mansfield

SIZES:

	Small	Medium	Large
Body Bust:	33″	37″	41″
Garment Measurements:			
bust	36″	40″	44″
length of underarm	14″	15″	16″

Size Note: Instructions are written for sizes as follows: Small(Medium-Large).

MATERIALS

American Thread Glencastle Heather Knitting Worsted Size yarn in 3-oz skeins: 6(8-10) skeins Cranberry

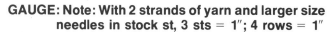

Sizes 9 and 11, 14″ straight knitting needles (or size required for gauge)
Medium stitch holder
6 Stitch markers
Materials Note: Yarn is used doubled throughout patt.

GAUGE: Note: With 2 strands of yarn and larger size needles in stock st, 3 sts = 1″; 4 rows = 1″

INSTRUCTIONS
Note: Use 2 strands of yarn throughout patt.

BACK
With smaller size needle, CO 55(61-67) sts *loosely*. **Row 1:** * K1, P1; rep from * to last st, K1. Rep Row 1 for 2½″ for seed st border. Change to larger size needles and work as follows. **Note:** You will now begin working 3 sections in seed st, each separated by 7 stock sts.

Row 1 (right side): † K7; *place marker for seed st side section*; P1, (K1, P1) 3(4-5) times, *place marker*; K7; † place marker for seed st center section; P1, (K1, P1) 6(7-8) times, place marker; rep from † to † once. **Note:** Sl markers on each following row.

Row 2: † P7; P1, (K1, P1) 3(4-5) times; P7; † P1, (K1, P1) 6(7-8) times; rep from † to † once.
Rep last 2 rows until piece measures 14(15-16)″ from CO edge, ending by working Row 2.

SLEEVES AND YOKE
CO 9(11-13) sts at end of prev row for sleeve (see **Figs 8, 9 and 10** of *Casting On, Method 1* on page 6). You should now have 64(72-80) sts. **Row 1:** P1, (K1, P1) 4(5-6) times; continue in seed st across next 14(16-18) sts (dropping marker) as follows: (K1, P1) 7(8-9) times; K7; P1, (K1, P1) 6(7-8) times; K7; P1, (K1, P1) 3(4-5) times; drop marker; K7; CO 9(11-13) sts (as before) for other sleeve = 73(83-93) sts.

Row 2 (wrong side): † P1, (K1, P1) 11(13-15) times; † P7; P1, (K1, P1) 6(7-8) times; P7; rep from † to † once.

Row 3: † P1, (K1, P1) 11(13-15) times; † K7; P1, (K1, P1) 6(7-8) times; K7; rep from † to † once. Rep last 2 rows until piece measures 3(3¼-3½)″ from CO edge of sleeve, ending by working a wrong-side row.

Shape Neck: Note: Change to stock st on next row, dropping markers. **Dividing Row:** K 23 (27-31), drop yarn but do not cut; sl next 27(29-31) sts to holder for neck; join 2 strands of new yarn and knit rem sts. Working across both sides of neck opening, continue in stock st (beg with a purl row) for 1½″. **Next Row (seed st row):** P1, * K1, P1; rep from * across. Work in seed st (rep prev row) for 1½(1 3/4-2)″. Then change to stock st and work 2½″ more. BO all sts.

Neckline: With right side facing and smaller size needles (remember to use 2 strands of yarn), pick up 14(16-18) sts along right neck shaping; sl sts from holder to free needle and work across these sts as follows: K1, (P1, K1) 13(14-15) times; pick up 14(16-18) sts along left neck shaping = 55(61-67) sts. **Next Row (seed st row):** * K1, P1; rep from * to last st, K1. Work in seed st (rep prev row) for 2″, ending by working last row on right side. BO all sts in knit.

FRONT
Work same as Back.

FINISHING
Sew shoulder and side seams. Weave in all ends. Lightly steam press on wrong side.

REVERSIBLE AFGHAN

designed by Doris England

The pattern stitch used in this beautiful afghan is reversible and works up quickly — using 3 strands of yarn and combining colors to produce a shaded effect.

SIZE: Approx 56″ x 72″
MATERIALS
Worsted weight yarn:
  10 oz dark brown;
  14 oz medium brown;
  14 oz light brown;
  14 oz medium beige;
  14 oz light beige;
  14 oz ecru;
  10 oz white
Size 15, 36″ circular knitting needle (or size required for gauge)
Materials Note: Three strands of yarn (combining colors) are used throughout patt.
GAUGE: With 3 strands of yarn in Butterfly Patt St, 7 sts = 4″

BUTTERFLY PATTERN STITCH

Note: Before starting your afghan, make a sample swatch to practice the butterfly st. Use 3 strands of yarn and CO 19 sts; knit 2 rows and then work as follows.
Row 1: K3 (garter st edge), purl to last 3 sts, K3 (garter st edge).
Row 2: Knit.
Row 3: Rep Row 1.
Row 4: Knit.
Row 5: K3; * K3, work butterfly st as follows: *insert right-hand needle in next st 6 rows below as to knit* **(Fig 1)** [you will be skipping 5 rows]; *keeping needle in this position, sl st above off left-hand needle and unravel this st down 5 rows; then insert left-hand needle in st with right-hand needle and knit this st, pulling up approx 1¼″ lp in front of unraveled strands* **(Fig 2)** [*butterfly st made*]; rep from * [Note: Keep yarn slack at back of work when working next st so strands will form a "V" as shown in **Fig 3.**] to last 4 sts, K4.
Rep Rows 1 through 5 for patt.

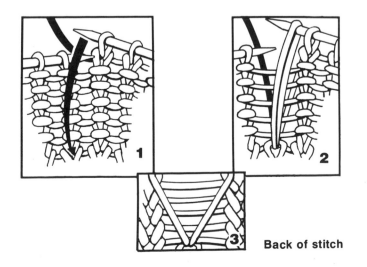

Back of stitch

INSTRUCTIONS

Note: Use 3 strands of yarn (combining colors as specified) throughout patt.
With 2 strands dk brown and 1 strand med brown, CO 115 sts *loosely.* Knit 4 rows. **Dec Row:** Knit across, decreasing 16 sts evenly spaced = 99 sts.
Continuing with same colors, work Rows 1 through 5, 3 times of Butterfly Patt St [3 patt repeats].
Continuing in Butterfly Patt St, work 4 patt repeats [rep Rows 1 through 5, 4 times] in each of the following 15 color combinations:
  1. 1 strand dk brown and 2 strands med brown
  2. 1 strand each dk, med and lt brown
  3. 2 strands med brown and 1 strand lt brown
  4. 1 strand med brown and 2 strands lt brown
  5. 1 strand each med brown, lt brown and med beige
  6. 2 strands lt brown and 1 strand med beige
  7. 1 strand med brown and 2 strands med beige
  8. 1 strand each lt brown, med and lt beige
  9. 2 strands med beige and 1 strand lt beige
  10. 1 strand med beige and 2 strands lt beige
  11. 1 strand each med beige, lt beige and ecru
  12. 2 strands lt beige and 1 strand ecru
  13. 1 strand lt beige and 2 strands ecru
  14. 1 strand each lt beige, ecru and white
  15. 2 strands ecru and 1 strand white

When last color combination is completed, continue with 1 strand ecru and 2 strands white in Butterfly Patt St and work 3 more patt repeats. Continuing with same colors, knit across next row, increasing 16 sts evenly spaced = 115 sts. Then knit 4 more rows. BO all sts *loosely.* Weave in all ends.

PONCHO COAT
designed by Mary Thomas
This beautiful garment is easy to make and a delight to
wear. We made ours with a lovely pure wool yarn that
gives a soft, easy-draping hand to the fabric. Worsted
weight synthetic yarn can also be used and will let you
machine wash and dry your garment.

**SIZE: Garment measures approx 41″ from bottom
edge to back of neck, and 52″ across back and arms
at shoulders.**
MATERIALS
**Chester Farms 2-ply pure wool yarn *or* any worsted
weight 4-ply yarn: 40 oz each Natural and Spice
Heather**
**Size 11, 14″ straight and 36″ circular knitting needles
(or size required for gauge)**
2 Small stitch holders
8 Buttons (1¼″ diameter)

Materials Notes: For yarn source (Chester Farms), see
page 4 . Yarn is used doubled (one strand of each color)
throughout patt.

**GAUGE: With 2 strands of yarn in stock st,
3 sts = 1″; 4 rows = 1″**

INSTRUCTIONS
Note: Use one strand each of Natural and Spice Heather
throughout patt.

BACK
With circular needle, CO 123 sts. Do not join; work back
and forth in rows. **Border Row:** Knit to last st, bring yarn
to front of work, sl 1 as to purl. **Note: Throughout patt
when row ends with a knit st, sl last st in this manner
for an even edge unless otherwise specified.** This will
not be mentioned again in instructions. Rep Border Row,
9 times more = garter st border. Now work as follows.

Row 1 (right side): Knit. **Row 2:** K5 (side garter st border), purl to last 5 sts; K5 (side garter st border). **Row 3 (inc row):** K6, work right increase **(Fig 1)**; knit to last 6 sts, work left increase **(Fig 2)**; K6 = 125 sts. **Row 4:** Rep Row 2. **Rows 5 through 10:** Rep Rows 1 and 2, 3 times. Rep Rows 3 through 10, 15 times more = 155 sts. Work even (rep Rows 1 and 2) until work measures 38" from CO edge, ending by working a wrong-side row.

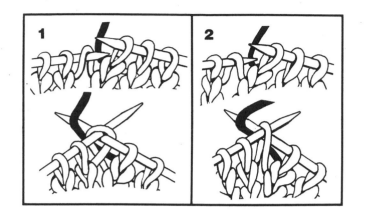

Top Shaping: Row 1: BO 15 sts in knit; knit rem sts = 140 sts. **Row 2:** BO 15 sts in purl; purl rem sts = 125 sts. **Row 3:** Sl 1 as to knit, K1, PSSO; BO 9 sts in knit, knit rem sts (do not sl last st) = 115 sts. **Row 4:** Sl 1 as to purl, P1, PSSO; BO 9 sts in purl, purl rem sts = 105 sts. Rep Rows 3 and 4, 4 times more. BO rem 25 sts for back of neck.

LEFT FRONT
With circular needle, CO 65 sts. Do not join; work back and forth in rows. Work garter st border (10 rows) same as Back. Then work as follows:
Row 1 (right side): Knit. **Row 2:** K7 (garter st front band), purl to last 5 sts; K5 (garter st side border). **Row 3 (inc row):** K4, work right increase **(Fig 1)**; knit rem sts = 66 sts. **Row 4:** Rep Row 2. **Rows 5 through 10:** Rep Rows 1 and 2, 3 times. Rep Rows 3 through 10, 8 times more; then rep Rows 3 and 4 once = 75 sts.

Work vertical buttonhole at side edge as follows. **Note:** Do not sl st at buttonhole edge. **First Half (worked on first 3 sts only): Row 1:** K3; leave rem sts unworked. **Row 2:** K3. **Row 3:** K3, cut yarn, leaving 4" ends for weaving in later. **Second Half (worked on rem 72 sts):** With right side facing, join yarn next to First Half. **Row 1:** Knit. **Row 2:** K7, purl to within 2 sts of buttonhole, K2. **Row 3:** Knit. **Joining Row:** K7, purl to within 2 sts of buttonhole, K2; continue with same yarn and knit across First Half (buttonhole completed).

Continue increasing at side edge as follows. Rep Rows 1 through 10 once; then rep Rows 3 through 10, 5 times more = 81 sts. Work even (rep Rows 1 and 2) until work measures 37½" from CO edge (½" less than Back), ending by working a knit row.
Top Shaping: Row 1 (wrong side): BO 7 sts of front band in knit; (one st now on right-hand needle) purl next 3 sts and sl these 4 sts to holder for front neck shaping; purl to last 5 sts, K5 = 70 sts. **Row 2:** BO 15 sts in knit; knit to last 2 sts, K2 tog = 54 sts. **Row 3:** Sl 1 as to purl, purl rem sts. **Row 4:** Sl 1 as to knit, K1, PSSO; BO 9 sts in knit, knit to last 2 sts; K2 tog = 43 sts. Rep Rows 3 and 4, 3 times more; then rep Row 3 once = 10 sts. **Last Row:** Sl 1 as to knit, K1, PSSO; BO rem sts in knit.

Measure and mark positions on front band for 6 buttons evenly spaced, with first button 17" above bottom edge and last button ½" below neck edge.

RIGHT FRONT
Work same as Left Front until garter st border (10 rows) is completed. Then work as follows. **Row 1 (right side):** Knit. **Row 2:** K5 (garter st side border), purl to last 7 sts, K7 (garter st front band). **Row 3 (inc row):** Knit to last 6 sts; work left increase **(Fig 2)**, K6 = 66 sts. **Row 4:** Rep Row 2. **Rows 5 through 10:** Rep Rows 1 and 2, 3 times. Rep Rows 3 through 10 until there are 81 sts on needle; then work even (rep Rows 1 and 2) AND AT THE SAME TIME work vertical buttonhole at side edge corresponding to Left Front *and* at each marked interval on front band as follows.

Front Band Buttonhole: Note: Beg on right side; do not sl st at buttonhole edge. **First Half (worked on first 4 sts only): Row 1:** K4; leave rem sts unworked. **Row 2:** K4. **Row 3:** K4; cut yarn, leaving 4" ends. **Second Half:** With right side facing, join yarn next to First Half. **Row 1:** Knit. **Row 2:** K5, purl to front band; K3. **Row 3:** Knit. **Joining Row:** K5, purl to front band, K3; continue with same yarn and knit across First Half (buttonhole completed).

Side Buttonhole: Note: Beg on wrong side; do not sl st at buttonhole edge. **First Half (worked on first 3 sts only): Row 1:** K3; leave rem sts unworked. **Row 2:** K3. **Row 3:** K3; cut yarn, leaving 4" ends. **Second Half:** With wrong side facing, join yarn next to First Half. **Row 1:** K2, purl to last 7 sts, K7. **Row 2:** Knit. **Row 3:** Rep Row 1.

Joining Row: Knit to buttonhole; continue with same yarn and knit across First Half (buttonhole completed).

When last buttonhole is completed, work even until work measures same as Left Front to first bind-off of Top Shaping, ending by working a wrong-side row.

Top Shaping: Row 1: BO 7 sts of front band in knit; (one st now on right-hand needle) knit *next* 3 sts and sl these 4 sts to holder for front neck shaping; knit rem sts = 70 sts. **Row 2:** BO 15 sts in purl; purl to last 2 sts, P2 tog = 54 sts. **Row 3:** Sl 1 as to purl, knit rem sts (do not sl last st). **Row 4:** Sl 1 as to purl, P1, PSSO; BO 9 sts in purl, purl to last 2 sts; P2 tog = 43 sts. Rep Rows 3 and 4, 3 times more; then rep Row 3 once = 10 sts. **Last Row:** Sl 1 as to purl, P1, PSSO; BO rem sts in purl.
Beg at side edge, sew top edges of fronts and back tog, ending at neck shaping.

HOOD
With right side facing and straight needles, join yarn (one strand of each color) at inside edge of right front band. **Row 1:** K4 from holder; pick up 12 sts along right neck shaping to seam; pick up 25 sts along BO sts at back of neck; pick up 12 sts along left neck shaping; K4 from holder (remember to sl last st) – 57 sts.
Row 2: K2, purl to last 2 sts; K2.

Row 3: K1, inc in next st [*to inc: knit in front and back of st*]; K 24, work right increase **(Fig 1)**; K5, work left increase **(Fig 2)**; knit rem sts = 60 sts.
Row 4: K1, inc in next st; purl to last 3 sts, K3 = 61 sts.
Row 5: K2, inc in next st; knit rem sts = 62 sts.
Row 6: K2, inc in next st; purl to last 4 sts, K4 = 63 sts.
Row 7: K3, inc in next st, K 24; work right increase **(Fig 1)**, K7, work left increase **(Fig 2)**; knit rem sts = 66 sts.
Row 8: K3, inc in next st, purl to last 5 sts; K5 = 67 sts.
Row 9: K4, inc in next st, knit rem sts = 68 sts.
Row 10: K4, inc in next st, purl to last 6 sts; K6 = 69 sts.
Row 11: K5, inc in next st, K 24; work right increase, K9, work left increase; knit rem sts = 72 sts.
Row 12: K5, inc in next st, purl to last 7 sts; K7 = 73 sts.
Row 13: K6, inc in next st, knit rem sts = 74 sts.
Row 14: K6, inc in next st, purl to last 8 sts; K8 = 75 sts.
Row 15: K7, inc in next st, K24; work right increase, K 11, work left increase; knit rem sts = 78 sts.
Row 16: K7, inc in next st, purl to last 9 sts; K9 = 79 sts.
Row 17: K8, inc in next st, knit rem sts = 80 sts.
Row 18: K8, inc in next st, purl to last 10 sts; K 10 = 81 sts.
Row 19: Knit.
Row 20: K 10, purl to last 10 sts; K 10.
Work even (rep Rows 19 and 20) until Hood measures 9″ from back neck edge, ending by working a knit row.
Top Shaping: Dividing Row: K 10, P 21; BO next 19 sts in purl; purl to last 10 sts, K 10. Continue working across each section (join new yarn to work left section) as follows. **Row 1:** Knit across both sections. **Row 2:** K 10, purl rem sts of left section; purl across sts of right section to last 10 sts, K 10. Rep last 2 rows until sections measure 3″ from BO sts of Top Shaping, ending by working a wrong-side row. Cut yarn, leaving approx 50″ length for weaving. Beg at outer edge and weave sts of sections tog (see *Weaving on Two Needles* on page 13). Sew edge of sections just joined to BO sts of Top Shaping at back of Hood.

LEFT POCKET
With straight needles (remember to use one strand of each color), CO 22 sts. **Row 1:** Inc in first st [*to inc: knit in front and back of st*]; knit rem sts = 23 sts. **Row 2:** Knit. **Row 3:** Rep Row 1 = 24 sts. **Row 4:** K2 (garter st edge), purl to last 2 sts; K2 (garter st edge). **Row 5:** Knit. Rep last 2 rows until piece measures 4″ from CO edge, ending by working a wrong-side row.

Dec Row (right side): K2, work dec as follows: sl next 2 sts knitwise to right-hand needle **(Fig 3)**; then insert tip of left-hand needle through same sts **(Fig 4)** and knit both sts tog in this position = dec made; knit rem sts = 23 sts.

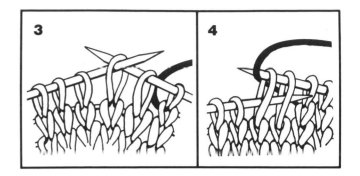

Work 7 rows even (rep Rows 4 and 5, 3 times; then rep Row 4 once more). Rep last 8 rows, 3 times more; then rep Dec Row once more = 19 sts. **Next Row:** Knit. **Last Row:** K1, K2 tog; knit rem sts = 18 sts. BO all sts in knit. Cut yarn, leaving approx 40″ sewing length.

RIGHT POCKET
With straight needles, CO 22 sts. **Row 1:** Knit to last 2 sts; inc in next st, K1 = 23 sts. **Row 2:** Knit. **Row 3:** Rep Row 1 = 24 sts. **Row 4:** K2, purl to last 2 sts; K2. **Row 5:** Knit. Rep last 2 rows until piece measures 4″ from CO edge, ending by working a wrong-side row.
Dec Row (right side): Knit to last 4 sts; K2 tog, K2 = 23 sts. Work 7 rows even (rep Rows 4 and 5, 3 times; then rep Row 4 once more). Rep last 8 rows, 3 times more; then rep Dec Row once more = 19 sts. **Next Row:** Knit. **Last Row:** Knit to last 3 sts; K2 tog, K1 = 18 sts. BO all sts in knit. Cut yarn, leaving approx 40″ sewing length.

FINISHING
Position corresponding pocket on each front, aligning straight side edge 2″ from front band and top (BO) edge approx 11½″ below neck edge. Sew pockets in place, leaving approx 8″ at decreased side shaping free for opening. Weave in all ends. Sew on buttons (at side edge, sew button on inside edge of back). Fold back approx 2″ cuff on hood.

CAR COAT
designed by Doris England

A dimensional textured effect is given to this garment with the alternating bands of garter stitch and a pattern stitch.

SIZES:	Small	Medium	Large
Body Bust:	33″	37″	41″
Garment Measurements:			
bust	39″	43″	47″
length to underarm	17″	17″	17″
sleeve length	18″	18″	18″

Size Note: Instructions are written for sizes as follows: Small(Medium-Large).

MATERIALS
Dawn Sayelle* **Knitting Worsted Size TWEED yarn in 3-oz skeins: 7(9-11) skeins each Sand Tones and Buckwheat**
Size 11, 14″ straight and 29″ circular knitting needles (or size required for gauge)
Stitch holders: 2 small and 1 medium
14 Stitch markers
4 Beige buttons (1″ diameter)
Materials Note: Yarn is used doubled (one strand of each color) throughout patt.

GAUGE: With 2 strands of yarn:
in garter st, 3 sts = 1″; 8 rows = 1½″
in stock st, 3 sts = 1″; 4 rows = 1″

PATTERN STITCHES

PATTERN A (worked on 24 sts and 14 rows)
Row 1 (right side): P8, K8, P8.
Row 2: Purl.
Row 3: K1, P8, K6, P8, K1.
Row 4: Purl.
Row 5: K2, P8; K4, P8, K2.
Row 6: P 10, K1; P2, K1, P 10.
Row 7: K 11, P2, K 11.
Row 8: Rep Row 6.
Row 9: Rep Row 5.
Row 10: Purl.
Row 11: Rep Row 3.
Row 12: Purl.
Row 13: Rep Row 1.
Row 14: Purl.

PATTERN B (worked on 14 sts and 14 rows)
Row 1 (right side): K3, P8, K3.
Rows 2, 4, 6, 8, 10, 12 and 14: Purl.
Row 3: K2, P4; K2, P4, K2.
Row 5: K1, P4; K4, P4, K1.
Row 7: P4, K2; P2, K2, P4.
Row 9: Rep Row 5.
Row 11: Rep Row 3.
Row 13: Rep Row 1.

PATTERN C (worked on 14 sts and 14 rows)
Row 1 (right side): K6, P8.
Rows 2, 4, 6, 8, 10, 12 and 14: Purl.
Row 3: K5, P8, K1.
Row 5: K4, P8, K2.
Row 7: K3, P8, K3.
Row 9: K2, P8, K4.
Row 11: K1, P8, K5.
Row 13: P8, K6.

INSTRUCTIONS
Note: Use 2 strands (one of each color) throughout patt.

POCKET LINING (make 2)
With straight needles, CO 20 sts. Work in stock st for 5½″. Cut yarn, leaving 30″ sewing length. Sl all sts to sm holder; set aside.

BODY
Note: Worked in one piece to underarms. With circular needle, CO 124(136-148) sts. Do not join; work back and forth in rows.

Garter St Band: Rows 1 through 6: Knit. **Row 7 (buttonhole row):** K3, YO (buttonhole), K2 tog; knit rem sts = 124(136-148) sts (YO counts as one st). **Row 8:** Knit.

Patt Band: Row 1 (right side): Knit. **Row 2 (marking row):** K7 (garter st front band), P1(4-7); place marker, P 24, place marker; * P4(6-8); place marker, P 24, place marker; rep from * twice more; P1(4-7), K7 (garter st front band). **Note:** Sl markers throughout patt, unless otherwise specified. **Rows 3 through 16:** Work Patt A on 24 sts between each set of markers, keeping 7 sts of each front band in garter st and rem sts in stock st.

Garter St Band: Note: Remove markers on next row. **Rows 1 through 7:** Work same as prev Garter St Band. **Row 8 (pocket openings):** K10(13-16); BO next 20 sts for pocket opening; knit to last 30(33-36) sts; BO next 20 sts for pocket opening; knit rem sts.

Patt Band: Row 1: K 10(13-16); † *sl sts of one pocket lining with knit-side facing you to left-hand needle, then knit across 20 sts of lining* †; knit to last 30(33-36) sts; rep from † to † once; knit rem sts = 124(136-148) sts. **Row 2 (marking row):** K7, PO(3-3); place marker, P 14, place marker; * P2(3-5); place marker, P 14, place marker; rep from * 5 times more; PO(3-3), K7. **Rows 3 through 16:** Work Patt B on 14 sts between each set of markers, keeping 7 sts of each front band in garter st and rem sts in stock st.

Garter St Band: Note: Keep markers (to be used in next patt band). **Rows 1 through 8:** Work same as beg Garter St Band.

Patt Band: Row 1: Knit. **Row 2:** K7, purl to last 7 sts, K7. **Rows 3 through 16:** Work Patt C on 14 sts between each set of markers, keeping 7 sts of each front band in garter st and rem sts in stock st.

Garter St Band: Note: Remove markers on next row. **Rows 1 through 8:** Work same as beg Garter St Band.

Dividing Row (right side): For collar: K6, inc in next st for collar shaping; place marker to separate sts of collar and front. For right front: K2 tog (dec made) for neck shaping, K 19(21-23); sl 28(30-32) sts on right-hand needle to sm holder for right front shaping to be worked later. BO next 12(14-16) sts for underarm. For back: knit *next* (one st already on right-hand needle) 43(47-51) sts and sl these 44(48-52) sts to med holder for back shaping to be worked later. BO next 12(14-16) sts for underarm. For left front: knit to last 9 sts, K2 tog for neck shaping; place marker to separate sts of front and collar. For collar: inc in next st for collar shaping, K6. **Note:** Sl collar markers on each following row; keep collar sts in garter st.

Left Front Shaping: Change to straight needles. Work the following bands AND AT THE SAME TIME continue neck and collar shaping as follows: dec one st *before* collar marker EVERY 6th row 6(6-7) times more *and* inc one st *after* collar marker EOR until front is completed.

Patt Band: Marking Row (wrong side): K8, P4(5-6); place marker, P 14, place marker; P2(3-4). **Next 14 Rows:** Work Patt B on 14 sts between markers and rem sts in stock st.

Garter St Band: Note: On next row, remove patt markers only; leave collar markers. Knit 8 rows.

Patt Band: Knit one row. **Marking Row:** Knit collar sts; P2(3-4); place marker, P 14, place marker; PO(1-2). **Next 14 Rows:** Work Patt C on 14 sts between markers and rem sts in stock st. **Note:** On next row, remove patt markers only. Work 0(2-6) rows in stock st.

Shoulder and Collar Shaping: Continuing in stock st and remembering to increase for collar shaping, BO from armhole edge as follows: 7(8-9) sts once; 7(8-8) sts once. You should now have 28(29-31) sts left for collar. Beg at outside edge and work collar shaping for back of neck as follows. **Row 1 (short row):** Knit to last 6 sts, TURN (leave 6 sts unworked). **Row 2:** Sl first st as to purl, knit rem sts. **Rows 3 and 4:** Knit across all sts. **Row 5 (short row):** Knit to last 7 sts, TURN (leave 7 sts unworked). **Rows 6 through 8:** Rep Rows 2 through 4. Rep last 4-row sequence having one more st left unworked each time until there are 13 sts left unworked. BO all sts in knit. Cut yarn, leaving approx 32″ sewing length.

Right Front Shaping: With wrong side facing and straight needles, sl sts from holder to needle; join yarn (one strand of each color). Work the following bands AND AT THE SAME TIME continue neck and collar shaping as follows: inc one st *before* collar marker EOR until front is completed *and* dec one st *after* collar marker EVERY 6th row, 6(6-7) times more.

Patt Band: Marking Row (wrong side): P2(3-4); place marker, P 14, place marker; P4(5-6), K8. **Next 14 Rows:** Work Patt B on 14 sts between markers and rem sts in stock st.

Garter St Band: Note: Remove markers on next row. Knit 8 rows.

Patt Band: Row 1: Knit. **Row 2 (marking row):** PO(1-2); place marker, P14, place marker; P2(3-4), knit collar sts. **Rows 3 through 16:** Work Patt C on 14 sts between markers and rem sts in stock st. **Note:** On next row, remove patt markers only. Work 1(3-7) rows in stock st.

Shoulder and Collar Shaping: Work same as in Left Front Shaping.

Back Shaping
With wrong side facing and straight needles, sl sts from holder to needle. Join yarn (one strand of each color) and work as follows.

Patt Band: Marking Row (wrong side): PO(1-3); place marker, P 14, place marker; * P1(2-2); place marker, P 14, place marker; rep from * once more; PO(1-3). **Next 14 Rows:** Work Patt B on 14 sts between each set of markers and rem sts in stock st.

Garter St Band: Note: Keep markers (to be used in next patt band). Knit 8 rows.

Patt Band: Row 1: Knit. **Row 2:** Purl. **Next 14 Rows:** Work Patt C on 14 sts between each set of markers and rem sts in stock st. **Note:** On next row, remove markers. Work 0(2-6) rows in stock st.

Shoulder Shaping: Continuing in stock st, BO 7(8-9) sts at beg of next 2 rows; BO 7(8-8) sts at beg of next 2 rows; BO rem 16(16-18) sts for back of neck.

SLEEVE (make 2)

With straight needles and 2 strands of yarn (one strand of each color), CO 56(60-64) sts.

Garter St Band: Knit 10 rows.

Patt Band: Row 1 (right side): Knit. **Row 2 (marking row):** P3(4-6); place marker, P 24, place marker; P2(4-4); place marker, P 24, place marker; P3(4-6). **Rows 3 through 16:** Work Patt A on 24 sts between each set of markers and rem sts in stock st.

Garter St Band: Note: Remove markers on next row. Knit 8 rows.

Patt Band: Row 1: Knit. **Row 2 (marking row):** P3(4-5); place marker, P 14, place marker; * P4(5-6); place marker, P 14, place marker; rep from * once more; P3(4-5). **Rows 3 through 16:** Work Patt B on 14 sts between each set of markers and rem sts in stock st.

Garter St Band: Note: Keep markers (to be used on next patt band). Knit 8 rows.

Patt Band: Row 1: Knit. **Row 2:** Purl. **Rows 3 through 16:** Work Patt C on 14 sts between each set of markers and rem sts in stock st.

Garter St Band: Note: Remove markers on next row. Knit 10 rows. BO all sts *loosely*.

FINISHING

Block pieces to measurements by pinning each piece out on a flat padded surface. Lightly spray with water; then let dry thoroughly before removing pins and assembling. Sew shoulder and sleeve seams. Sew BO edge of sleeves into armholes, aligning center of sleeve with shoulder seam and 6(7-8) sts on each side of sleeve seam with BO sts at underarm. Sew BO edges of collar tog at back of neck; then sew collar to back neck edge. Sew pocket linings in place; sew on buttons.

Fashion Show

Chapter 4

Knitted fashions are beautiful — and this chapter gives you a wide selection of patterns for garments such as a two-piece dress, an authentic Shetland shawl, and an innovative pullover that combines knitting with a fur-like fabric. We've also included a vest, wrap sweater and jacket with matching scarf for the larger-sized woman.

Two-piece DRESS

designed by Mary Thomas

This beautiful dress has a soft, easy fit, and is a breeze to knit. The top by itself makes a fashionable sweater. Be sure your gauge is exactly that specified, and check it again every few inches as you work the pieces.

SIZES:

Body Measurements:	Petite	Small	Medium	Large
bust	32″	34″	36″	38″
waist	24″	26″	28″	30″
hip	34″	36″	38″	40″
Garment Measurements:				
Skirt:				
waist (before inserting elastic)	30″	32″	34″	36″
hip	36″	38″	40″	42″
length	26″	26″	26″	26″
Pullover:				
bust	34″	36″	38″	40″
length to underarm	13″	13½″	14″	14″
sleeve length to underarm	16½″	17″	17½″	17½″

Size Note: Instructions are written for sizes as follows: Petite(Small-Medium-Large).

MATERIALS

"Concorde" sport weight yarn in 1¾ oz-balls:
    12(13-15-16) balls Brique
Sizes 4 and 6, 14″ straight knitting needles (or size required for gauge)
Stitch holders: 1 small and 1 medium
6 Stitch markers
¾″ Elastic (1 yd length)
Materials Note: For yarn source (Joseph Galler Inc.), see page 4.

GAUGE: With larger size needles in stock st,
6 sts = 1″; 8 rows = 1″

SKIRT INSTRUCTIONS

BACK

Waistline Casing: With larger size needles, CO 90(96-102-108) sts *loosely*. Knit one row. Change to smaller size needles; beg with a purl row and work in stock st for 1″, ending by working a knit row. **Next Row (turning ridge):** Knit.
Change to larger size needles. Beg with a knit row and work 8 rows in stock st. Continuing in stock st, inc one st at each end of next row and then EVERY following 6th row, 8 times = 108(114-120-126) sts. Now inc one st at each end EVERY 8th row, 15 times = 138(144-150-156) sts. Work even until skirt measures approx 26″ from turning ridge or desired length, ending by working a knit row.
Hem: Change to smaller size needles. **Next Row (turning ridge):** Knit. Beg with a knit row and work in stock st for ¾″. Change to larger size needles and work one more row. BO all sts *loosely*.

FRONT

Work same as Back.

FINISHING

Block pieces to measurements. Sew side seams. Fold hem to inside and slip stitch *loosely* in place. Fold waistline casing to inside and slip stitch *loosely* in place, leaving approx 2″ free at either side seam for elastic insertion. Cut elastic to waist measurement and then insert through casing. Sew ends of elastic securely; sew rem 2″ of casing in place.

PULLOVER INSTRUCTIONS

BACK

With smaller size needles, CO 102(108-114-120) sts *loosely*. Work in K1, P1 ribbing for 3″, increasing one st at end of last row = 103(109-115-121) sts. **Eyelet Row:** K1; * YO, K2 tog; rep from * across = 103(109-115-121) sts (counting each YO as one st). Change to larger size needles. Beg with a purl row and work even in stock st until piece measures 13(13½-14-14)″ from CO edge or desired length to underarm, ending by working a purl row.
Shape Armholes: Continuing in stock st, BO 5(7-8-9) sts at beg of next 2 rows = 93(95-99-103) sts. Dec one st at each armhole edge EOR 5(5-6-6) times = 83(85-87-91) sts. Work even until armhole measures 7¾(8-8¼-8½)″, ending by working a purl row.
Shape Neck and Shoulders: Row 1 (dividing row): BO 6 sts, (one st now on right-hand needle) knit *next* 23(24-24-26) sts; sl next 23(23-25-25) sts to med holder for back of neck; join new ball of yarn and knit rem 30(31-31-33) sts of left shoulder. **Row 2:** BO 6 sts, purl to neck edge; BO 3 sts at right neck edge, purl rem sts. **Row 3:** BO 5(6-6-6) sts, knit to neck edge; BO 3 sts at left neck edge, knit rem sts. **Row 4:** BO 5(6-6-6) sts, purl to neck edge; BO 3 sts at right neck edge, purl rem sts. **Row 5:** BO 5(5-5-6) sts, knit to neck edge; BO 3 sts at left neck edge, knit rem sts. **Row 6:** BO 5(5-5-6) sts, purl to neck edge; BO 3 sts at right neck edge, purl rem sts. **Row 7:** BO rem 5(5-5-6) sts of right shoulder; BO 3 sts at left neck edge, knit rem sts. BO rem 5(5-5-6) sts.

FRONT

Work same as Back until Eyelet Row is completed. Change to larger size needles. Purl one row; then work in patt as follows.

Row 1 (right side): K 18(21-23-26); † *place marker for side pattern stitch and work as follows on next 13 sts:* P1, K1, P1; RT (right twist) **[to make RT: K2 tog but do not remove from left-hand needle (Fig 1); knit first st on left-hand needle again (Fig 2); then sl both sts off left-**

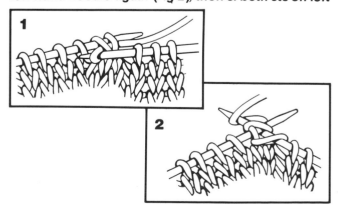

hand needle = **RT made**]; *P3, RT; P1, K1, P1; place marker;* † K 15(15-16-16); place marker for center pattern stitch and work as follows on next 11 sts; *P1, K1, P1; RT, P1, RT; P1, K1, P1;* place marker; K 15 (15-16-16); rep from † to † once; K 18 (21-23-26). **Note:** Sl markers on each following row.

Row 2: † *Purl to marker; K3, P7, K3;* † purl to next marker, K3, P2, K1; P2, K3; rep from † to † once; purl rem sts. Rep last 2 rows until piece measures same as Back to underarm, ending by working a wrong-side row.

Shape Armholes, Neck and Shoulders: Row 1 (dividing row): BO 6 sts, knit to marker; work in established patt st across next 13 sts, purl to next marker; P1, K1, P1; RT, sl next (center) st to sm holder; join new ball of yarn to work other side; RT, P1, K1, P1; knit to next marker, work in established patt st across next 10 sts, knit rem sts. **Row 2:** BO 6 sts, purl to marker; work in established patt st across next 13 sts, purl to next marker; K3, P2; work across other side as follows: P2, K3, purl to next marker; work in established patt st across next 13 sts, purl rem sts. Continuing to work in this manner across each side with a separate ball of yarn, keeping continuity of pattern sts, work shaping as follows. Dec one st at each armhole edge EOR 5(5-6-6) times AND AT THE SAME TIME dec one st at each neck edge EVERY 3rd row. Then keeping armhole edges even, continue to dec one st at each neck edge EVERY 3rd row until 21(22-22-24) sts rem on needle. Work even (if necessary) until armhole measures same as Back to shoulder; then BO from each armhole edge EOR as follows: 6 sts once; 5(6-6-6) sts once; 5(5-5-6) sts twice.

SLEEVE (make 2)
With larger size needles, CO 48(50-52-54) sts. Change to smaller size needles and work in K1, P1 ribbing for 3″, increasing one st at end of last row = 49(51-53-55) sts. **Eyelet Row:** K1; * YO, K2 tog; rep from * across = 49(51-53-55) sts (counting each YO as one st). Change to larger size needles. **Next Row:** Purl across, increasing 4 sts evenly spaced = 53(55-57-59) sts. Now work in patt as follows.

Row 1 (right side): K 20(21-22-23); place marker for center pattern stitch and work as follows on next 13 sts: P1, K1, P1; RT, P3, RT; P1, K1, P1; place marker, knit rem 20(21-22-23) sts. **Note:** Sl markers on each following row.
Row 2: Purl to marker; K3, P7, K3; purl rem sts.
Working in patt as established (rep Rows 1 and 2), inc one st at each end EVERY 8th row, 9(10-11-11) times = 71(75-79-81) sts. Then work even until sleeve measures 16½(17-17½-17½)″ or desired length to underarm.
Shape Cap: Continuing in patt as established, BO 5(7-8-9) sts at beg of next 2 rows = 61(61-63-63) sts. Then dec one st at each end EOR until 17(15-15-15) sts rem on needle. BO all sts.

FINISHING
Block pieces to measurements. Sew right shoulder seam.
Neck Ribbing: Beg at left front neck edge with right side facing and smaller size needles; pick up 54(56-58-60) sts along left front neck edge; knit st from holder and mark this st with a piece of contrasting yarn or sm safety pin; pick up 54(56-58-60) sts along right front neck edge to shoulder seam; pick up 12 sts along right back neck edge; K 23(23-25-25) from back neck holder; pick up 12 sts along left back neck edge = 156(160-166-170) sts.
Note: Continue to mark center front st on each following row. **Row 1 (wrong side):** * K1, P1; rep from * across.
Row 2: * K1, P1; rep from * to within 2 sts of marked st; sl 1 as to knit, K1, PSSO; knit marked st, K2 tog, P1; ** K1, P1; rep from ** across rem sts. **Row 3:** * K1, P1; rep from * to within 2 sts of marked st; K2 tog, purl marked st; K2 tog, P1; ** K1, P1; rep from ** across rem sts. **Rows 4 and 5:** Rep Rows 2 and 3. **Row 6 (eyelet row):** K1, YO; * K2 tog, YO; rep from * to within one st of marked st; K2 tog and mark this st for center st, YO; ** K2 tog, YO; rep from ** to last st, P1. **Note:** On next row, work each YO as one st.
Row 7: * K1, P1; rep from * to within 2 sts of marked st; P2 tog, purl marked st, P2 tog; ** K1, P1; rep from ** across rem sts. BO all sts in ribbing.
Sew left shoulder seam and weave ends of neck ribbing tog. Sew side and sleeve seams; sew sleeves into armholes. Weave in all ends.

Two-piece Dress — page 63

Reversible Afghan — page 55

Vest — page 49

Triangular Shawl — page 82

Cable Cardigan Vest — page 42

Jacket Sweater — page 27

Jacket Sweater — page 27

Boot Toppers — page 96

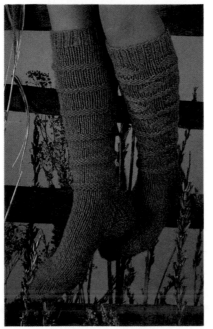

Knee Socks — page 98

Knit-in Design for Jacket Sweater — page 27

Fitted Vest — page 83

Ski Sweater and Hat — page 33

Bargello Afghan — page 143

Heirloom Bedspread — page 152

Long Stitch Vest — page 85

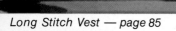

Irish Islands Afghan — page 138

Sport Headband — page 100

Pillows: Fisherman — page 139 and Norwegian — page 140

Cardigan Sweater — page 40

riped Pullover — page 86

be Knee Socks — page 97

Pullover Vest — page 38

Argyle Vest — page 38

2-needle Mittens and Hat — page 100

Fisherman Cardigan — page 35

Fair Isle Pullover and Hat —

Furry Jacket — page 87

Christmas Afghan — page 149

70

Norwegian Pullover — page 25   Raglan Pullover and Hat — page 44   Raglan Pullover and Hat — page 44

Raglan Pullover and Hat — page 44   Dutch Tiles Afghan — page 144

Tube Dolls — page 124

Owl Sweater — page 133

Helmet and Mittens — page 123

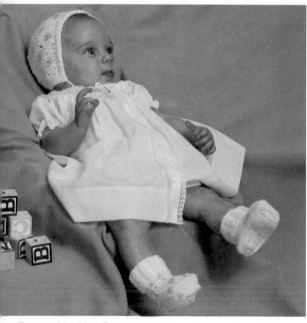

Forget Me Not Bonnet and Booties — page 121

Baby Layette — page 116

Twist Bonnet and Booties — page 120

Toddler Scarf — page 128

Christening Dress and Bonnet — page 114

alentine Baby Afghan — page 132

Gingerbread Boy — page 129

Dog Coat — page 110

73

Shoulderette Bed Jacket — page 52

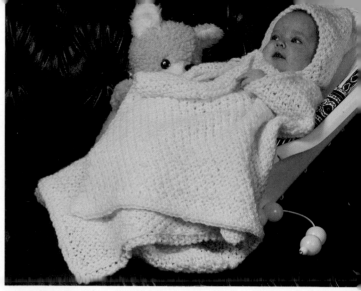

Infant Seat Hooded Wrap — page 131

Tam — page 105

Quick Knit Top — page 51

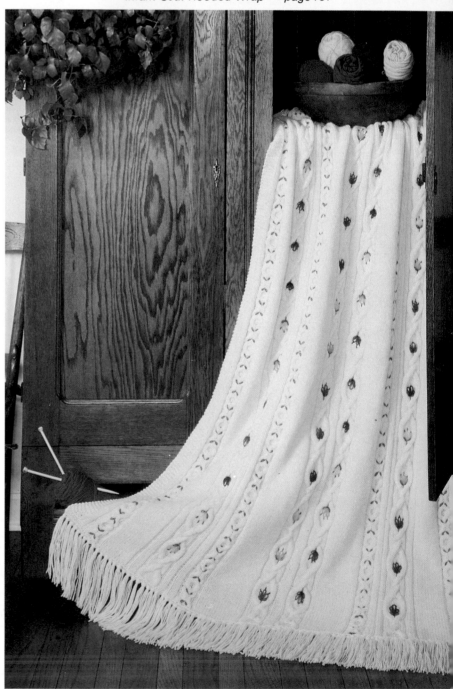

Cable Garden Afghan — page 147

at, Scarf and Mittens — *page 53*

Striped Bonnet and Booties — *page 119*

Seascape Afghan — *page 137*

etland Lace Shawl — **page 81**

Cardigan Vest — *page 89*

75

Car Coat — page 59

Summer Skies Afghan — page 142

Doily — page 153

Golf Club Covers — page 112

Mopsies Slippers — page 109

Ballet Leg Warmers — pa

76

Poncho Coat — page 56

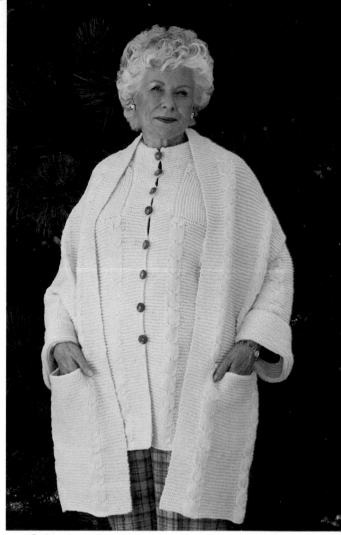

Cable Jacket and Scarf — page 92

Cable Pullover (Version A) — page 23

T-Sweater — page 54

Potholders — page 158

Table Runner — page 155

World's Greatest Dishcloth — page 160

Sunrise Afghan — page 136

Pincushion — page 158

Snug Snake Draft Chaser — page 157

ce Edgings — page 156

Jute Handbag — page 103

Knitter's Pin — page 107

cy Mohair Afghan — page 141

Gloves — page 106

Cable Pullover (Version B) — page 23

Cable Pullover (Version A) — page 23   Dickey — page 108

Chenille Hat and Scarf — page 104   Striped Hat and Mittens — page 102   Wrap Sweater — page 90

SHETLAND LACE SHAWL

designed by Jean Leinhauser

Lace knitting is an ancient art which reached its peak on the Shetland Islands off the coast of Scotland. There the island women spun the native wool into gossamer threads which they worked on fine steel needles to create delicate and elaborate shawls of great beauty. These shawls, especially popular during the Victorian period, were often called "wedding ring shawls" as they were fine enough to draw through a gold wedding band.
Our version, made with baby weight yarn and size 10 needle, features a traditional old Shetland pattern, called "Horseshoe", which is easy to knit yet gives a lovely, lacy effect.

SIZE: Approx 52″ wide x 45″ long with edging

MATERIALS
Baby weight yarn: 12 oz ecru
Size 10, 36″ circular knitting needle (or size required for gauge)

GAUGE: In "Horseshoe" patt st, 10 sts = 2″

INSTRUCTIONS

CO 201 sts. Do not join; work back and forth in rows. Knit first row; then work in patt as follows.
"Horseshoe" Pattern Stitch
Row 1 (wrong side): K1; * P9, K1; rep from * across.
Row 2: P1; * K3, YO, sl 1 as to knit, K2 tog, PSSO; YO, K3, P1; rep from * across.
Row 3: Purl.
Row 4: K1; * YO, K3; sl 1 as to knit, K2 tog, PSSO; K3, YO, K1; rep from * across.
Row 5: Purl.
Row 6: P1; * K1, YO, K2; sl 1 as to knit, K2 tog, PSSO; K2, YO, K1, P1; rep from * across.
Row 7: K1; * P9, K1; rep from * across.
Row 8: P1; * K2, YO, K1; sl 1 as to knit, K2 tog, PSSO; K1, YO, K2, P1; rep from * across.
Rep Rows 1 through 8 until piece measures approx 38″ long. Then rep Rows 1 and 2 once more. BO all sts *loosely*.

EDGING (make 4 pieces)
Note: Edging is worked separately in 4 pieces; then sewn to shawl and joined at corners.
CO 283 sts. Do not join; work back and forth in rows.
Row 1 (right side): Knit in back lp (**Fig 1**) of first st [abbreviated K1-b]; * P2, K1-b; rep from * across.

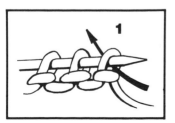

Row 2: P1; * K1-b, K1, P1; rep from * across.
Rep last 2 rows until piece measures 2½″ from CO edge, ending by working Row 2. Then work last 3 rows as follows.
Row 1: K1-b; * drop next st off needle, P1, K1-b; rep from * across.
Row 2: P1; * K1-b, P1; rep from * across.
Row 3: K1-b; * P1, K1-b; rep from * across.
BO all sts *loosely*. Unravel each dropped st all the way down to the CO edge.

FINISHING
With right sides of shawl and edging facing up, sew BO edge of edging pieces to sides of shawl. Then weave ends of edging tog at corners. Weave in all ends.

TRIANGULAR SHAWL
designed by Mary Thomas

SIZE: Approx 60″ wide x 28″ deep before fringing

MATERIALS
Worsted weight yarn: 18 oz white
Size 11, 14″ straight knitting needles (or size required for gauge)

**GAUGE: In garter st,
          7 sts = 2″; 6 rows (3 ridges) = 1″**

INSTRUCTIONS
Note: Each YO counts as one st throughout patt.
CO 211 sts.
Row 1 (wrong side): Knit.
Row 2: Knit.
Row 3: K2 tog, knit to last 2 sts, K2 tog = 209 sts.
Row 4: Knit.

Rows 5 through 10: Rep Rows 3 and 4, 3 times = 203 sts.
Row 11: K2 tog, K2; * YO, K2 tog; rep from * to last 3 sts, K1, K2 tog = 201 sts.
Row 12: K2 tog, K1; * YO, sl 1 as to knit, K1, PSSO; rep from * to last 2 sts, K2 tog = 199 sts.
Rows 13 through 16: Rep Rows 11 and 12, twice = 191 sts.
Rep Rows 1 through 16, 9 times more (**Note:** You will be decreasing 20 sts every 16 rows.) = 11 sts. Then rep Rows 1 through 10 once = 3 sts. BO rem sts. Weave in all ends.

FRINGE
Follow *Basic Fringe Instructions* on page 16 and make Single Knot Fringe. Cut 20″ strands of yarn and use 4 strands for each knot of fringe. Tie 63 knots of fringe evenly spaced across each side of shawl.

FITTED VEST

designed by Mary Thomas

SIZES:

	Petite	Small	Medium	Large
Body Bust:	29"	33"	37"	41"
Garment Measurements:				
bust	31"	35"	39"	43"
length to underarm	8"	8"	8"	8"

Size Note: Instructions are written for sizes as follows: Petite(Small-Medium-Large).

MATERIALS
Worsted weight yarn: 7(8-10-12) oz beige heather
Size 7, 14″ straight knitting needles (or size required for gauge)
Size F aluminum crochet hook (for edging only)
2 Stitch markers
4 Buttons (⅝″ diameter)

GAUGE: In stock st, 5 sts = 1″; 7 rows = 1″

PATTERN STITCH (worked on 9 sts)
Note: Each YO counts as one st.
Rows 1, 3 and 5 (wrong side): Purl.
Row 2: K2 tog, K2; YO, K1, YO; K2, sl 1 as to knit, K1, PSSO.
Row 4: K2 tog, K1; YO, K3, YO; K1, sl 1 as to knit, K1, PSSO.
Row 6: K2 tog; YO, K5, YO; sl 1 as to knit, K1, PSSO.
Rep Rows 1 through 6 for patt.

INSTRUCTIONS

BACK
CO 70(76-84-94) sts. Work 6 rows even in stock st. Continuing in stock st, dec one st at each end EOR twice = 66(72-80-90) sts. Work 2 rows even. Now inc one st at each end of next row and then each following 6(4-4-4)th row, 5(7-8-8) times = 78(88-98-108) sts. Work even until piece measures 8″ from CO edge or desired length to underarm, ending by working a purl row.
Shape Armholes: Continuing in stock st, BO 4(5-6-8) sts at beg of next 2 rows = 70(78-86-92) sts. Dec one st at each end EOR 3(4-5-6) times = 64(70-76-80) sts. Work even until armhole measures 8½(9-9½-10)″, ending by working a purl row.
Shape Neck and Shoulders: Row 1 (dividing row): K 25(27-29-30) sts; BO next 14(16-18-20) sts for back of neck; knit rem sts. **Row 2:** Purl across both sides of neck opening (join another ball of yarn to work right shoulder). Continuing to work across each side with a separate ball of yarn, BO 2 sts at each neck ege EOR twice AND AT THE SAME TIME shape shoulders as follows: BO 7(8-9-9) sts at beg of next 2 rows; BO 7(8-8-9) sts at beg of next 2 rows; BO 7(7-8-8) sts at beg of next 2 rows.

LEFT FRONT
CO 3 sts. Beg bottom V-shaping as follows.
Row 1: Knit.
Row 2: Purl to last st, inc in last st = 4 sts.
Row 3: Inc in first st, knit to last 2 sts; inc in next st, K1 = 6 sts.
Rep last 2 rows, 9(6-2-1) time(s) more = 33(24-12-9) sts.

Sizes (Small-Medium-Large) ONLY: Continue V-shaping as follows. **Row 1:** Purl to last st, inc in last st = (25-13-10) sts. **Row 2:** CO one st, then inc in CO st; knit to last 2 sts, inc in next st, K1 = (28-16-13) sts. Rep these 2 rows, (2-6-8) times more = (36-40-45) sts.

ALL SIZES: Establish Patt St and continue shaping as follows.

Row 1 (wrong side): P7(7-7-8); place marker for Patt St, work Row 1 of Patt St on next 9 sts, place marker; purl rem sts. **Note:** Sl markers on each following row.
Row 2: Knit to marker; work in Patt St across next 9 sts; knit to last 2 sts, inc in next st, K1 = 34(37-41-46) sts.
Row 3: Purl.
Rows 4 and 5: Rep Rows 2 and 3 = 35(38-42-47) sts. Bottom V-shaping is now completed; continue with side shaping (corresponding to shaping on Back) as follows.
Row 6: K2 tog, knit to marker; work in Patt St across next 9 sts; knit rem sts = 34(37-41-46) sts.
Row 7: Purl.
Rows 8 and 9: Rep Rows 6 and 7 = 33(36-40-45) sts.
Row 10: Knit to marker; work in Patt St across next 9 sts; knit rem sts.
Row 11: Purl.
Row 12: Inc in first st, knit to marker; work in Patt St across next 9 sts; knit rem sts = 34(37-41-46) sts.
Keeping 9 sts between markers in Patt St and rem sts in stock st, continue to inc one st at side edge EVERY 6(4-4-4)th row, 5(7-8-8) times more = 39(44-49-54) sts.

Work even until piece measures same as Back to underarm, ending by working a **purl** row, AND AT THE SAME TIME when 9 repeats of Patt St have been completed (54 rows total), drop markers and work 9 sts in stock st.

Shape Armhole, Neck and Shoulder: Continuing in stock st, BO 4(5-6-8) sts at beg of row for underarm, work across to last 2 sts at neck edge, dec = 34(38-42-45) sts. Dec one st at armhole edge EOR 3(4-5-6) times AND AT THE SAME TIME continue to dec one st at neck edge EVERY 6th row, 9(10-10-10) times = 22(24-27-29) sts. Then dec one st at neck edge EVERY 4th row, 1(1-2-3) time(s) AND AT THE SAME TIME when armhole measures same as Back to shoulder, BO at armhole edge EOR as follows: 7(8-9-9) sts once; 7(8-8-9) sts once; 7(7-8-8) sts once.

RIGHT FRONT

CO 3 sts. Beg bottom V-shaping as follows.
Row 1: Knit.
Row 2: Inc in first st, purl rem sts = 4 sts.
Row 3: Inc in first st, knit to last st, inc in last st = 6 sts. Rep last 2 rows, 9(6-2-1) time(s) more = 33(24-12-9) sts.

Sizes (Small-Medium-Large) ONLY: Continue V-shaping as follows. **Row 1:** CO one st, then inc in CO st; purl rem sts = (26-14-11) sts. **Row 2:** Inc in first st, knit to last st, inc in last st = (28-16-13) sts. Rep these 2 rows, (2-6-8) times more = (36-40-45) sts.

ALL SIZES: Establish Patt St and continue shaping as follows.
Row 1 (wrong side): P 17(20-24-29); place marker for Patt St, work Row 1 of Patt St on next 9 sts, place marker; purl rem sts. **Note:** Sl markers on each following row.
Row 2: Inc in first st, knit to marker; work in Patt St across next 9 sts; knit rem sts = 34(37-41-46) sts.
Row 3: Purl.
Rows 4 and 5: Rep Rows 2 and 3 = 35(38-42-47) sts. Bottom V-shaping is now completed; continue with side shaping (corresponding to shaping on Back) as follows.
Row 6: Knit to marker; work in Patt St across next 9 sts; knit to last 2 sts, K2 tog = 34(37-41-46) sts.

Row 7: Purl.
Rows 8 and 9: Rep Rows 6 and 7 = 33(36-40-45) sts.
Row 10: Knit to marker; work in Patt St across next 9 sts; knit rem sts.
Row 11: Purl.
Row 12: Knit to marker; work in Patt St across next 9 sts; knit to last st, inc in last st = 34(37-41-46) sts.
Continue working in same manner as Left Front to underarm, ending by working a **knit** row.
Shape Armhole, Neck and Shoulder: Follow instructions for Left Front.

FINISHING

Sew shoulder and side seams.
Body Edging: Beg on right side at either shoulder seam. With crochet hook, work one rnd in sc evenly spaced around entire edge of vest, adjusting sts to keep work flat. Mark right front center edge for 4 button lps evenly spaced and then work one more rnd in reverse sc (see **Figs 1 and 2**) as follows. * Work one st in each sc to marked st; work (one reverse sc, sl st, ch 8 for button lp, sl st) all in marked st; rep from * 3 times more; work one st in each rem sc. Finish off.

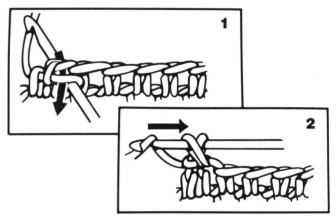

Armhole Edging (make 2): Beg on right side at underarm seam. With crochet hook, work one rnd in sc evenly spaced around armhole edge; then work one more rnd in reverse sc. Finish off; weave in all ends. Sew on buttons.

Long Stitch VEST

designed by Doris England

SIZES:	Petite	Small	Medium	Large
Body Bust:	29″	32″	35″	38″
Garment Width (across back at underarms):	16″	17½″	18¾″	20¼″

Size Note: Instructions are written for sizes as follows: Petite(Small-Medium-Large).

MATERIALS
Worsted weight yarn: 6(7-8-9) oz blue
Size 9, 24″ circular knitting needle (or size required for gauge)
Stitch holders: 2 small and 1 medium

GAUGE: In garter st, 4 sts = 1″
In Patt St, 7 sts = 2″

PATTERN STITCH
Rows 1 and 2: Knit.
Row 3: * K1, YO twice; rep from * to last st, K1.
Row 4: Knit across, dropping each YO (forming long sts).
Rep Rows 1 through 4 for patt.

INSTRUCTIONS
BODY
[**Note:** Worked in one piece to underarms.] CO 152(164-176-188) sts *loosely.* Do not join; work back and forth in rows. Knit one row; then work Patt St Rows 1 through 4 twice. **Next Row:** Knit.
Beading Row: K2 tog; * YO, (K2 tog) twice; rep from * to last 2 sts; YO, K2 tog = 114(123-132-141) sts. **Note:** On next row, work each YO as one st. Work Patt St Rows 1 through 4, 6 times. **Next Row:** Knit.
Dividing Row: K 29(31-33-35) and sl these sts to sm holder for one front; K 56(61-66-71) and sl these sts to med holder for back; knit rem sts for other front.

Front Shaping: Continuing on 29(31-33-35) sts, work Patt St Rows 3 and 4. **Shape Armhole: Rows 1 through 4:** Work Patt St Rows 1 through 4 AND AT THE SAME TIME dec one st at armhole edge EVERY row twice = 27(29-31-33) sts. **Rows 5 through 8:** Work Patt St Rows 1 through 4 AND AT THE SAME TIME dec one st at armhole edge once = 26(28-30-32) sts. Rep last 8 rows, 3 times more = 17(19-21-23) sts.
Medium and Large Sizes ONLY: Work Patt St Rows 1 through 4 once more (without decreases).
ALL SIZES: Knit one more row; then sl rem sts to sm holder for neck.

Back Shaping
Sl sts from med holder to needle; join yarn next to front just worked. Work Patt St Rows 3 and 4. **Shape Armholes: Rows 1 through 4:** Work Patt St Rows 1 through 4 AND AT THE SAME TIME dec one st at each armhole edge EVERY row twice = 52(57-62-67) sts. **Rows 5 through 8:** Work Patt St Rows 1 through 4 AND AT THE SAME TIME dec one st at each armhole edge once = 50(55-60-65) sts. Rep last 8 rows, 3 times more = 32(37-42-47) sts.

Now work Patt St Rows 1 through 4 (without decreases), 1(1-2-2) time(s) more. **Last Row:** Knit. Sl rem sts to med holder for neck. **Note:** Back Shaping has 4 more rows than Front Shaping.

Rem Front Shaping
Sl sts from holder to needle; join yarn next to back just worked. Work same as other Front Shaping. At end of last row, do not sl sts to holder; continue with neck shaping as follows.

Neck Shaping
Row 1: K 17(19-21-23) across front just worked; K 32(37-42-47) from back neck holder; K 17(19-21-23) from front neck holder = 66(75-84-93) sts. **Next Row:** Knit. **Beading Row:** K2(1-2-1); * YO, K2; rep from * across = 98(112-125-139) sts. **Note:** On next row, work each YO as one st. Work Patt St Rows 1 through 4 once. **Last Row:** Knit. BO all sts *loosely* in knit.

FINISHING
Weave in all ends. **Ties:** Use 3 strands of yarn and make 2 twisted cords (see *Twisted Cord* instructions on page 15): one approx 40″ long for tie at neckline and the other approx 60(66-70-74)″ long for tie at waistline *or* use a crochet hook (size H) and 2 strands of yarn and make 2 chains to same measurements. Knot each end of tie; trim ends. Weave each tie through corresponding beading row. Gather neckline to desired size, then knot tie in a single loop at each side. Fringe ends of ties if desired.

STRIPED PULLOVER

designed by Doris England

The unique striping design of this sweater is created by the variegated colors of the yarn. The garment is worked in rnds on the body and in rows on the sleeves and yoke.

SIZES:	Small	Medium	Large
Body Bust:	32″	35″	39″
Garment Measurements:			
bust	34″	37″	41″
length to underarm	15″	16″	16″
sleeve length	19″	20″	21″

Size Note: Instructions are written for sizes as follows: Small(Medium-Large).

MATERIALS
Unger's "Foliage" yarn in 1⁷/₁₀ oz balls: 11(12-14) balls rust/gray shades
Sizes 7 and 9, 29″ circular knitting needles (or size required for gauge)
Stitch marker
2 Medium stitch holders
Materials Note: For yarn source (William Unger & Co.), see page 4.

GAUGE: With larger size needle in stock st, 15 sts = 4″; 20 rows = 4″

INSTRUCTIONS

BODY
With smaller size needle, CO 128(140-156) sts. Place marker for end of rnd; join, being careful not to twist sts.

Note: Sl marker on each following rnd. Work in K1, P1 ribbing for 10 rnds. Change to larger size needle and work in stock st (knit each rnd) until piece measures 15(16-16)″ from CO edge or desired length to underarm. Use sm safety pin or piece of contrasting yarn and mark first st and 65(71-79)th st for sewing Body to Yoke later. BO all sts.

RIGHT SLEEVE, RIGHT FRONT YOKE AND BACK YOKE
Note: Section is worked all in one piece.

Right Sleeve: With smaller size needle, CO 32(36-40) sts *loosely*. Do not join; work back and forth in rows. Work in K1, P1 ribbing for 15 rows. **Inc Row:** * K1, knit in front and back of next st [inc made]; rep from * across = 48(54-60) sts. Change to larger size needle. Beg with a purl row and work in stock st, increasing one st at each end EVERY 6th row, 12(13-14) times = 72(80-88) sts. Continuing in stock st, work even until sleeve measures 19(20-21)″ from CO edge or desired length to yoke edge, ending by working a **purl** row.

Right Front Yoke: Row 1 (dividing row): (K1, P1) 18(20-22) times; sl rem 36(40-44) sts to holder to be worked later for Back Yoke. Continuing in K1, P1 ribbing, work 26(28-30) more rows, ending last row at inside edge (neck edge). Use sm safety pin or piece of contrasting yarn and mark last st worked to be used later for sewing shoulder seam. Continue in ribbing and work 16(16-18) more rows, ending last row at neck edge. You should now have a total of 43(45-49) rows of ribbing. BO all sts in ribbing.

Back Yoke: Sl sts from holder to larger size needle. Join yarn next to Right Front Yoke just worked. **Row 1:** * K1, P1; rep from * across. Continuing in K1, P1 ribbing, work 85(89-97) more rows. Sl sts to holder. Cut yarn, leaving approx 36″ length for weaving sts later to Left Sleeve.

LEFT SLEEVE AND LEFT FRONT YOKE
Note: Section is worked in one piece.

Left Sleeve: Work same as Right Sleeve to Right Front Yoke, ending by working a **knit** row.

Left Front Yoke: Row 1 (dividing row): (P1, K1) 18(20-22) times; sl rem 36(40-44) sts to holder to be woven later to sts of back yoke. **Row 2 (right side):** * P1, K1; rep from * across. Continuing in ribbing as established (rep Row 2), work 25(27-29) more rows, ending last row at neck edge. Mark last st worked to be used later for sewing shoulder seam. Continue in ribbing and work 15(15-17) more rows, ending last row at outside edge. You should now have a total of 42(44-48) rows of ribbing [one row less than Right Front Yoke]. BO all sts in ribbing.

FINISHING
Weave sts of Back Yoke and Left Sleeve tog (see *Weaving on Needles* on page 13). Sew each shoulder seam to marker, leaving center 32(32-36) rows of Back Yoke free for neck edge. Beg at cuff edge and sew sleeve seams, carefully matching stripes. Matching markers on Body with sleeve seams, sew Yoke to Body easing in fullness. Weave in all ends. Lightly steam front neck edges back to form front "collar".

FURRY JACKET

designed by Doris England

This unusual jacket combines rectangles of fur-like fabric with knitting for a striking affect. Its over-sized collar can be pulled up to make a cozy hood. The garment works up quickly with a gauge of only 2 sts per inch. But that also means that any variation from the specified gauge will change the garment size drastically. Be sure to check your gauge as you work the pieces.

SIZES:

	Small	Medium	Large
Body Bust:	32″	36″	40″
Garment Measurements:			
bust	40″	44″	48″
length to underarm	17″	17″	17″
sleeve length to underarm	18″	19″	19″

Size Note: Instructions are written for sizes as follows: Small(Medium-Large).

MATERIALS
**Bulky weight yarn or 2 strands of worsted weight yarn: 21(24-27) oz black;
8(10-12) oz white**
Sizes 10½, 11 and 13, 24″ circular knitting needles (or size required for gauge)
Fur fabric: ²/₃ yd (38″ minimum width)

**GAUGE: With largest size needle in Patt St,
2 sts = 1″**

PATTERN STITCH
Row 1: * K1, knit next st in row below (**Fig 1**); rep from * across.

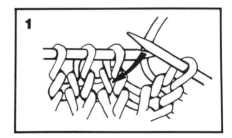

Rep Row 1 for patt. **Note:** To change colors in Patt St, always change colors after an even number of rows have been completed.

INSTRUCTIONS
KNITTED PIECES
Note: Use single strand of bulky weight yarn *or* two strands of worsted weight yarn throughout patt.

Bottom Ribbing (make 2): With size 11 needle and black, CO 30(32-36) sts. Do not join; work back and forth in rows. Work in K1, P1 ribbing for 2″. BO all sts in ribbing.

Side Band (make 2): With size 11 needle and black, CO 10(12-12) sts. Do not join; work back and forth in rows. Work in K1, P1 ribbing for 2″. Then change to size 13 needle (or size required for gauge) and work in Patt St until piece measures 17″ from CO edge. BO all sts *loosely.*

Right Sleeve: With size 10½ needle and black, CO 22(24-24) sts. Do not join; work back and forth in rows. Work in K1, P1 ribbing for 3″. **Inc Row:** K1, P1; * knit in front and back of next st [inc made], P1; rep from * to last 0(2-2) sts; (K1, P1) 0(1-1) time = 32(34-34) sts. Now work in Patt St in the following Striping Sequence (remember to change color only after completing an even number of Patt St rows).
Black Stripe: 4(4½-4½)″.
Note: On next row, change to size 11 needle.
White Stripe: 4(4½-4½)″.
Black Stripe: 3″.
Note: On next row, change to size 13 needle (or size required for gauge).
White Stripe: 2″.
Black Stripe: Work until piece measures 18(19-19)″ from CO edge or desired length to underarm.
Striping Sequence is now completed; continue with black in Patt St and work as follows. **Shape Cap:** BO 2 sts at beg of next 2 rows = 28(30-30) sts; BO 3 sts at beg of next 2 rows = 22(24-24) sts; BO 4 sts at beg of next 4(2-2) rows = 6(16-16) sts; BO 5 sts at beg of next 0(2-2) rows = 6 sts. BO rem sts.

Left Sleeve: Work same as Right Sleeve until K1, P1 ribbing and Inc Row have been completed = 32(34-34) sts. Then work in Patt St in the following Striping Sequence (remember to change color only after completing an even number of Patt St rows).
Black Stripe: 2″.
White Stripe: 2(2½-2½)″; change to size 11 needle and work 1″ more.
Black Stripe: 5½(6-6)″.
Note: On next row, change to size 13 needle (or size required for gauge).
White Stripe: 3½″.
Black Stripe: Work until piece measures same as Right Sleeve to underarm.

Striping Sequence is now completed; continue with black in Patt St and work Shape Cap same as in Right Sleeve.

Cowl Neck: With size 13 needle (or size required for gauge) and black, CO 57(61-65) sts. Do not join; work back and forth in rows.
Row 1: * K1, P1; rep from * to last st, K1.
Row 2 (beading row): * K2 tog, YO; rep from * to last st, K1. **Note:** On next row, work each YO as one st.
Row 3: K2 tog; * P1, K1; rep from * to last st, K1 = 56(60-64) sts.
Now work in Patt St in the following Striping Sequence (remember to change color only after completing an even number of Patt St rows).
Black Stripe: 3".
Note: On next row, change to size 11 needle.
White Stripe: 2½".
Black Stripe: 2".
White Stripe: 1".
Note: On next row, change to size 10½ needle.
Black Stripe: Work until piece measures 14" from CO edge. BO all sts *loosely*.

FUR PIECES

Front and Back: Enlarge diagram in **Fig 2** on paper for desired size, having each square equal to 1". Make one pattern piece for Back using solid line for neckline and another pattern piece for Front using broken line for neckline. Place fur piece right side down with pile in downward direction. Trace pattern pieces side by side on wrong side of fur piece with chalk; then cut out both pieces. Use small safety pins and mark each side edge of both pieces 15" from bottom edge for underarms.

ASSEMBLING

Use black sewing thread and sew ¼" shoulder seams on fur pieces, either by hand (use backstitching); or by machine (use light tension with loose pressure on pressure foot and 8-10 sts to the inch). Reduce seam bulkiness by shaving or clipping away the pile on seam allowances; then use a pin to pull out long fibers caught in the line of stitching.

Using 2-plies of black bulky weight yarn *or* single strand of black worsted weight yarn, sew knitted pieces to fur pieces with overcast stitching as follows. Sew BO edge of each bottom ribbing knitted piece to bottom edge of each fur piece, having knitted edge slightly under fur edge. With knitted edge slightly overlapping fur edge, sew knitted side band pieces to fur front and back pieces, aligning BO edge of each knitted piece at markers on fur pieces and carefully matching rows of bottom ribbing. Sew sleeve seams, carefully matching stripes. Then with knitted edge slightly overlapping fur edge, sew sleeves into armholes, aligning sleeve seam with center of side band and center of sleeve BO edge at shoulder seam. Sew side edges of knitted cowl neck piece tog to form a tube, carefully matching stripes. With knitted edge slightly overlapping fur edge, sew BO edge of cowl neck piece into neck opening, aligning cowl seam at center back of fur piece.

FINISHING

Weave in all ends. **Drawstring:** Use 2 strands of black bulky weight or 4 strands of black worsted weight yarn and make a twisted cord (see *Twisted Cord* instructions on page 15) 60" long or desired length. Weave drawstring through beading row on cowl neck piece, beg and ending at center front.

Fig 2

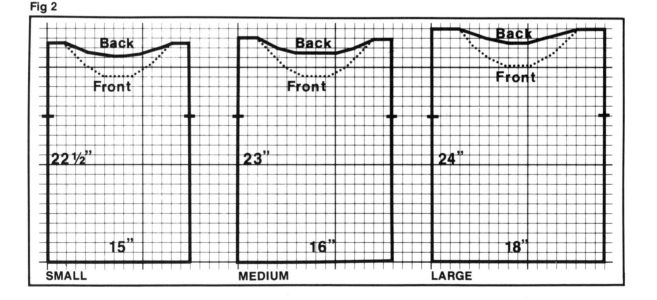

CARDIGAN VEST
in larger sizes
designed by Louise O'Donnell and Mary Thomas

SIZES

Body Bust:	38"	40"	42"	44"
Garment Measurements:				
bust	40"	42"	44"	46"
length to underarm	12"	12"	12"	12"

Size Note: Instructions are written for bust sizes as follows: 38(40-42-44)".

MATERIALS
American Thread Glencastle Heather Knitting Worsted Size yarn in 3-oz skeins: 4(5-6-6) skeins Mulberry
Size 8, 14" straight and 36" circular knitting needles (or size required for gauge)
Stitch holders: 1 medium and 1 large
Cable needle
6 Buttons (5/8" diameter)

GAUGE: In stock st, 9 sts = 2"; 6 rows = 1"

INSTRUCTIONS
BODY
[**Note:** Work in one piece to underarms.] With circular needle, CO 180(190-200-210) sts *loosely.* Do not join; work back and forth in rows. Knit 4 rows for bottom garter st border; then work in patt as follows. **Note:** On following rows, Cable Patt St is worked from * to * in instructions on 9 sts.
Row 1 (right side): K 12; *P1, K7, P1 *; knit to last 21 sts; rep from * to * once, K 12.
Row 2: K3 for garter st edge, P9; *K1, P7, K1 *; purl to last 21 sts; rep from * to * once; P9, K3 for garter st edge.
Row 3 (cable twist row): K 12; * P1, sl next 2 sts onto cable needle and hold at **back** of work; K1, then K2 from cable needle; K1, sl next st onto cable needle and hold at **front** of work; K2, then K1 from cable needle, P1 *; knit to last 21 sts; rep from * to * once, K 12.
Row 4: Rep Row 2.
Rep Rows 1 through 4, twice more = 3 cable twist rows.
Now work **button lp** as follows: * knit first st, turn and knit same st again; rep from * 3 times more = button lp made.
Note: Beg next row with last st of button lp.
Continue to rep Rows 1 through 4 AND AT THE SAME TIME work button lp EVERY 12th row, 4 times more. When 5th button lp is completed, rep Rows 1 through 4, twice more. You should now have 17 cable twist rows. Now work as follows, discontinuing Cable Patt Sts.
Row 1 (right side): Knit.
Row 2: K3, P 34(36-38-40); K 16(17-18-19), P 74(78-82-86); K 16(17-18-19), P 34(36-38-40); K3.
Row 3: Knit.
Row 4 (dividing row): K3, P 33(35-37-39), K3; now sl these 39(41-43-45) sts just worked to med holder for left front; BO next 12(13-14-15) sts for underarm [one st now on right-hand needle]; K2, P 72(76-80-84), K3; now sl these 78(82-86-90) sts just worked to lge holder for back; BO next 12(13-14-15) sts for underarm [one st now on right-hand needle]; K2, P 33(35-37-39), K3.

Right Front Shaping
Change to straight needles. Work one more button lp; then continue on 39(41-43-45) sts as follows.
Shape Armhole: Row 1 (dec row): Knit to last 5 sts; K2 tog, K3 = 38(40-42-44) sts. **Row 2:** K3, purl to last 3 sts, K3. Rep last 2 rows, 4 times more = 34(36-38-40) sts.

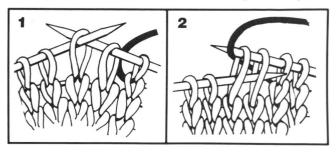

Shape Neck: Row 1 (dec row): K3; dec over next 2 sts as follows: sl each of the next 2 sts *knitwise* to right-hand needle **(Fig 1);** insert tip of left-hand needle through same 2 sts **(Fig 2)** and knit both sts tog in this position [dec made]; knit rem sts = 33(35-37-39) sts. Keeping 3 sts at each end in garter st and rem sts in stock st, continue to dec one st after center garter st edge (as in **Figs 1 and 2)** EVERY 4th row, 11(12-13-14) times more = 22(23-24-25) sts. Work even until armhole measures 10(10½-11-11)", ending by working a knit row.

Shape Shoulder and Back Neckband: Maintaining sts as established, BO from armhole edge EOR as follows: 7(7-7-8) sts once; 6(7-7-7) sts once; 6(6-7-7) sts once. Continuing on rem 3 sts for back neckband, work in garter st for 3½(3½-3¾-3¾)" more. BO all sts in knit.

Back Shaping
With right side facing and straight needles, sl sts from lge holder to needle; join yarn at right armhole edge and work as follows.

Shape Armhole: Row 1 (right side): K3, dec over next 2 sts (as in **Figs 1 and 2**); knit to last 5 sts; K2 tog, K3 = 76(80-84-88) sts. **Row 2:** K3, purl to last 3 sts, K3. Rep last 2 rows, 4 times more = 68(72-76-80) sts. Keeping 3 sts at each end in garter st and rem sts in stock st, work even until armhole measures ½" less than Right Front Shaping to shoulder, ending by working a wrong side row.

Shape Neck and Shoulders: Row 1 (right side): K 25(26-27-28); BO next 18(20-22-24) sts for neck opening; knit rem sts. **Row 2:** K3, purl to neck edge; join new ball of yarn at right neck edge, BO 2 sts, purl to last 3 sts, K3. **Row 3:** Knit to neck edge; BO 2 sts at left neck edge, knit rem sts. **Row 4:** K3, purl to neck edge; BO 2 sts at right neck edge, purl to last 3 sts, K3. **Row 5:** BO 7(7-7-8) sts, knit to neck edge; BO 2 sts at left neck edge, knit rem sts. **Row 6:** BO 7(7-7-8) sts, purl to neck edge; BO 2 sts at right neck edge, purl rem sts. **Row 7:** BO 6(7-7-7) sts, knit to neck edge; BO 2 sts at left neck edge, knit rem sts. **Row 8:** BO 6(7-7-7) sts, purl across each side. **Row 9:** BO rem 6(6-7-7) sts of right shoulder; knit across sts of left shoulder. BO rem 6(6-7-7) sts.

Left Front Shaping
With right side facing and straight needles, sl sts from holder to needle; join yarn at armhole edge and work as follows.

Shape Armhole: Row 1 (dec row): K3, dec over next 2 sts (as in **Figs 1 and 2**); knit rem sts = 38(40-42-44) sts. **Row 2:** K3, purl to last 3 sts, K3. Rep last 2 rows, 4 times more = 34(36-38-40) sts.

Shape Neck: Row 1 (dec row): Knit to last 5 sts; K2 tog, K3 = 33(35-37-39) sts. Keeping 3 sts at each end in garter st and rem sts in stock st, continue to dec one st before center garter st edge (as before) EVERY 4th row, 11(12-13-14) times more = 22(23-24-25) sts. Work even until armhole measures same as Right Front Shaping to shoulder, ending by working a wrong-side row.

Shape Shoulder and Back Neckband: Work same as in Right Front Shaping.

FINISHING
Sew shoulder seams. Weave bound-off edges of back neckband tog; then sew neckband to back neck edge. Weave in all ends; sew on buttons.

WRAP SWEATER
in larger sizes
designed by Nancy Dent

SIZES:

	Small	Medium	Large
Body Bust:	38"	42"	46"
Garment Measurements:			
bust	44"	48"	52"
length to underarm	22"	21½"	20½"

Size Note: Instructions are written for sizes as follows: Small(Medium-Large).

MATERIALS
Dawn Sayelle* Knitting Worsted Size yarn in 4-oz skeins: 10(11-12) skeins Amber
Size 9, 14" straight and 36" circular knitting needles (or size required for gauge)
Medium stitch holder

GAUGE: In Patt St, 5 sts = 1"

PATTERN STITCH
Row 1: K1 (garter st edge); * K2, P2; rep from * to last 3 sts; K2, K1 (garter st edge).
Row 2: K1 (garter st edge), P2; * K2, P2; rep from * to last st, K1 (garter st edge).

Rows 3 through 8: Rep Rows 1 and 2, 3 times.
Row 9: Rep Row 2.
Row 10: Rep Row 1.
Rows 11 through 16: Rep Rows 9 and 10, 3 times. Rep Rows 1 through 16 for patt.

INSTRUCTIONS
BODY
Note: Body is worked in one piece, beginning at back lower edge and ending at front lower edge.
Back: With straight needles, CO 112(120-132) sts. Work in Patt St for 22(21½-20½)". Mark first and last st of row for underarms (use sm safety pins or pieces of yarn in contrasting color). Continue in patt as established until work measures 8½(9-10)" above markers (for underarms), ending by working an even-numbered row of Patt St.
Shape Neck and Shoulders: Dividing Row (right side): Work across first 39(43-47) sts in patt as established, K1 (garter st neck edge); sl next 32(32-36) sts to holder for back of neck; join another skein of yarn, K1 (garter st neck edge), work across rem sts in patt as established = 40(44-48) sts each shoulder. Continuing to work across each shoulder with a separate ball of yarn, keep one st at each neck edge in garter st and rem sts in patt as established and work 3" more, ending last row at armhole edge of right shoulder.

Fronts: Row 1 (right side): Work across sts of right shoulder in patt as established, then continue with same yarn and CO 12 sts (see *Casting On, Method 2* on page 12) for right front neck shaping; now with yarn from left shoulder, CO 12 sts (in same manner) onto left-hand needle for left front neck shaping; knit across these CO sts, then work in patt as established across rem sts of left shoulder = 52(56-60) sts each front. **Row 2:** Work across first 39(43-47) sts in patt as established, then continue in Patt St across rem 13 sts of left front; knit across CO sts of right front neck shaping, then work in patt as established across rem sts of right front. **Row 3:** Work across first 39(43-47) sts in patt as established, then continue in Patt St across rem 13 sts of right front; work in patt as established across sts of left front. **Row 4:** Work across each front in patt as established. **Row 5 (inc row):** Work in patt as established across right front to within 2 sts of neck edge, inc in next st [to inc: knit (if st is a knit st) or purl (if st is a purl st) in front and back of st], K1; inc in first st at left neck edge [to inc: knit in front and back of st], then work in patt as established across rem sts. Continuing in patt

as established and working increase sts in Patt St, continue to inc one st each neck edge (as in Row 5) EVERY 4th row, 7 times more = 60(64-68) sts each front. Mark last increase at each neck edge for working trim later. Continue working in patt as established until fronts measure same as back, measuring from center of shoulders. BO all sts in patt.

SLEEVE (make 2)
With straight needles, CO 100(104-112) sts. Work in Patt St for 20". BO all sts in patt.

HOOD
With right side facing, beg at right front center neck edge. Using straight needles, pick up one st in each CO st and in each row to holder; sl sts from holder to free needle and then knit across these 32(32-36) sts; pick up one st in each row and in each CO st to left front center neck edge. Count the sts and divide by 4. On next row, if necessary, inc to the nearest number of sts divisible by 4 to make Patt St come out evenly. Work even in Patt St for approx 17", ending by working either Row 4 or Row 12 of Patt St. BO all sts in patt.

FINISHING
If desired, steam very lightly on wrong side. Fold hood in half, with right sides tog, and overcast BO sts.

Trim: With right side facing, beg at lower right front edge. With circular needle, pick up 2 sts every 3 rows along right front, hood and left front edges, ending at lower left

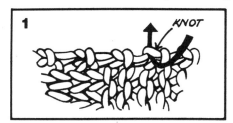

front edge as follows: * one st in "knot" (**Fig 1**), one st in next row; sk next "knot", one st in next row; one st in next "knot", sk next row; rep from * around. You should have a number of sts divisible by 4; if necessary, decrease to the nearest number of sts divisible by 4 on next row. [**Note:** Do not join; work back and forth in rows.] **Next Row:** Knit to first marker, purl to next marker, knit rem sts. Work in Patt St for 23 rows. BO all sts in Patt St.

Mark front armholes to correspond to back armholes; then sew BO edge of sleeves into armholes (between markers), aligning center of sleeve with center of shoulder. Sew side and sleeve seams, ending halfway to cuff edge of sleeves. Try on sweater and turn back cuff edge of sleeve to desired length. Mark and then finish sewing sleeve seam with wrong sides tog so seam will not show on right side of cuff. Weave in all ends.

Belt: With straight needles, CO 20 sts. * Yarn to back of work, K1; yarn to front of work, sl 1 as to purl; rep from * across. Rep this row until belt measures 30" longer than desired waist measurement, or 63(67-71)". BO as follows: K1, * K2 tog, pass first st over 2nd st on right-hand needle; rep from * to last st, sl last st as to knit, pass first st over sl st on right-hand needle. Weave in yarn ends.

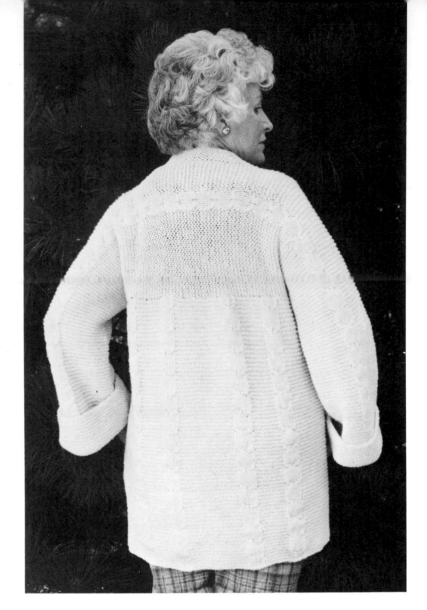

CABLE JACKET and SCARF
in larger sizes
designed by Nancy Dent

An interesting yoke treatment and a separate scarf with pockets add interest to this well-tailored jacket.

SIZES:	Small	Medium	Large
Body Bust:	38″	42″	46″
Garment Measurements:			
bust	44″	48″	52″
length to underarm	22″	22″	22″

Size Note: Instructions are written for sizes as follows: Small(Medium-Large).

MATERIALS
Dawn Sayelle* Knitting Worsted Size yarn in 4-oz skeins: 11(12-13) skeins Fisherman
Size 9, 14″ straight knitting needles (or size required for gauge)
Size H aluminum crochet hook (for edging only)
Stitch holders: 3 small and 2 medium
8 Stitch markers
Cable needle
8 Buttons (7/8″ diameter)

GAUGE: In garter st, 9 sts = 2″

PATTERN STITCHES

Cable Pattern (worked on 6 sts)
Row 1 (right side): Knit.
Row 2: Purl.
Rows 3 and 4: Rep Rows 1 and 2.
Row 5 (cable twist row): Sl next 2 sts to cable needle and hold at *back* of work; knit next st, then K2 from cable needle; sl next st to cable needle and hold at *front* of work; knit next 2 sts, then K1 from cable needle.
Row 6: Purl.
Rows 7 through 10: Rep Rows 1 through 4.
Rep Rows 1 through 10 for patt.

Cable Reverse Pattern (worked on 6 sts)
Rows 1 through 4: Rep Rows 1 through 4 of Cable Pattern.
Row 5 (cable twist row): Sl next st to cable needle and hold at *front* of work; knit next 2 sts, then K1 from cable needle; sl next 2 sts to cable needle and hold at *back* of work; knit next st, then K2 from cable needle.
Rows 6 through 10: Rep Rows 6 through 10 of Cable Pattern.
Rep Rows 1 through 10 for patt.

JACKET INSTRUCTIONS

SLEEVES AND YOKE

Note: Section is worked all in one piece; beginning at cuff edge of left sleeve and ending at cuff edge of right sleeve.

Left Sleeve: CO 76(80-88) sts. Work in garter st (knit each row) for 6". Then work in patt as follows.
Row 1 (right side): K 22(24-28); * *place marker for patt sts, work Row 1 of Cable Patt over next 6 sts; place marker,* * K 20; rep from * to * once; K 22(24-28). **Note:** Sl markers on each following row.
Row 2: K 22(24-28); * *work Row 2 of Cable Patt over next 6 sts;* * K 20, rep from * to * once; K 22(24-28).
Work in patt as established [keep 6 sts between each set of markers in Cable Patt and rem sts in garter st] until piece measures 19(18-17)" from CO edge, ending by working a wrong-side row. Mark first and last st of row for underarms (use sm safety pins or pieces of contrasting yarn). Then continue as follows.

Yoke: First Half (worked to center of neck opening): Continue in patt as established until piece measures 7(8-9)" from markers, ending by working a wrong-side row. **Dividing Row (right side):** Work in patt as established across first 38(40-44) sts for back; BO next 4 sts for neck opening; work in patt as established across rem sts = 34(36-40) sts for left front. **Next Row:** Work across left front in patt as established to within 2 sts of neck edge, K2 tog; join another skein of yarn and work across back in patt as established. Continue to work across each side of neck opening in patt as established AND AT THE SAME TIME dec one st at front neck edge EVERY row 4 times more = 29(31-35) sts for left front. Mark last decrease for working neck shaping on right front later. Continue in patt as established until work measures approx 9(10-11)" from markers (for underarms), ending by working Row 9 of Cable Patt. **Next Row (wrong side):** BO 29(31-35) sts of left front in purl; with same yarn from left front, CO 29(31-35)sts onto right-hand needle (free needle) for right front; now work across back in patt as established. You are now at center of neck opening and will begin working Cable Reverse Patt on 6 sts between each set of markers.

Second Half: Work across sts of back as follows: knit to marker, work Row 1 of Cable Reverse Patt over next 6 sts, knit to neck edge. Then work across CO sts of right front as follows: K1, place marker for patt sts; work Row 1 of Cable Reverse Patt over next 6 sts; place marker, knit rem sts. Work in patt as established [keep 6 sts between each set of markers in Cable Reverse Patt and rem sts in garter st] until right front measures same as left front from center of neck opening to marker at last neck decrease, ending by working a right-side row. Continue in patt as established (work inc sts in garter st) AND AT THE SAME TIME inc one st at front neck edge EVERY row 5 times = 34(36-40) sts for right front. **Joining Row (right side):** Work across back in patt as established; continue with same yarn (finish off yarn from right front) and CO 4 sts, then work across right front in patt as established = 76(80-88) sts. Continue in patt as established (work CO sts in garter st) until right front measures same as left front from center of neck opening to marker (for underarm). Mark first and last st of row for underarms.

Right Sleeve: Continue in patt as established until sleeve measures same as left sleeve from underarm marker to garter st cuff. Work in garter st (drop markers) for 6". BO all sts.

BACK

Hold Sleeves and Yoke with right side facing and back yoke edge across top. Pick up 100(108-118) sts along back yoke edge between markers (for underarms). **Next Row (wrong side):** K 18(22-27); * *place marker for patt sts, work Row 2 of Cable Reverse Patt over next 6 sts; place marker, K 10, place marker for patt sts; work Row 2 of Cable Reverse Patt over next 6 sts, place marker;* * K 20, rep from * to * once; K 18(22-27). Work in patt as established [keep 6 sts between each set of markers in Cable Reverse Patt and rem sts in garter st] until piece measures 22" from yoke edge, ending by working a right-side row. BO all sts in patt.

LEFT FRONT

CO 10 sts for front band. Work in garter st until piece measures same length as center edge of left front on yoke. Continuing with same yarn and needle with sts of front band, beg on right side at lower left front center edge on yoke and pick up 40(44-49) sts across edge of left yoke to marker (for underarm) = 50(54-59) sts. **Next Row (wrong side):** K 18(22-27); * *place marker for patt sts, work Row 2 of Cable Reverse Patt over next 6 sts, place marker;* * K 10, rep from * to * once; K 10. Work in patt as established [keep 6 sts between each set of markers in Cable Reverse Patt and rem sts in garter st] until piece measures same as Back, ending by working a right-side row. BO all sts in patt.

RIGHT FRONT

CO 10 sts for front band. Work in garter st until piece measures same length as center edge of right front on yoke. Cut yarn, leaving 4" end for weaving in later; leave sts on needle. With new ball of yarn and free needle, beg on right side at marker (for underarm) and pick up 40(44-49) sts across edge of right yoke to center edge; knit sts of front band from other needle = (50-54-59) sts.
Next Row (wrong side): K 10; *place marker for patt sts, work Row 2 of Cable Reverse Patt over next 6 sts, place marker;* K 10, rep from * to * once; K 18(22-27). Complete in same manner as Left Front.

FINISHING

Weave in all ends. Lightly steam press on wrong side to desired measurements. Overcast side and sleeve seams. Sew front bands to yoke.

Neck Trim: With right side facing, beg at right front center neck edge. Pick up 10 sts across CO sts of front band; pick up one st EOR and one st in each st around neck edge to front band at left front neck edge; pick up 10 sts across CO sts of front band. Work in garter st for 2¼", decreasing sts as needed for neck shaping. End last row on right side; then BO all sts in knit.

Left Front Edging: With right side facing and crochet hook, join yarn with a sl st in top row at left front neck edge. Ch 1, work sc in same place and in each ridge along center edge, ending at bottom edge. Finish off; weave in ends.

Right Front Edging: Mark right front center edge for 8 buttonholes evenly spaced, having first one 11" from bottom edge and last one ½" from neck edge. With right side facing and crochet hook, join yarn with a sl st in row at lower right front center edge. Work sc in same place; *work sc in each ridge along center edge to marker; sk marked ridge, ch 3 tightly for buttonhole; rep from * 7 times more, sc in each ridge to neck edge. Finish off; weave in ends. Sew on buttons.

SCARF INSTRUCTIONS

POCKET LINING (make 2): CO 32 sts. Work in stock st for 8". Cut yarn, leaving approx 30" sewing length. Sl all sts to sm holder; set aside.

First Half [**Note:** Scarf is worked in 2 sections; then woven tog at center back.] CO 52 sts. Work in patt as follows. K 10, * place marker for patt sts; work Row 1 of Cable Patt over next 6 sts, place marker;* K 20, rep from * to * once; K 10. Continue in patt as established [keep 6 sts between markers in Cable Patt and rem sts in garter st] until piece measures approx 14" from CO edge, ending by working Row 4 of Cable Patt.

Pocket Opening: K 10, sl next 32 sts with markers to sm holder to be worked later for pocket band; sl sts of one pocket lining with knit-side facing you to left-hand needle behind sts on holder; now work across sts of lining as follows: * place marker for patt sts, work Row 5 of Cable Patt over next 6 sts, place marker;* K 20, rep from * to * once; then knit rem 10 sts.
Continue in patt as established until piece measures approx 40" from CO edge or desired length to center back, ending by working Row 9 of Cable Patt. Sl all sts to med holder.

Second Half: Work same as First Half.

FINISHING

Pocket Bands (make 2): With right side facing, sl sts of pocket from holder to needle. Join yarn and work Cable Patt Rows 5 through 9. BO all sts in patt.

Weave sts at center back tog (see *Weaving on Needles* on page 13). Sew ends of pocket bands to scarf. Weave in all ends.

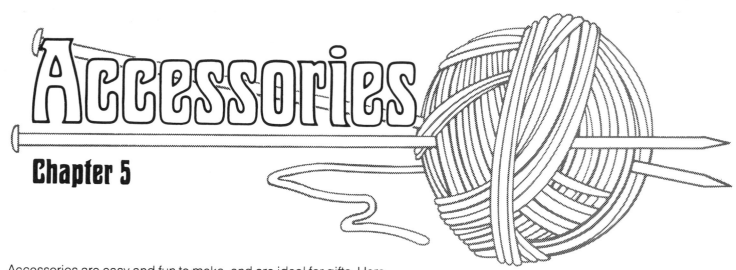

Accessories

Chapter 5

Accessories are easy and fun to make, and are ideal for gifts. Here you'll find leg warmers for your favorite ballerina; hats, scarves, gloves and mittens; slippers that look just like an old-fashioned dust mop; a set of colorful golf club covers; and a lapel pin that lets you proudly proclaim that you're a knitter.

BALLET LEG WARMERS
designed by Mary Thomas

These leg warmers — suitable both for dancers and for adding an extra layer of warmth for outdoor sports — are shaped by changing needle sizes, rather than increasing and decreasing.

SIZE: Written in one size; length measures approx 24″ long.

MATERIALS
Worsted weight yarn: 5 oz medium blue
Sizes 7, 8, 10, 10½, 10″ straight knitting needles (or sizes required for gauge)

GAUGE: In stock st:
          with size 7 needles, 5 sts = 1″
          with size 8 needles, 4½ sts = 1″
          with size 10 needles, 4 sts = 1″
          with size 10½ needles, 7½ sts = 2″

INSTRUCTIONS
(Make 2)
With size 7 needles (or size required for gauge of 5 sts = 1″), CO 40 sts. Work in K1, P1 ribbing for 3″. Then work in stock st for 3″ more [6″ from CO edge]. Continuing in stock st, work as follows.

Change to size 8 needles (or size required for gauge of 4½ sts = 1″) and work 5″ more [11″ from CO edge].

Change to size 10 needles (or size required for gauge of 4 sts = 1″) and work 6″ more [17″ from CO edge].

Change to size 10½ needles (or size required for gauge of 7½ sts = 2″) and work 4″ more [21″ from CO edge].

Continue with same size needles and work in K1, P1 ribbing for 3″. BO VERY LOOSELY in ribbing. Sew side seam neatly; weave in all ends.

BOOT TOPPERS

designed by Mary Thomas

The cuff makes the difference—Version A is worked with cables and Version B cuff is worked in moss stitch.

SIZE: Written in one size.

MATERIALS
Dawn Sayelle* Knitting Worsted Size TWEED yarn in 3-oz skeins: For Version A: 2 skeins Sand Tones
For Version B: 2 skeins Buckwheat
Size 8, 7" double pointed needles [dpn] (or size required for gauge)
Small stitch holder
Cable needle (for Version A only)

GAUGE: In stock st, 5 sts = 1"; 13 rnds = 2"

VERSION A INSTRUCTIONS
(Make 2)
With Sand Tones, CO 42 sts *loosely* onto one needle; then divide sts evenly onto 3 needles. Join, being careful not to twist sts. Work in garter st (knit one rnd, purl one rnd) for 4 rnds. Then work cuff design as follows.

Cuff Design (with cables): Rnd 1 (inc rnd): * K2, inc in next st; K3, inc in next st; rep from * around = 54 sts. **Rnds 2 through 4:** Knit. **Rnd 5:** * K2, sl next 2 sts to cable needle and hold at *back* of work; knit next 2 sts, then K2 from cable needle; rep from * around. **Rnds 6 through 8:** Knit. **Rnd 9:** * Sl next 2 sts to cable needle and hold at *front* of work; knit next 2 sts, then K2 from cable needle, K2; rep from * around. **Rnds 10 through 17:** Rep Rnds 2 through 9. **Rnds 18 and 19:** Knit. **Rnd 20 (dec rnd).** * K2, K2 tog; K3, K2 tog; rep from * around = 42 sts. Cuff design is now completed; continue as follows.

Leg: Beg and end with a purl rnd and work 5 rnds in garter st. **Next Rnd:** * K2, P4; rep from * around. Rep last rnd until piece measures 15" from CO edge or desired length to heel.

Foot Strap: Dividing Rnd: BO 11 sts; knit *next* (one st already on needle) 9 sts, then sl these 10 sts to holder to be worked later for 2nd Half; BO next 11 sts, knit rem sts. **First Half:** Continuing on 10 sts and working back and forth in rows, knit 6 rows. **Dec Row:** K2 tog; knit to last 2 sts, K2 tog = 8 sts. Continue in garter st (knit each row) until strap measures 3" from Dividing Rnd. BO all sts. **2nd Half:** Sl sts from holder to needle; join yarn and work same as First Half.

FINISHING
Sew BO edge of straps tog; weave in all ends. Turn right side out and fold down approx 3½" cuff.

VERSION B INSTRUCTIONS
(Make 2)
With Buckwheat, work same as Version A instructions, substituting the following Cuff design.

Cuff Design (moss st): Rnds 1 and 2: * K1, P1; rep from * around. **Rnds 3 and 4:** * P1, K1; rep from * around. **Rnds 5 through 20:** Rep Rnds 1 through 4, four times more. Cuff design is now completed; continue with Leg instructions.

TUBE KNEE SOCKS
designed by Mary Thomas

These socks have no heel to turn—they're knitted as a tube, yet fit the ankle and leg nicely, and fit any size woman's or girl's foot.

SIZE: Written in one size.

MATERIALS
Sport weight yarn: 4 oz red
Sizes 1 and 3, 7″ double pointed needles [dpn] (or size required for gauge)

GAUGE: With larger size needles in stock st,
13 sts = 2″; 9 rnds = 1″

INSTRUCTIONS

(Make 2)
With larger size dpn, CO 56 sts *loosely* onto one needle; change to smaller size dpn and divide sts onto 3 needles (16-20-20). Join, being careful not to twist sts. Work in K1, P1 ribbing for 1½″. Change to larger size dpn and work in patt as follows.

Rnd 1: * P2, K2; rep from * around.

Rnd 2: * P2, right twist (abbreviated RT) [*to make RT: K2 tog but do not remove from left-hand needle* **(Fig 1)**;*insert tip of right-hand needle into first st* **(Fig 2)** *and knit it again, then sl both sts off left-hand needle = RT made*]; rep from * around.

Rnds 3 through 5: Rep Rnd 1, 3 times.

Rnd 6: Rep Rnd 2.

Rnd 7: Rep Rnd 1.

Rnd 8: * K2, P2; rep from * around.

Rnd 9: * RT, P2; rep from * around.

Rnds 10 through 12: Rep Rnd 8, 3 times.

Rnd 13: Rep Rnd 9.

Rnd 14: Rep Rnd 8.
Rep Rnds 1 through 14 until sock measures approx 20″ from CO edge or 2″ less than desired length.

Shape Toe: Rnd 1: * K6, K2 tog; rep from * around = 49 sts. **Rnds 2 and 3:** Knit. **Rnd 4:** * K5, K2 tog; rep from * around = 42 sts **Rnds 5 and 6:** Knit. **Rnd 7:** * K4, K2 tog; rep from * around = 35 sts. **Rnds 8 and 9:** Knit. **Rnd 10:** * K3, K2 tog; rep from * around = 28 sts. **Rnds 11 and 12:** Knit. **Rnd 13:** * K2, K2 tog; rep from * around = 21 sts. **Rnds 14 and 15:** Knit. **Rnd 16:** * K1, K2 tog = 14 sts. **Rnd 17:** Knit. Cut yarn, leaving 20″ end for weaving.

FINISHING
Thread end into tapestry or yarn needle. Divide sts on 2 needles and weave sts tog (see *Weaving on Needles* on page 13). Weave in all ends.

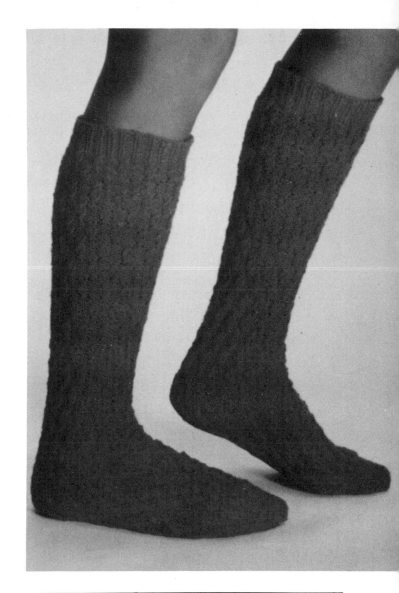

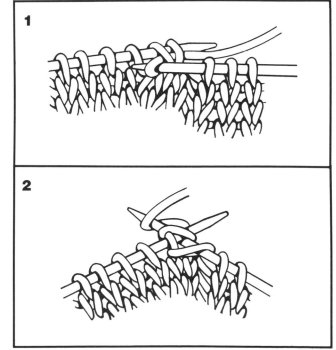

KNEE SOCKS

designed by Mary Thomas

The circular bands of reverse stock st highlight the leg portion of these socks, shown in two versions. Version A is worked in 2 colors while Version B is worked in one color with an added touch—textured stitch design worked between the circular bands.

SIZE: Written in one size, measuring approx 13″ above heel to knee, with adjustable foot length.

MATERIALS
Dawn Sayelle* Knitting Worsted Size TWEED yarn in
   3-oz skeins: 2 skeins Harvest for each version;
        1 skein Pumpkin (for Version A only)
Sizes 6 and 8, 7″ double pointed needles (or size required for gauge)

GAUGE: With larger size needles in stock st,
       5 sts = 1″; 13 rnds = 2″

VERSION A INSTRUCTIONS
(Make 2)

LEG
With Harvest and larger size dpn, CO 40 sts *loosely* onto one needle; change to smaller size dpn and divide sts onto 3 needles (14-14-12). Join, being careful not to twist sts. Work in K1, P1 ribbing for 1½″. Change to larger size dpn and work in patt as follows.

Rnds 1 through 10: With Harvest, knit 10 rnds.

Rnds 11 through 13 (circular band): With Pumpkin, purl 3 rnds.

Rep Rnds 1 through 13, twice more. Then with Harvest, knit 9 more rnds. **Dec Rnd.** Continuing with Harvest, * K8, K2 tog; rep from * around = 36 sts. Now rep Rnds 11 through 13, once; then rep Rnds 1 through 13, twice more. Continue with Harvest and knit 7 more rnds; then work as follows.

HEEL

Divide sts as follows: 18 sts on first needle for heel; 9 sts each on 2nd and 3rd needles for instep. Continuing with 18 sts on first needle *only* (leave sts on 2nd and 3rd needles unworked), use Pumpkin and work back and forth in rows as follows.

Row 1: * K1, sl 1 as to purl; rep from * 8 times more.

Row 2: Purl.
Rep last 2 rows until heel measures 2", ending by working Row 1. Change to Harvest and turn heel as follows.

Turn Heel: [**Note:** Heel is turned by working short rows; when instructions say "TURN", leave rem sts unworked, turn your work and begin next row.] **Row 1 (wrong side):** P 11, P2 tog, P1; TURN. **Row 2:** Sl 1 as to purl, K5; sl 1 as to knit, K1, PSSO, K1; TURN. **Row 3:** Sl 1 as to purl, P6, P2 tog; P1; TURN. **Row 4:** Sl 1 as to purl, K7; sl 1 as to knit, K1, PSSO, K1; TURN. **Row 5:** Sl 1 as to purl, P8, P2 tog, P1. **Row 6:** Sl 1 as to purl, K9; sl 1 as to knit, K1, PSSO, K1 = 12 sts. Heel is now turned; continue with Harvest and work in rnds as follows.

GUSSET AND FOOT

Rnd 1 (joining rnd): With right side facing, use needle with 12 heel sts and pick up 9 sts along side of heel; with free needle, knit across 18 sts from next 2 needles (instep); with free needle, pick up 9 sts along other side of heel, then K6 from first needle (heel sts). You should now have 48 sts (15-18-15); next rnd begins at center of heel.

Rnd 2: Knit to last 3 sts on first needle, K2 tog, K1; knit across sts on 2nd needle; knit first st on 3rd needle, sl 1 as to knit, K1, PSSO; knit rem sts = 46 sts (14-18-14).

Rnd 3: Knit.
Rep Rnds 2 and 3, five times more = 36 sts (9-18-9). Now knit even in rnds until sock measures approx 2" less than desired foot length. Change to Pumpkin and work as follows.

TOE SHAPING

Rnd 1: Knit to last 3 sts on first needle, K2 tog, K1; knit first st on 2nd needle, sl 1 as to knit, K1, PSSO; knit to last 3 sts on same (2nd) needle, K2 tog, K1; knit first st on 3rd needle, sl 1 as to knit, K1, PSSO; knit rem sts = 32 sts (8-16-8).

Rnd 2: Knit.
Rep Rnds 1 and 2, five times more = 12 sts (3-6-3). Now knit 3 sts from first needle and sl these sts on 3rd needle; you should now have 2 needles with 6 sts on each. Cut yarn, leaving approx 20" length for weaving.

FINISHING

Thread yarn end into tapestry or yarn needle and weave sts tog (see *Weaving on Needles* on page 13). Weave in all ends.

VERSION B INSTRUCTIONS
(Make 2)

Work same as Version A until 1½" of K1, P1 ribbing have been completed. Change to larger size dpn and work in patt bands as follows. **Note:** Continue with Harvest throughout patt.

Textured Stitch Band 1: Rnds 1 and 2: Knit. **Rnd 3:** K4, (P2, K8) 3 times; P2, K4. **Rnd 4:** K3, (P4, K6) 3 times; P4, K3. **Rnds 5 and 6:** K2, (P6, K4) 3 times; P6, K2. **Rnd 7:** Rep Rnd 4. **Rnd 8:** Rep Rnd 3. **Rnds 9 and 10:** Knit.

Circular Band: Purl 3 rnds.

Textured Stitch Band 2: Rnds 1 and 2: Knit. **Rnd 3:** P1, (K8, P2) 3 times; K8, P1. **Rnd 4:** P2, (K6, P4) 3 times; K6, P2. **Rnds 5 and 6:** P3 (K4, P6) 3 times; K4, P3. **Rnd 7:** Rep Rnd 4. **Rnd 8:** Rep Rnd 3. **Rnds 9 and 10:** Knit.

Circular Band: Purl 3 rnds.

Textured Stitch Band 3: Rep Textured Stitch Band 1.

Circular Band: Purl 3 rnds.

Textured Stitch Band 4: Rnds 1 through 8: Rep Rnds 1 through 8 of Textured Stitch Band 2. **Rnd 9:** Knit. **Rnd 10:** (K8, K2 tog) 4 times = 36 sts.

Circular Band: Purl 3 rnds.

Textured Stitch Band 5: Rnds 1 and 2: Knit. **Rnd 3:** K4, (P2, K7) 3 times; P2, K3. **Rnd 4:** K3, (P4, K5) 3 times; P4, K2. **Rnds 5 and 6:** K2, (P6, K3) 3 times; P6, K1. **Rnd 7:** Rep Rnd 4. **Rnd 8:** Rep Rnd 3. **Rnds 9 and 10:** Knit.

Circular Band: Purl 3 rnds.

Textured Stitch Band 6: Rnds 1 and 2: Knit. **Rnd 3:** (P1, K8) 4 times. **Rnd 4:** P2, (K6, P3) 3 times; K6, P1. **Rnds 5 and 6:** P3, (K4, P5) 3 times; K4, P2. **Rnd 7:** Rep Rnd 4. **Rnd 8:** Rep Rnd 3. **Rnds 9 and 10:** Knit.

Circular Band: Purl 3 rnds.

Knit 7 more rnds; then beg with Heel instructions and complete in same manner as Version A.

SPORT HEADBAND
designed by Mary Thomas

SIZE: Written in one size.

MATERIALS
Worsted weight yarn: 2 oz red
Size 7, 10″ straight knitting needles (or size required for gauge)

GAUGE: In stock st, 5 sts = 1″

INSTRUCTIONS

CO 32 sts. **Row 1:** * YB (yarn to back of work), K1; YF (yarn to front of work), sl 1 as to purl, rep from * across. Rep Row 1 until piece measures 5½″ from CO edge.

Next Row: * YB, K1; YF, sl 1 as to purl; P1, sl 1 as to purl; rep from * across. Rep this row until piece measures 10½″ from CO edge.

Now rep Row 1 until piece measures 16″ from CO edge. BO in K1, P1 ribbing. Sew BO and CO edges tog. Weave in all ends.

2-needle MITTENS and HAT
designed by Mary Thomas

These 2-needle mittens are unique and quick to make — they're knitted sideways in one piece, including the thumb. The matching hat features a thick cuff with bright stripes.

SIZES: Written in four sizes: child's small (4-5 yrs), child's medium (6-8 yrs), child's large (10-12 yrs) or adult small (glove size 6½-7), and adult average (glove size 7½-8).
Size Note: Instructions are written for smallest size with changes for larger sizes in parentheses.

MATERIALS
Worsted weight yarn: 5(6-8-8) oz medium blue; ¼ oz each orange, yellow, green, white and red
Sizes 7 and 9, 14″ straight knitting needles (or size required for gauge)
Small stitch holder

GAUGE: With smaller size needles in stock st,
                              5 sts = 1″; 7 rows = 1″

MITTEN INSTRUCTIONS

(Make 2)

[**Note:** Throughout patt, slip each sl st as to purl, keeping an even tension (sl st should not be loose).] Beg at little finger edge of hand, CO 34(40-48-54) sts loosely. Work in patt as follows.

Patt Row 1: Knit across all sts.

Patt Row 2: Purl to last 10(12-16-16) sts, knit rem sts (for garter st cuff).

Patt Row 3: Knit to last st, TURN [rem st is left unworked].

Patt Row 4: Sl first st, purl to last 10(12-16-16) sts, knit rem sts.

Rep Patt Rows 1 through 4, 3(4-4-5) times more; then rep Patt Rows 1 and 2, 0(0-1-1) more time. ALL SIZES: Rep Patt Row 1, once more = 17(21-23-27) rows total.

Gusset and Thumb: [**Note:** Shaping is worked in short rows; when instructions say "TURN", leave rem sts on needle unworked, turn your work and begin next row.] Work first half of shaping as follows.

Row 1: P 18(20-22-26) and sl these sts to holder; purl next 2 sts, TURN.

Row 2: Sl first st, K1; CO 7(9-12-14) sts (see *Casting On, Method 2* on page 12) for thumb.

Row 3: P 11(13-16-18), TURN.

Row 4: Sl first st, knit to last st, TURN [last st is left unworked].

Row 5: Sl first st, P 10(13-16-18), TURN.

Row 6: Sl first st, knit across all rem sts.

Row 7: P 13(16-20-22), TURN.

CHILD'S MEDIUM SIZE ONLY

Row 8: Rep Row 4. **Row 9:** Sl first st, P 15, TURN.

CHILD'S LARGE and ADULT SMALL or (ADULT AVERAGE) SIZES ONLY:

Row 8: Rep Row 4. **Row 9:** Sl first st, P 19(22), TURN.

Row 10: Rep Row 6. **Row 11:** P 22(26), TURN.

ALL SIZES: Rep Row 6, then work second half as follows.

Row 1: P 13(17-22-26), knit rem 10(12-16-16) sts of cuff.

Row 2: Knit to last st, TURN.

Row 3: Sl first st, P 11(15-20-20), TURN.

Row 4: Sl first st, knit across all rem sts.

Row 5: P 12(16-21-24), TURN.

Row 6: Sl first st, knit to last st, TURN.

Row 7: Sl first st, P 9(13-18-20), TURN.

Row 8: Rep Row 4.

CHILD'S MEDIUM SIZE ONLY

Row 9: P 13, TURN. **Row 10:** Rep Row 4.

CHILD'S LARGE and ADULT SMALL or (ADULT AVERAGE) SIZES ONLY

Row 9: P 18(20), TURN. **Row 10:** Rep Row 6. **Row 11:** Sl first st, P 14(16), TURN. **Row 12:** Rep Row 4.

ALL SIZES: BO 7(9-12-14) thumb sts, purl next st, TURN.

Next Row: Sl first st, K1; sl sts from holder to free needle and knit across these sts to last st, TURN. Work Patt Row 4, once. Now work Patt Rows 1 through 4, 4(5-5-6) times; then work Patt Rows 1 and 2, 0(0-1-1) more time. BO all sts loosely, leaving approx 20" sewing length.

FINISHING

Thread sewing length into tapestry or yarn needle and weave through sts at top of mitten. Draw up tightly and fasten securely; then sew side seam (CO and BO edges tog). Finish top of thumb and sew thumb seam in same manner. Weave in all ends.

HAT INSTRUCTIONS

With med blue and smaller size needles, CO 85(90-95-100) sts. Work even in stock st for 3". Change to larger size needles. Continuing in stock st, work 2 rows each in the following color sequence: orange, yellow, green, med blue, white and red.

When 12 rows of color sequence are completed, continue with blue in stock st until piece measures 15(16-17-17)" from CO edge, ending by working a purl row. Now shape top as follows.

Row 1: * K2 tog, K3; rep from * across = 68(72-76-80) sts.

Rows 2, 4 and 6: Purl.

Row 3: * K2 tog, K2; rep from * across = 51(54-57-60) sts.

Row 5: * K2 tog, K1; rep from * across = 34(36-38-40) sts.

Row 7: * K2 tog; rep from * across = 17(18-19-20) sts.

FINISHING

Cut yarn, leaving approx 24" sewing length. Thread into tapestry or yarn needle; draw through all sts. Draw up tightly and fasten securely; then sew side seam, carefully matching stripes. Turn under CO edge to inside to form 6" hem and sl st loosely in place. Turn up 3" of hem to outside for striped cuff. Weave in all ends.

4-needle STRIPED HAT and MITTENS

designed by Barbara Retzke and Mary Thomas

SIZES

For Hat: Small   Large
  approx head size   19-20"   20-21"
For Mittens: Small   Medium   Large
  approx ages   6-8 yrs   10-12 yrs   14-16 yrs

Size Note: Instructions are written for smallest size with changes for larger size(s) in parentheses.

MATERIALS

Worsted weight yarn: 6 oz red; ½ oz each black, yellow, blue, orange and green

Sizes 4 and 6, 7″ double pointed needles [dpn] (or sizes required for gauge)

2 Stitch markers

GAUGE: In stock st:

with smaller size needles, 6 sts = 1″; 8 rnds = 1″
with larger size needles, 5 sts = 1″; 7 rnds = 1″

HAT INSTRUCTIONS

With red and **larger** size dpn, CO 99(108) sts. Divide sts evenly onto 3 needles. Join, being careful not to twist sts. **Rib Rnd:** * P2, K1; rep from * around. Rep Rib Rnd for 2(2½)″. Change to **smaller** size dpn and work in stock st (knit each rnd) until piece measures 4½(5½)″ from CO edge. Continuing in stock st, work the following 30-rnd Stripe Sequence:

  1 rnd black;

  5 rnds yellow;

  1 rnd black;

  5 rnds blue;

  1 rnd black;

  5 rnds orange;

  1 rnd black;

  5 rnds green;

  1 rnd black;

  5 rnds red

When Stripe Sequence (30 rnds) is completed, continue with red in stock st and work top shaping as follows.

Rnd 1: * K2 tog, K9(10); rep from * 8 times = 90(99) sts.

Rnd 2 and all even-numbered rnds: Knit.

Rnd 3: * K2 tog, K8(9); rep from * 8 times = 81(90) sts.

Rnd 5: * K2 tog, K7(8); rep from * 8 times = 72(81) sts.

Rnd 7: * K2 tog, K6(7); rep from * 8 times = 63(72) sts.

Rnd 9: * K2 tog, K5(6); rep from * 8 times = 54(63) sts.

Rnd 11: * K2 tog, K4(5); rep from * 8 times = 45(54) sts.

Rnd 13: * K2 tog, K3(4); rep from * 8 times = 36(45) sts.

Rnd 15: * K2 tog, K2(3); rep from * 8 times = 27(36) sts.

Rnd 17: * K2 tog, K1(2); rep from * 8 times = 18(27) sts.

Rnd 19: * K2 tog, K0(1); rep from * 8 times = 9(18) sts.

For Larger Size Only: Rnd 21: * K2 tog; rep from * 8 times = 9 sts.

FINISHING

Cut yarn, leaving approx 8″ end. Thread into tapestry or yarn needle; draw through all sts twice. Draw up tightly and fasten securely on inside. Weave in all ends. Fold cuff up to right side of hat. **Pompon:** With equal amounts of each color, make a 3″ diameter pompon (see *Pompon* instructions on page 17) and attach firmly to top of hat.

MITTEN INSTRUCTIONS

(Make 2)

With red and smaller size dpn, CO 33(39-45) sts loosely onto one needle. Then divide onto 3 needles as follows: 12(12-15) sts on each of first 2 needles, and 9(15-15) sts on 3rd needle. Join, being careful not to twist sts. **Rib Rnd:** * K2, P1; rep from * around. Rep Rib Rnd, 5 times more. Continuing to rep Rib Rnd, work the following 13-rnd Stripe Sequence:

> 1 rnd black;
> 2 rnds yellow;
> 1 rnd black;
> 2 rnds blue;
> 1 rnd black;
> 2 rnds orange;
> 1 rnd black;
> 2 rnds green;
> 1 rnd black

When Stripe Sequence (13 rnds) is completed, continue with red and work 6(7-8) rnds in stock st (knit each rnd).

Thumb Gusset: Rnd 1: K 15(18-21), place marker for thumb sts; inc in next st, K1, inc in next st; place marker, knit rem sts = 5 thumb sts (between markers). **Note:** Sl markers on each following rnd. **Rnds 2 and 3:** Knit. **Rnd 4:** Knit to first marker; inc in next st, knit to within one st of next marker; inc in next st, knit rem sts = 7 thumb sts. **Rnds 5 and 6:** Knit. Rep Rnds 4 through 6, 3(4-5) times more = 13(15-17) thumb sts.

Dividing Rnd: K 15(18-21), drop marker; sl next 13(15-17) thumb sts to holder to be worked later; drop marker, CO 2(3-4) sts (see *Casting On, Method 2* on page 12); knit rem sts = 32(39-46) sts. Continue in stock st until mitten (including cuff) measures 7(8-9)" or ½" less than desired length.

Top Shaping: Rnd 1: K0(3-2); * K2 tog, K2; rep from * around = 24(30-35) sts. **Rnd 2:** Knit. **Rnd 3:** K0(0-2); * K2 tog, K1; rep from * around = 16(20-24) sts. **Rnd 4:** Knit. **Rnd 5:** * K2 tog; rep from * around = 8(10-12) sts. Finish off, leaving approx 8" end. Thread into tapestry or yarn needle; draw through all sts twice. Draw up tightly and fasten securely on inside.

Thumb: With smaller size dpn, sl 13(15-17) sts from holder to 2 needles. Join red yarn; with free needle, pick up 2(3-4) sts over CO sts at base of thumb. Dividing these 15(18-21) sts evenly onto 3 needles, knit even in rnds for 1¼(1½-1¾)" or approx ¼" less than desired length. Then shape top as follows. **Rnd 1:** * K2 tog, K1; rep from * around = 10(12-14) sts. **Rnd 2:** * K2 tog; rep from * around = 5(6-7) sts. Cut yarn leaving approx 6" end. Thread into tapestry or yarn needle and draw through all sts twice. Draw up tightly and fasten securely on inside. Weave in all ends.

JUTE HANDBAG
designed by Mary Thomas

SIZE: Approx 12" wide x 10" deep (without handles)

MATERIALS
Jute macrame cord (3 ply): 150 yds
Size 13, 10" straight knitting needles (or size required for gauge)
1 Set bamboo purse handles (8¼" x 6½")
Materials Note: Jute macrame cord and purse handles are available through craft stores.

GAUGE: In patt st, 4 sts = 1"

INSTRUCTIONS
CO 36 sts.
Row 1 (right side): Knit.
Row 2: * † *P2 tog, leaving both sts on left-hand needle; purl first st on left-hand needle again; then sl both sts off left-hand needle* †; rep from * across.
Row 3: Knit.
Row 4: P1; rep from † to † (in Row 2) to last st, P1.
Rep Rows 1 through 4 until piece measures approx 20" from CO edge, ending by working Row 2. BO all sts in knit.

FINISHING
Fold piece in half lengthwise with wrong sides tog. Use single strand of cord and overcast side seams, leaving approx 2" free at open edge. Use 2 strands of cord and overcast CO edge to one handle and then BO edge to other handle. Weave in all ends. Lining optional.

CHENILLE HAT and SCARF

designed by Mary Thomas

SIZE: Hat is written in one size; scarf measures approx 6″ wide x 60″ long.

MATERIALS
Chenille yarn: 10¼ oz (287 grams) red
Sizes 6 and 7, 14″ straight knitting needles (or size required for gauge)
Materials Note: For hat, 3½ oz (98 grams) of yarn are required; for scarf, 6¾ oz (189 grams) of yarn are required.

GAUGE: With larger size needles in K1, P1 ribbing, 7 sts = 2″ (without stretching)

SPECIAL NOTE: Before beginning your hat or scarf, we suggest working a swatch to become familiar with the techniques of knitting with chenille yarn. This yarn is difficult to unravel.

PATTERN STITCH
(worked on even number of sts)
Row 1 (right side): K1, * wrap yarn twice around needle as in **Fig 1**, P1; wrap yarn twice around needle as in **Fig 2**, K1; rep from * to last st, wrap yarn twice around needle as in **Fig 1**, P1.

Row 2: K1, drop both wraps, P1; * drop both wraps, K1; drop both wraps, P1; rep from * across.
Row 3: * K1, P1; rep from * across.
Rows 4 through 6: Rep Row 3, three times.
Rep Rows 1 through 6 for patt.

HAT INSTRUCTIONS

With smaller size needles, CO 70 sts. Work 4 rows in K1, P1 ribbing. Change to larger size needles and work in Patt St until piece measures 7½″ from CO edge, ending by working Row 6.

Shape Top: Row 1: K3 tog; P1, K1, P1; * K3 tog, P1; (K1, P1) twice; rep from * across = 52 sts. **Row 2, 4 and 6:** * K1, P1; rep from * across. **Row 3:** K3, tog, P1; * K3 tog, P1, K1, P1; rep from * across = 34 sts. **Row 5:** K1, P1; * K3 tog, P1; rep from * across = 18 sts.

FINISHING
Cut yarn, leaving approx 24″ sewing length. Thread into tapestry or yarn needle; draw through all sts. Draw up tightly and fasten securely; then sew side seam, carefully matching rows of long sts. Weave in all ends.

SCARF INSTRUCTIONS

With smaller size needles, CO 20 sts. Work 4 rows in K1, P1 ribbing. Change to larger size needles and work in Patt St until scarf measures approx 60″ from CO edge or desired length, ending by working Row 2. Change to smaller size needles and work 3 rows in K1, P1 ribbing. BO all sts in ribbing. Weave in all ends.

TAM

designed by Mary Thomas

SIZE: Written in one size.

MATERIALS
Mohair-blend yarn: 2 oz yellow
Sizes 6 and 8, 14″ straight knitting needles (or size required for gauge)

GAUGE: With larger size needles in stock st,
5 sts = 1″; 6 rows = 1″

INSTRUCTIONS

With smaller size needles, CO 100 sts loosely. Work 3 rows in K1, P1 ribbing. Change to larger size needles and work increase shaping as follows.

Row 1 (right side): * Inc in next st, K9; rep from * across = 110 sts.

Rows 2, 4, 6, 8 and 10: Purl.

Row 3: * Inc in next st, K 10; rep from * across = 120 sts.

Row 5: * Inc in next st, K 11; rep from * across = 130 sts.

Row 7: * Inc in next st, K 12; rep from * across = 140 sts.

Row 9: * Inc in next st, K 13; rep from * across = 150 sts.

Row 11: * Inc in next st, K 14; rep from * across = 160 sts.

Beg with a purl row and work 5 rows even in stock st. Then work decrease shaping as follows.

Row 1: * K2 tog, K 28, K2 tog; rep from * across = 150 sts.

Row 2 and all even-numbered rows: Purl.

Row 3: * K2 tog, K 26, K2 tog; rep from * across = 140 sts.

Row 5: * K2 tog, K 24, K2 tog; rep from * across = 130 sts.

Row 7: * K2 tog, K 22, K2 tog; rep from * across = 120 sts.

Row 9: * K2 tog, K 20, K2 tog; rep from * across = 110 sts.

Row 11: * K2 tog, K 18, K2 tog; rep from * across = 100 sts.

Row 13: * K2 tog, K 16, K2 tog; rep from * across = 90 sts.

Row 15: * K2 tog, K 14, K2 tog; rep from * across = 80 sts.

Row 17: * K2 tog, K 12, K2 tog; rep from * across = 70 sts.

Row 19: * K2 tog, K 10, K2 tog; rep from * across = 60 sts.

Row 21: * K2 tog, K8, K2 tog; rep from * across = 50 sts.

Row 23: * K2 tog, K6, K2 tog; rep from * across = 40 sts.

Row 25: * K2 tog, K4, K2 tog; rep from * across = 30 sts.

Row 27: * K2 tog, K2, K2 tog; rep from * across = 20 sts.

Row 29: * K2 tog; rep from * across = 10 sts.

Row 30: Purl.

FINISHING

Cut yarn, leaving 24″ sewing length. Thread into tapestry or yarn needle; draw through rem sts twice. Draw up tightly and fasten securely. Then sew seam to CO edge. Weave in all ends. To block tam, dampen and then insert 10″ diameter china plate inside tam. Let dry thoroughly before removing plate. This method gives an even and rounded circumference to the tam.

GLOVES *for women*

designed by Mary Thomas

These gloves are a basic design to complement your wardrobe, and can be made with worsted weight yarn or sport weight yarn.

SIZE: Written in one size and will fit glove sizes 6½-7½.

MATERIALS
For Worsted Weight Version:
    Worsted weight yarn: 3 oz brown/black tweed
    Size 7, 7″ double pointed needles (or size
        required for gauge)
For Sport Weight Version:
    Sport weight yarn: 2 oz copper heather
    Size 6, 7″ double pointed needles (or size
        required for gauge)
For Both Versions:.
    Stitch marker
    6 Safety pins (med size for sm stitch holders)

GAUGE: In Stock st:
            **with worsted weight yarn and size 7
            needles,**
                5 sts = 1″; 7 rnds = 1″
            with sport weight yarn and size 6 needles,
                6 sts = 1″; 8 rnds = 1″

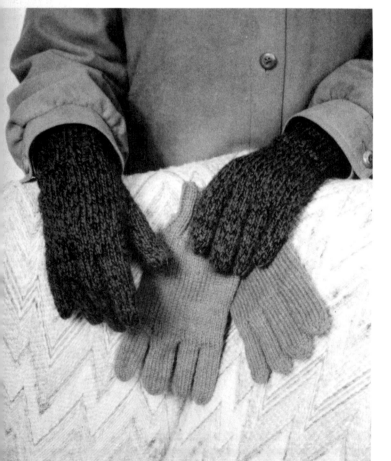

INSTRUCTIONS

Notes: Instructions are written for Worsted Weight Version with changes for Sport Weight Version in parentheses. Use size 7 needles with worsted weight yarn; or size 6 needles with sport weight yarn (or size required for gauge).

RIGHT GLOVE
CO 36(44) sts *loosely* on one needle. Divide sts on 3 needles as follows: 12-12-12(16-16-12). Join, being careful not to twist sts. **Note:** Beg yarn end identifies end of rnd [falls between first and 3rd needles]. Work in K2, P2 ribbing for 2″. Then knit 3 rnds even.

Thumb Gusset: Rnd 1 (marking rnd): Knit to last 2 sts on 3rd needle; place marker to separate sts of hand and thmb; inc in next st [*to inc: knit in front and back of st = inc made*], K1 = 3 thumb sts. **Note:** Sl marker on each following rnd.

Rnds 2 and 3: Knit.

Rnd 4: Knit to marker; inc in each of next 2 sts, K1 = 5 thumb sts.

Rnds 5 and 6: Knit.

Rnd 7: Knit to marker; inc in next st, knit to last 2 sts; inc in next st, K1 = 7 thumb sts.

Rnds 8 and 9: Knit.
Rep last 3 rnds, 2(3) times more = 11(13) thumb sts.

Dividing Rnd (for thumb): Knit to marker; remove marker, sl rem 11(13) sts to holder [safety pin] to be worked later for thumb; CO 2 sts (see *Casting On, Method 2* on page 12) over thumb sts at end of 3rd needle = 36(44) sts. Continuing in rnds, knit even until work measures 1½″ above thumb or desired length to fingers.

Dividing Rnd (for fingers): K2, then CO 2 sts and leave these 4 sts on needle for part of index finger; sl next 5(6) sts to holder for one side of middle finger; sl next 4(5) sts to holder for one side of ring finger; sl next 8(10) sts to holder for little finger; sl next 4(5) sts to holder for other side of ring finger; sl next 5(6) sts to holder for other side of middle finger; divide rem sts on 2 needles for rem part of index finger as follows: 4-4(4-6). Sts for index finger should now be divided on 3 needles as follows: 4-4-4(4-4-6).

Index Finger: Join and knit even in rnds until finger measures 2½″ or desired length. **Dec Rnd:** * K2 tog; rep from * around = 6(7) sts. Cut yarn, leaving approx 6″ end. Thread into tapestry or yarn needle; draw through all sts. Draw up tightly and fasten securely.

Middle Finger: Sl sts from holders [one on each side of index finger] to 2 needles. With free needle, pick up and knit 2 sts over CO sts at base of index finger. With free needle, knit next 5(6) sts [sts from one holder]; then CO 1 st. With rem free needle, knit next 5(6) sts [sts from other holder]. Now divide these 13(15) sts on 3 needles as follows: 4-4-5(5-5-5). Join and knit even in rnds until finger measures 2¾″ or desired length. **Dec Rnd:** * K2 tog; rep from * to last st, K1 = 7(8) sts. Finish in same manner as index finger.

Ring Finger: Sl sts from holders [one on each side of middle finger] to 2 needles. With free needle, pick up and knit 2 sts over CO st at base of middle finger. With free needle, knit next 4(5) sts [sts from one holder]; then CO 1 st. With rem free needle, knit next 4(5) sts [sts from other holder]. Now divide these 11(13) sts on 3 needles as follow: 4-4-3(4-4-5). Join and knit even in rnds until finger measures 2½" or desired length. **Dec Rnd:** * K2 tog; rep from * to last st, K1 = 6(7) sts. Finish in same manner as index finger.

Little Finger: Sl sts from holder to 2 needles. With free needle, pick up and knit 2 sts over CO st at base of ring finger. Now divide these 10(12) sts on 3 needles as follows: 4-4-2(4-4-4). Join and knit even in rnds until finger measures 2¼" or desired length. **Dec Rnd:** * K2 tog; rep from * around = 5(6) sts. Finish in same manner as index finger.

Thumb: Sl sts from holder to 2 needles. With free needle, pick up and knit 3 sts over CO sts. Now divide these 14(16) sts on 3 needles as follows: 4-4-6(6-6-4). Join and knit even in rnds until thumb measures 2¼" or desired length. **Dec Rnd:** * K2 tog; rep from * around = 7(8) sts. Finish in same manner as index finger. Weave in all ends.

LEFT GLOVE
Work same as Right Glove to Dividing Rnd (for fingers). **Dividing Rnd (for fingers):** K8(10), then CO 2 sts and leave these 10(12) sts on needle for part of index finger; sl next 5(6) sts to holder for one side of middle finger; sl next 4(5) sts to holder for one side of ring finger; sl next 8(10) sts to holder for little finger; sl next 4(5) sts to holder for other side of ring finger; sl next 5(6) sts to holder for other side of middle finger; leave last 2 sts on needle for rem part of index finger. Now divide sts for index finger on 3 needles as follows: 4-4-4(4-4-6). Work fingers and thumb same as Right Glove.

KNITTER'S PIN
designed by Mary Thomas

MATERIALS
Sport weight yarn: 10 yds bright yellow (or color of your choice)
Size 2, 10" straight knitting needles
2 Round wooden toothpicks
2 Beads (5 mm diameter) in white (or color of your choice)
Small safety pin

GAUGE: None specified

INSTRUCTIONS
CO 8 sts, leaving approx ½" end. Knit 13 rows. **Next Row (right side):** K3, sl rem 5 sts to right-hand needle. Cut yarn, leaving 36" end; wind into a small ball, leaving approx 2" free between knitted piece and ball. With right side facing, sew small yarn ball in place at lower right-hand corner (opposite beg yarn end).

Cut one end off each toothpick, leaving toothpick approx 1¾" long. Sl bead over cut end of each toothpick (if necessary, twist or glue beads to secure in place). Beg at outside edge and insert one toothpick through 3 sts and the other toothpick through 5 sts, ending at yarn end. Then with right side facing, insert tip of right-hand toothpick into 4th st and bring yarn around point as to knit. Sew safety pin on wrong side for attaching pin to wearing apparel.

TURTLE-NECK DICKEY
designed by Mary Thomas

SIZE: Written in one size.

MATERIALS
Sport weight yarn: 3 oz red
Size 4, 16″ circular knitting needle or 7″ double
pointed needles (for neckband only)
Size 6, 10″ straight knitting needles (or size required
for gauge)
Small stitch holder

GAUGE: With straight needles in stock st,
6 sts = 1″; 8 rows = 1″

INSTRUCTIONS

[**Note:** Dickey is worked in one piece, beginning at front lower edge.] With straight needles, CO 72 sts. Knit 4 rows for garter st border. Then work as follows.

Row 1 (right side): Knit.

Row 2: K2 for garter st edge, purl to last 2 sts; K2 for garter st edge.

Rep last 2 rows until piece measures 10″ from CO edge, ending by working Row 2.

Shape Neck and Shoulders: Row 1 (dividing row): K 25, knit next 22 sts and sl these sts to holder for front of neck; knit rem sts. Continue working across each side of neck opening as follows. **Row 2:** K2, purl to neck edge; join new ball of yarn at left neck edge and purl to last 2 sts, K2. **Row 3:** Knit to within 2 sts of neck edge, K2 tog; then K2 tog at right neck edge, knit rem sts = 24 sts each side. **Row 4:** K2, purl to neck edge; then purl across other side to last sts, K2. **Rep Rows 3 and 4,** 5 times more = 19 sts

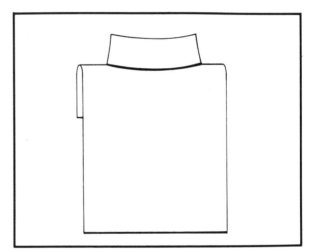

each side. **Joining Row:** Knit to neck edge; continue with same yarn (cut yarn from other side, leaving 4″ end for weaving in later) and CO 34 sts (see *Casting On, Method 2* on page 12) for back of neck; then knit across other side = 72 sts. Now work as follows.

Row 1 (wrong side): K2, purl to last 2 sts, K2.

Row 2: Knit.

Rep last 2 rows until piece measures 4″ from CO sts at back of neck. Knit 4 more rows for garter st border. BO all sts in knit.

Neckband: With right side facing, beg at right back neck edge. Use circular needle or double pointed needles (dividing sts onto 3 needles) and pick up 34 sts along CO sts at back neck edge; pick up 24 sts along left neck edge; K 22 from holder; pick up 24 sts along right neck edge = 104 sts. Join and work K1, P1 ribbing in rnds for 5″. BO all sts in ribbing. Fold ribbing in half to outside. Weave in all ends.

MOPSIES SLIPPERS

These slippers are a breeze to make and fun to wear, and would make a good item for bazaar sales.

SIZES: Small   Medium
    fits shoe sizes   6-7   8-9
Size Note: Instructions are written for sizes as follows: Small(Medium).

MATERIALS
**American Thread Dawn Sayelle* Knitting Worsted
    Size Ombre yarn in 3½ oz skeins: 2 skeins
    Shaded Pinks**
**Size 11, 10″ straight knitting needles (or size
    required for gauge)**
Size G or H aluminum crochet hook (for fringing)
Materials Note: Yarn is used doubled throughout patt.

GAUGE: With 2 strands of yarn in stock st,
                               3 sts = 1″

INSTRUCTIONS

(Make 2)
Beg at heel, use 2 strands of yarn and CO 19(23) sts. Then work as follows. [**Note:** Sl each sl st as to purl.]

Row 1 (wrong side): K2; (sl 1, K1) 3(4) times; sl 1, P1, YB (yarn at back of work); (sl 1, K1) 3(4) times; sl 1, K2.

Row 2. K8(10), inc in next st [*to inc: knit in front and back of st*]; K1, inc in next st; K8(10) = 21(25) sts.

Row 3: K2; (sl 1, K1) 3(4) times; sl 1, inc in next st [*to inc: purl in front and back of st*]; P1, inc in next st, YB; (sl 1, K1) 3(4) times; sl 1, K2 = 23(27) sts.

Row 4: K9(11); inc in next st [*to inc: knit in front and back of st*]; K3, inc in next st; K9(11) = 25(29) sts.

Row 5: K2; (sl 1, K1) 3(4) times; sl 1, P7, YB; (sl 1, K1) 3(4) times; sl 1, K2.

Row 6: Knit.
Rep Rows 5 and 6 until garter st section measures 5½(6½)″ from CO edge. Then shape toe as follows.

Row 1: * K1, P1; rep from * to last st, K1.

Row 2: K2 tog; * P1, K1; rep from * to last st, P1 = 24(28) sts.

Continuing in K1, P1 ribbing as established, dec one st at beg of each row until 17(19) sts rem on needle.

FINISHING
Cut yarn, leaving approx 18″ sewing length. Thread into tapestry or yarn needle; draw through all sts, removing knitting needle. Pull up tightly and fasten securely. Turn slipper inside out and sew seam at top of toe section (from tip to where rib section began). Sew seam at heel. Weave in all ends.

Fringe: Cut 8″ strands of yarn. Use 2 strands for each knot of fringe. With right side facing and crochet hook, tie knots (see *Basic Fringe Instructions* on page 16) around sts and work 6 rows of fringe around side section of each slipper.

DOG COAT
designed by Mary Thomas

SIZES:

	Small	Medium	Large
Length (base of tail to neck):	10"	14"	20"
Width (without side tabs):	9"	12"	18"

Size Note: Instructions are written for sizes as follows: Small(Medium-Large).

MATERIALS
Worsted weight yarn: 2(3-6) oz each red and gray
Size 10, 14" straight knitting needles (or size required for gauge)
Small stitch holder
Black Velcro (12" length)

GAUGE: In Patt St, 19 sts = 4"

PATTERN STITCH
To practice stitch, use red and CO 19 sts. Drop red (do not cut); join gray. **Note:** Colors are carried along side of work.
Row 1 (right side): With gray, * K1, YB (yarn to back of work), sl 1 as to purl; rep from * to last st, K1.
Row 2: Knit. Drop gray.
Row 3: With red, K2; * YB, sl 1 as to purl, K1; rep from * to last st, K1.
Row 4: Knit. Drop red.
Rep Rows 1 through 4 for patt. [For swatch, rep Rows 1 through 4, 4 times more; your piece should measure 4" wide.]

INSTRUCTIONS

[**Note:** Throughout patt, slip each sl st as to purl.] With red, CO 19(25-45) sts. Drop red (do not cut), join gray (colors are carried along side of work).

Row 1 (right side): With gray, * K1, YB, sl 1; rep from * to last st, K1.

Row 2 (inc row): Inc in first st [*to inc: knit in front and back of st*]; knit to last 2 sts, inc in next st, K1 = 21(27-47) sts. Drop gray.

Rows 3 and 4: With red (pick up red in back of work — behind dropped color), rep Rows 1 and 2 = 23(29-49) sts. Drop red.

Rep Rows 1 through 4, 5(7-9) times more = 43(57-85) sts.

Now work in Patt St (beg with Row 1) until piece measures 10(14-20)" from CO edge or desired length, ending by working Row 3.

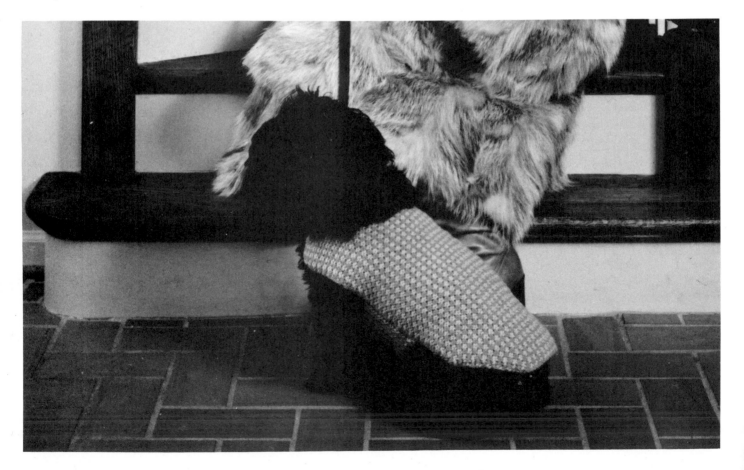

Dividing Row (wrong side): With red, K 14(17-25) and sl these sts to holder for shoulder; BO next 15(23-35) sts for neck opening; knit rem sts for other shoulder. Drop red.

Shoulder Shaping: Row 1: With gray, K1; * YB, sl 1, K1; rep from * to last 2 sts, K2 tog = 13(16-24) sts. **Row 2:** Knit. Drop gray. **Row 3:** With red, K2; * YB, sl 1, K1; rep from * to last 2 sts, K2 tog = 12(15-23) sts. **Row 4:** Knit. Drop red. Now work in Patt St (beg with Row 1) until shoulder measures approx 2(3-4)″ from BO sts at neck opening, ending by working Row 3. Now work end shaping as follows. **Row 1 (wrong side):** With red, knit to last 2 sts, K2 tog = 11(14-22) sts. Drop red. **Row 2:** With gray, K2 tog; * YB, sl 1, K1; rep from * across = 10(13-21) sts. **Row 3:** Knit to last 2 sts, K2 tog = 9(12-20) sts. Drop gray. **Row 4:** With red, K2 tog, K1; * YB, sl 1, K1; rep from * to last st, K1 = 8(11-19) sts. **Row 5:** Rep Row 3 = 7(10-18) sts. Drop red. **Row 6:** Rep Row 2 = 6(9-17) sts. **Row 7:** Rep Row 3 = 5(8-16) sts. Cut gray, leaving approx 4″ end for weaving in later. **Row 8:** Rep Row 4 = 4(7-15) sts. BO all sts.

Other Shoulder Shaping: With right side facing, sl sts from holder to needle; join gray at left neck edge. **Row 1 (right side):** With gray, K2 tog, K1; * YB, sl 1, K1; rep from * across = 13(16-24) sts. **Row 2:** Knit. Drop gray. **Row 3:** With red, K2 tog, K1; * YB, sl 1, K1; rep from * to last st, K1 = 12(15-23) sts. **Row 4:** Knit. Drop red. Now work in Patt St (beg with Row 1) until shoulder measures approx 2(3-4)″ from BO sts at neck opening, ending by working Row 3. Now work end shaping as follows. **Row 1 (wrong side):** With red, K2 tog, knit rem sts = 11(14-22) sts. Drop red. **Row 2:** With gray, K1; * YB, sl 1, K1; rep from * to last 3 sts, YB, sl 1, K2 tog = 10(13-21) sts. **Row 3:** K2 tog, knit rem sts = 9(12-20) sts. Drop gray. **Row 4:** With red, K2; * YB, sl 1, K1; rep from * to last 2 sts, K2 tog = 8(11-19) sts. **Row 5:** Rep Row 3 = 7(10-18) sts. Drop red. **Row 6:** Rep Row 2 = 6(9-17) sts. **Row 7:** Rep Row 3 = 5(8-16) sts. Cut gray, leaving approx 4″ end. **Row 8:** Rep Row 4 = 4(7-15) sts. BO all sts.

Side Tab (make 2): With right side facing, use straight pins and mark off center 2(4-6)″ along side edge between neck opening and last increase row. With gray, pick up 11(19-29) sts along center marked edge. **Next Row (wrong side):** Knit. Drop gray. Work in Patt St (beg with Row 3) until tab measures approx 2(3-4)″ from side edge or desired length, ending by working Row 3. Now work end shaping as follows. **Row 1 (wrong side):** With red, K2 tog; knit to last 2 sts, K2 tog = 9(17-27) sts. Drop red. **Row 2:** With gray, K2 tog; * YB, sl 1, K1; rep from * to last 3 sts, YB, sl 1, K2 tog = 7(15-25) sts. **Row 3:** K2 tog; knit to last 2 sts, K2 tog = 5(13-23) sts. (For Small and Medium Sizes Only: Cut gray, leaving 4″ end.) **Row 4:** With red, K2 tog, K1; * YB, sl 1, K1; rep from * to last 2 sts, K2 tog = 3(11-21) sts. **Sizes Small and Medium Only:** BO all sts.

Size Large Only: Row 5: K2 tog, knit to last 2 sts, K2 tog = 19 sts. Drop red. **Row 6:** With gray, K2 tog; * YB, sl 1, K1; rep from * to last 3 sts, YB, sl 1, K2 tog = 17 sts. **Row 7:** K2 tog, knit to last 2 sts, K2 tog = 15 sts. Cut gray, leaving 4″ end. **Row 8:** With red, K2 tog; * K1, YB, sl 1; rep from * to last 3 sts, K1, K2 tog = 13 sts. BO all sts.

FINISHING
Weave in all ends. Sew pieces of Velcro at shoulder edges and side tab edges to close coat on front of chest and under stomach.

GOLF CLUB COVERS

designed by Mary Thomas

MATERIALS

Worsted weight yarn: 4 oz yellow;
½ oz blue;
½ oz green;
¼ oz red;
¼ oz brown

Size 7, 10″ straight knitting needles (or size required for gauge)

PATTERN STITCH

Row 1 (right side): Knit across all sts.
Row 2: P 25, K20.
Row 3: Knit to last st, leave last st unworked.
Row 4: Sl 1 as to purl, P 23, K 20.
Rep Rows 1 through 4 for patt.

INSTRUCTIONS

[**Note:** Cover is worked sideways.] Work each cover (set of four) as follows. With yellow, CO 45 sts. Work in Patt St using Stripe Sequence in **Fig 1** for the cover you are making (1-Stripe Cover for #1 wood, 2-Stripe Cover for #2 wood, etc.).

When Stripe Sequence is completed, continue with yellow in Patt St until piece measures approx 8″ from CO edge (measure in center of stock st portion). BO all sts, leaving approx 24″ sewing length.

FINISHING

Thread sewing length into tapestry or yarn needle; weave through end sts of stock st edge. Draw up tightly and fasten securely for top. Continue with same yarn and with wrong sides tog, sew CO and BO edges tog for side seam. Weave in all ends. **Chain:** With yellow, CO 3 sts. Work in garter st (knit each row) for 30″. Cut yarn, leaving approx 8″ end. Thread into tapestry or yarn needle; draw through all sts. Draw up tightly and sew to top of 1-Stripe Cover. Sew opposite end of chain to top of 4-Stripe Cover. Then sew tops of rem 2 covers to chain (between other covers) evenly spaced and in numerical order. **Pompons:** Make one 3″ diameter pompon (see *Pompon* instructions on page 17) for each cover, using equal amounts of each color yarn used in that cover. Sew matching pompon to top of corresponding cover.

Fig 1

1-Stripe	Cover	2-Stripe	Cover	3-Stripe	Cover	4-Stripe	Cover
Rows	Color	Rows	Color	Rows	Color	Rows	Color
1-16:	Yellow	1-14:	Yellow	1-12:	Yellow	1-10:	Yellow
17-20:	Blue	15-18:	Blue	13-16:	Blue	11-14:	Blue
21-24:	Yellow	19-20:	Yellow	17-18:	Yellow	15-16:	Yellow
		21-24:	Green	19-22:	Green	17-20:	Green
		25-28:	Yellow	23-24:	Yellow	21-22:	Yellow
				25-28:	Red	23-26:	Red
				29-32:	Yellow	27-28:	Yellow
						29-32:	Brown
						33-36:	Yellow

Tiny Treasures

Chapter 6

A delicate christening dress and bonnet; bonnet and bootie sets; colorful tube dolls; a shaped wrap designed especially to fit the popular infant seats; and a sweater with cables forming appealing owls are among the patterns in this chapter.

CHRISTENING DRESS AND BONNET

designed by Nancy Dent

This delicate, lacy christening dress is easy to make, and works up quickly. Its pretty stitch is formed by wrapping the yarn around the needle several times on one row, then dropping the wraps on the next row. If baby's busy fingers pull at the loops, you can get them back in place easily, simply by giving the area a good tug lengthwise.

SIZE: Written in one size to fit newborn to 9 months (approx 20 pounds); garment chest measures approx 19½".

MATERIALS
Dawn Wintuk* Baby yarn: 5 oz White
Size 3, 10″ straight knitting needles (or size required for gauge)
Size 5, 10″ straight and 24″ circular knitting needles
Stitch holders: 2 small and 1 large
Stitch marker
2 White buttons (½″ diameter)
White satin ribbon (1″ width): 1¾ yd
Size 20 tapestry needle (for button loops)

GAUGE: With smaller size needles in garter st,
13 sts = 2″

DRESS INSTRUCTIONS
YOKE AND SLEEVES

Note: Section is worked in garter st all in one piece, beginning at lower back yoke edge and ending at lower front yoke edge. With smaller size straight needles, CO 64 sts. Knit 3 rows. **Dividing Row:** [**Note:** Mark this row for right side of work.] K 32 for one side of back center opening; join another skein of yarn and knit rem sts for other side. Continue to work across each side with a separate skein of yarn as follows. Knit one row. At beg of next 2 rows, CO 8 sts (see *Casting On, Method 2* on page 12) for each sleeve = 40 sts each side. Continuing in garter st (knit each row), work until piece measures 3¼″ from beg CO edge, ending by working a wrong-side row. Place work flat on a table and measure width, well below needles; each side should measure approx 6¼″ wide.

Neck and Shoulder Shaping: Row 1 (right side): K 26, sl rem 14 sts of this side to sm holder for back of neck; sl next 14 sts of other side to sm holder for back of neck, cut yarn from this side, rejoin yarn and knit rem 26 sts. **Rows 2 and 3:** Knit. Now mark first and last st of row (use sm safety pins or pieces of contrasting yarn) for center of shoulders and sleeves. Continue in garter st until piece measures 1½″ from holders at back of neck, ending by working a wrong-side row. **Joining Row (right side):** Knit across 26 sts of first side; continue with same yarn (finish off yarn from other side) and CO 28 sts for front of neck, then knit across sts of other side = 80 sts.

Continuing in garter st, work until you have the same number of rows from marker (for center of sleeves and shoulders) to CO sts for sleeves, ending by working a wrong-side row. At beg of next 2 rows, BO 8 sts of each sleeve = 64 sts. Knit 4 more rows. Sl all sts to lge holder to be worked later for skirt. [**Note:** Width of front should now measure 9¾″.]

Neckband: With right side facing, beg at left back center neck edge. Using smaller size straight needles, join yarn and knit sts from holder; pick up one st in each ridge (EOR) along left front neck shaping to CO sts at front of neck; pick up one st in each CO st along front of neck; pick up one st in each ridge along right front neck shaping to holder sts at right back neck edge; knit sts from holder. Knit 4 rows. Then BO all sts with a medium tight tension in knit.

Sleeve Band (make 2): With right side facing and smaller size straight needles, join yarn and pick up one st in each ridge across outer sleeve edge. Work in same manner as Neckband.

SKIRT

Hold Yoke and Sleeves section with right side facing and back lower yoke edge across top. Using circular needle, join yarn at upper right-hand corner and pick up one st in each CO st along back yoke edge (64 sts); sl sts from holder to straight needle, then knit these 64 sts onto circular needle = 128 sts. Place marker to indicate beg of rnd; sl marker on each following rnd. Join and purl one rnd. **Inc Rnd:** K9, inc in each of next 46 sts; K 18, inc in each of next 46 sts; knit rem 9 sts = 220 sts. Now work in pattern stitch as follows.

Rnd 1: Purl.

Rnd 2: * YO twice, K1; YO 3 times, K1; YO 4 times, K1; YO 3 times, K1; YO twice, K6; rep from * around.

Rnd 3: Purl, dropping all YO's from needle.

Rnd 4: Knit.

Rnd 5: Purl.

Rnd 6: * K6, YO twice, K1; YO 3 times, K1; YO 4 times, K1; YO 3 times, K1, YO twice; rep from * around.

Rnd 7: Rep Rnd 3.

Rnd 8: Knit.

Rep Rnds 1 through 8 until skirt measures 11" from Inc Rnd, ending by working Rnd 4 or Rnd 8. BO all sts in purl, adjusting tension to keep work flat.

FINISHING

Do not steam garter st yoke. On wrong side, steam press skirt, stretching lengthwise firmly to show off pattern. Overcast side and sleeve seams. Weave in all ends.

Button Loops: With right side facing, work first button lp at top of right back center edge as follows. Thread yarn into size 20 tapestry needle doubled; secure on wrong side. Insert needle again slightly below first fastening, leaving sufficient size loop to fit button; tack in place. Continue with same yarn and reinforce loop by working buttonhole sts **(see Fig 1)** around loop until completely covered **(Fig 2).** Secure and weave in yarn end. Work a second button lp approx 1" below in same manner.

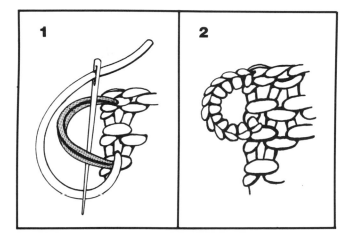

BONNET INSTRUCTIONS

BACK CENTER SECTION

Beg at neck edge, use larger size straight needles and CO 16 sts. Work in pattern stitch as follows.

Rows 1 and 2: Knit.

Row 3 (right side): K6; * YO twice, K1; YO 3 times, K1; YO 4 times, K1; YO 3 times, K1; YO twice, K6. [**Note:** For working pattern stitch on Crown later, rep from * across.] **Row 4:** Knit, dropping all YO's from needle.

Rows 5 and 6: Knit.

Row 7: K1; * YO twice, K1; YO 3 times, K1; YO 4 times, K1; YO 3 times, K1; YO twice, K6; rep from * across, ending last rep by working K1 instead of K6.

Row 8: Rep Row 4.

Rep Rows 1 through 8 until piece measures (slightly stretched) approx 5" from CO edge, ending by working Row 4 or Row 8. Leave sts on needle; cut yarn, leaving approx 4" end for weaving in later.

CROWN

With right side facing, beg at right neck edge of Back Center Section. With free needle, join yarn and pick up 20 sts along side edge to sts on needle; K 16 from needle; pick up 20 sts along opposite side edge to neck edge = 56 sts. Continue in pattern stitch as established in Back Center Section (beg with Row 6 or Row 2) and work until piece (slightly stretched) measures approx 5" from Back Center Section, ending by working Row 1 or Row 5. Change to smaller size straight needles and BO all sts in knit.

NECKBAND

Hold bonnet with right side facing and neck edge across top. With smaller size straight needles, join yarn at upper right-hand corner and pick up 20 sts along neck edge of crown to back center section; pick up 12 sts along neck edge of back section; pick up 20 sts along neck edge of crown to front edge = 52 sts. Knit 4 rows. BO all sts in knit. Weave in all ends.

FINISHING

Steam press on wrong side, stretching pattern rows firmly. For ease in pressing, place bonnet over a folded towel. **Ties:** Cut ribbon in half. Make folded rosette **(Fig 3)** on one end of each piece and sew (use sewing thread) firmly to each side of bonnet.

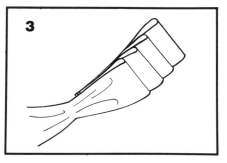

Ripple Lace
BABY LAYETTE

SIZE: Garments are designed to fit newborn to 3 months; afghan measures approx 36″ square.

MATERIALS
For Jacket, Bonnet, Booties and Mittens:
Dawn Wintuk* Baby yarn: 4 oz. pink
Size 2, 7″ double pointed needles (dpn)
Size 4, 7″ double pointed needles and 10″ straight knitting needles (or size required for gauge)
2 Small stitch holders
8 Stitch markers
Pink satin ribbon: 3 yds, ¼″ width;
1¼ yds, ¾″ width

For Afghan:
Dawn Sayelle* Knitting Worsted Size yarn: 14 oz pink
Size 9, 29″ circular knitting needle (or size required for gauge)

GAUGE: With baby weight yarn and size 4 needles in stock st, 7 sts = 1″; 9 rows = 1″
With worsted weight yarn and size 9 needle in Ripple Lace Patt, 20 sts = 4¾″

JACKET INSTRUCTIONS
YOKE
Beg at neck edge, with size 4 straight needles and baby weight yarn, CO 64 sts.
Row 1 (right side): K 14, YO; place marker for end of left front; K1 (raglan seam st); place marker for beg of left sleeve; YO, K6, YO; place marker for end of left sleeve; K1 (seam st); place marker for beg of back; YO, K 20, YO; place marker for end of back; K1 (seam st); place marker for beg of right sleeve; YO, K6, YO; place marker for end of right sleeve; K1 (seam st); place marker for beg of right front; YO, K 14 = 72 sts (counting each YO as one st).
Note: Sl markers on each following row.
Row 2: K3 (garter st border); purl across to last 3 sts, K3 (garter st border).
Row 3: * Knit to marker; YO, K1 (seam st), YO; rep from * 3 times more, knit rem sts. You should have 8 increases (YO's).
Rep last 2 rows, 13 times more (total of 26 more rows). You should now have 184 sts (29 sts for each front, 36 sts for each sleeve, 50 sts for back and one st for each seam st (between YO increases). **Next Row:** Rep Row 2, removing markers.

BODY
Dividing Row: K3; * K2, inc in next st [to inc: K1, P1 all in same st]; rep from * 7 times more, K2 [completes sts for left front]. Sl next 38 sts to holder for left sleeve. CO 3 sts for underarm. K3, (K2, inc in next st) 15 times, K2 [completes sts for back]. Sl next 38 sts to holder for right sleeve. CO 3 sts for underarm. K2, (inc in next st, K2) 8 times, K3 [completes sts for right front]. You should now have 145 sts. **Next Row:** K3, purl to last 3 sts, K3. Now work in patt as follows.

Ripple Lace Pattern
Row 1 (right side): K3; * YO, K2 tog; K5, K2 tog; YO, K1; rep from * to last 2 sts, K2. **Note:** Each YO counts as one st.
Rows 2, 4, 6 and 8: K3, purl to last 3 sts, K3.
Row 3: K4, * YO, K2 tog; K3, K2 tog; YO, K3; rep from * across, ending last rep with K4 instead of K3.
Row 5: K5, * YO, K2 tog; K1, K2 tog; YO, K5; rep from * across.
Row 7: K6, * YO; sl 1 as to knit, K2 tog, PSSO; YO, K7; rep from * across, ending last rep with K6 instead of K7.
Rep last 8 rows, 5 times more. Garment should now measure approx 8¾″ from CO edge. Knit 5 more rows for garter st border. BO all sts loosely in knit.

SLEEVE
(Make 2)
With size 4 dpn, sl 38 sts from sleeve holder to one needle; then divide sts on 3 needles (12-14-12). With free needle, pick up 2 sts along CO sts at underarm, placing one st at beg of first needle and one st at end of third needle = 40 sts (13-14-13). Join baby weight yarn at underarm and work patt in rnds as follows.

Ripple Lace Pattern
Rnd 1: * YO, K2 tog; K5, K2 tog; YO, K1; rep from * around.
Rnds 2, 4, 6 and 8: Knit.
Rnd 3: K1, * YO, K2 tog; K3, K2 tog; YO, K3; rep from * around, ending last rep with K2 instead of K3.
Rnd 5: K2, * YO, K2 tog; K1, K2 tog; YO, K5; rep from * around, ending last rep with K3 instead of K5.
Rnd 7: K3, * YO; sl 1 as to knit, K2 tog, PSSO; YO, K7; rep from * around, ending last rep with K4 instead of K7.
Rep last 8 rnds, 4 times more. Sleeve should now measure approx 4″ from underarm. Now work garter st border as follows: (purl one rnd, knit one rnd) twice. BO all sts loosely in purl.

COLLAR
With wrong side facing you and using size 4 straight needles and baby weight yarn, pick up 64 sts around neck edge (CO edge).
Beading Row: K3, P1; * YO, P2 tog; rep from * to last 4 sts; YO, P1, K3 = 65 sts.
Next Row: [Note: Right side of collar; wrong side of jacket.] Knit.
Inc Row: K6; * P2, inc in next st [to inc: purl in front and back of st]; rep from * 5 times more; P1, (P1, inc in next st) 8 times; P1, (inc in next st, P2) 6 times, K5 = 85 sts.
Work Rows 1 through 8 of Ripple Lace Pattern in Jacket Body instructions, once. Knit 5 more rows for garter st border; then BO all sts loosely in knit.

FINISHING
Weave in all ends. Lightly steam seams and garter st bands if needed. Cut a 40″ piece of ¼″ satin ribbon and weave through beading row for tie at neckline.

BOOTIE INSTRUCTIONS
(Make 2)

Beg at cuff, with size 2 dpn and baby weight yarn, CO 40 sts loosely on one needle. Then divide sts on 3 needles (14-14-12). Join, being careful not to twist sts. Purl first rnd; (knit one rnd, purl one rnd) twice for garter st border. Now work Rnds 1 through 8 of Ripple Lace Pattern in Jacket Sleeve instructions, twice (total of 16 rnds). Then knit 2 more rnds. **Beading Rnd:** K2 tog; * YO, K2 tog; rep from * around = 39 sts. Knit 3 more rnds. **Dividing Rnd:** K 13 and sl these sts to first holder; K 13 for instep; sl rem 13 sts to 2nd holder.

Instep: Working back and forth in rows on center 13 sts only, beg with a purl row and work in stock st until instep measures 2″ from Beading Rnd, ending by working a purl row. Leaving sts on needle, cut yarn (leave 4″ end for weaving in later).

Foot and Sole: Joining Rnd: Sl 13 sts from first holder to one needle. Join yarn and with same needle, pick up 11 sts along side of instep. With next needle, K 13 of instep. With next needle, pick up 11 sts along opposite side of instep; then K 13 from 2nd holder = 61 sts (24-13-24). Sl 4 sts from first and 3rd needles to 2nd needle [sts should now be divided 20-21-20 on 3 needles]. Join and continue in rnds as follows: (knit one rnd, purl one rnd) 5 times [5 ridges].

Toe and Heel Shaping

Rnd 1: K3, K2 tog; K 20; K2 tog, K7, K2 tog; K20; K2 tog, K3 = 57 sts.
Rnd 2: Purl.
Rnd 3: Knit.
Rnd 4: Purl.
Rnd 5: K2, K2 tog; K 20, K2 tog; K5, K2 tog; K 20, K2 tog, K2 = 53 sts.
Rnds 6 through 8: Rep Rnds 2 through 4.
Rnd 9: K1, K2 tog; K 20, K2 tog; K3, K2 tog; K 20, K2 tog, K1 = 49 sts.
Rnds 10 through 12: Rep Rnds 2 through 4.
Rnd 13: K2 tog, K 20; K2 tog, K1, K2 tog; K 20, K2 tog = 45 sts.
Rnd 14: Purl. BO all sts in knit.

FINISHING
Sew sole seam; weave in all ends. Cut two 17" pieces of ¼" satin ribbon; weave through beading rnd and tie in a bow.

THUMBLESS MITTEN INSTRUCTIONS
(Make 2)
Work same as Bootie until **8 rnds only** of Ripple Lace Pattern have been completed. Knit 2 more rnds. **Beading Rnd:** * YO, K2 tog; rep from * around. Now work in stock st (knit each rnd) until mitten measures 3½" from CO edge. Then shape top as follows.
Rnd 1: * K3, K2 tog; rep from * around = 32 sts.
Rnds 2 through 10: Knit 9 rnds.
Rnd 11: * K2 tog; rep from * around = 16 sts.

FINISHING
Cut yarn, leaving 12" end. Thread into tapestry or yarn needle and draw through rem sts. Pull up tightly and fasten securely on inside. Weave in all ends. Cut two 17" pieces of ¼" satin ribbon; weave through beading rnd and tie in a bow.

BONNET INSTRUCTIONS
Beg at center back, with size 4 straight needles and baby weight yarn, CO 9 sts.
Row 1 and all odd-numbered rows: Purl.
Row 2: * K1, YO; rep from * to last st, K1 = 17 sts.
Row 4: * K2, YO; rep from * to last st, K1 = 25 sts.
Row 6: * K3, YO; rep from * to last st, K1 = 33 sts.
Row 8: * K4, YO; rep from * to last st, K1 = 41 sts.

Continue to increase in this manner, working one more knit st before each YO on every knit row, until there are 105 sts on needle, ending by working a purl row.

Continuing in stock st, BO 13 sts at beg of next 2 rows for back of neck = 79 sts. Work even until piece measures 3¾" from BO sts (at back of neck), ending by working a knit row. Then work in reverse stock st (knit one row, purl one row) until piece measures 4½" from BO sts, ending by working a knit row.

Turn-Back Cuff
Turning Ridge: Inc in first st [to inc: knit in front and back of st]; knit across to last st, inc in last st = 81 sts. Now work in patt as follows.

Ripple Lace Pattern
Row 1 (right side): K1; * YO, K2 tog; K5, K2 tog; YO, K1; rep from * across.
Rows 2, 4 and 6: Purl.
Row 3: K2; * YO, K2 tog; K3, K2 tog; YO, K3; rep from * across, ending last rep with K2 instead of K3.
Row 5: K3; * YO, K2 tog; K1, K2 tog; YO, K5; rep from * across, ending last rep with K3 instead of K5.
Row 7: K4, * YO; sl 1 as to knit, K2 tog, PSSO; YO, K7; rep from * across, ending last rep with K4 instead of K7.
Row 8: Purl.
Knit 5 more rows for garter st border. BO all sts loosely in knit.

FINISHING
Sew seam at back of bonnet. Turn cuff back at turning ridge. **Neckband:** With right side facing, use size 4 straight needles and baby weight yarn and pick up 54 sts around neck edge, working through both layers at turn-back edges. Knit 6 rows. BO all sts in knit. Weave in all ends.

Cut ¾" satin ribbon in half. Make a bow at one end of each piece and sew (use sewing thread) to each side of bonnet front.

AFGHAN INSTRUCTIONS
With worsted weight yarn and circular needle, CO 151 sts. Do not join; work back and forth in rows. Knit 8 rows for bottom garter st. border. Then work in patt as follows.

Ripple Lace Pattern
Row 1 (right side): K6; * YO, K2 tog; K5, K2 tog; YO, K1; rep from * across, ending last rep with K6 instead of K1.
Rows 2, 4, 6 and 8: K5 (garter st side border); purl to last 5 sts, K5 (garter st side border).
Row 3: K7; * YO, K2 tog; K3, K2 tog; YO, K3; rep from * across, ending last rep with K7 instead of K3.
Row 5: K8; * YO, K2 tog; K1, K2 tog; YO, K5; rep from * across, ending last rep with K8 instead of K5.
Row 7: K9, * YO; sl 1, K2 tog, PSSO; YO, K7; rep from * across, ending last rep with K9 instead of K7.
Rep Rows 1 through 8 until work measures approx 35" from CO edge, ending by working Row 7. Knit 8 more rows for top garter st border. BO all sts in knit. Weave in all ends; lightly steam garter st borders.

STRIPED BONNET and BOOTIES

designed by Nancy Dent

SIZE: Written in one size to fit newborn to 6 months (approx 15 pounds).

MATERIALS
Baby weight yarn: 2 oz each blue and white
Size 3, 10″ straight knitting needles (or size required for gauge)
Size 1 steel crochet hook (for bootie ties only)
2 Small stitch holders (for booties only)

GAUGE: In garter st, 13 sts = 2″

STRIPING PATTERN
Row 1 (right side): Knit.
Rows 2 and 3: Purl.
Row 4: Knit.
Row 5: Purl.
Row 6: Knit. Change color.
Rep Rows 1 through 6 for patt, alternating colors at end of each patt rep.
Changing Color Notes: Colors are carried along side of work; do not finish off color at end of row unless specified. Change colors by picking up new color in back and to the right of the color used on prev row. Carry color not in use at edge of work by bringing color to front of work, over and to the left of yarn being used (twisting colors).

BONNET INSTRUCTIONS
With white, CO 35 sts. Beg with Row 2 and work in Striping Pattern (alternating white and blue) until 25 stripes (13 white and 12 blue) have been completed. Piece should now measure approx 5¼″ wide by 10″ long without stretching. With white, BO all sts. Cut yarns, leaving white 16″ sewing length. Thread into tapestry or yarn needle and sew yarn-twisted edges tog for back seam, carefully matching stripes.

FRONT BAND
With white, CO 75 sts. Beg with Row 1 and work in Striping Pattern until 3 stripes have been completed (white, blue and white). Finish off white; continue with blue and shape rolled hem as follows. **Row 1:** Knit. **Row 2:** * P 20, P2 tog; rep from * to last 9 sts, P9 = 72 sts. **Rows 3 through 8:** Beg with a purl row and work 6 rows in stock st. BO all sts loosely in purl.

FINISHING
Do not block. With right sides tog, pin CO edge of front band to front edge of hood; then sew edges tog. Allow free edge of band to roll inside of hood; tack loosely in place on each side.
Neckband and Ties: With blue, CO 60 sts for left tie; with right side of hood facing you and neck edge across top, continue with same needle and yarn, and pick up 80 sts across neck edge of hood; then using same yarn, CO 60 sts on same needle for right tie = 200 sts. Beg with a knit row and work 6 rows in stock st. BO all sts in knit, leaving approx 24″ sewing length. Thread into tapestry or yarn needle; fold ties and neckband in half lengthwise and sew across. Weave in all ends.

BOOTIE INSTRUCTIONS
(Make 2)
Beg at cuff, with blue, CO 39 sts. Knit one row. Then beg with Row 3 and work in Striping Pattern until 4 stripes have been completed (2 blue and 2 white). Piece should now measure approx 6″ wide by 2″ long without stretching. Finish off white; continue with blue. **Next Row:** Knit.
Beading Row: * P2 tog, YO; rep from * to last st, P1.
Dividing Row: K 13 and sl these sts to first holder; knit next 13 sts for instep; sl rem 13 sts to second holder.

Instep: Continuing on center 13 sts with blue, beg with Row 3 and work in Striping Pattern until 4 stripes have been completed (2 blue and 2 white). Leaving sts on needle, cut yarns (leave 4″ ends for weaving in later).

Foot and Sole: Joining Row: With right side facing, sl 13 sts from first holder to free needle; continuing with same needle, join blue yarn and pick up 12 sts along right side of instep; knit across 13 instep sts; pick up 12 sts along left edge of instep; K 13 from second holder = 63 sts. Beg with Row 2 and work in Striping Pattern until 2 stripes have been completed (1 blue and 1 white). Finish off white; continue with blue and shape toe and heel as follows.
Row 1: P4, P2 tog; P 19, P2 tog; P9, P2 tog; P 19, P2 tog; P4 = 59 sts.
Row 2: K3, K2 tog; K 19, K2 tog; K7, K2 tog; K 19, K2 tog; K3 = 55 sts.
Row 3: K2, K2 tog; K 19, K2 tog; K5, K2 tog; K 19, K2 tog; K2 = 51 sts.
Row 4: P1, P2 tog; P 19, P2 tog; P3, P2 tog; P 19, P2 tog; P1 = 47 sts.
Row 5: K2 tog; K 19, K2 tog; K1, K2 tog; K19, K2 tog = 43 sts. BO all sts in purl.

FINISHING
Sew sole and back seam. Allow 2 rows at cuff edge to roll over to form a hem (needs no tacking). Weave in all ends.
Ties: With crochet hook and 2 strands of blue, make 2 chains each 12″ long. Weave one tie through beading row of each bootie.
Pompons: Make 4 blue pompons (1″ diameter) [see *Pompon* instructions on page 17] and attach one pompon to each end of ties.

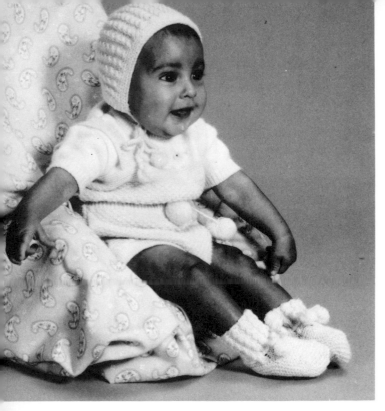

LEMON TWIST
Bonnet and Booties
designed by Nancy Dent

SIZE: Written in one size to fit newborn to 3 months (approx 12 pounds).

MATERIALS
Pompadour baby weight yarn: 3 oz yellow
Sizes 2 and 3, 10″ straight knitting needles (or size required for gauge)
Size F aluminum crochet hook (for ties only)
2 Small stitch holders (for booties only)

GAUGE: With smaller size needles in garter st, 7 sts = 1″

PATTERN STITCH
Row 1 (wrong side): K2; * P2, K2; rep from * across.
Row 2 (RT row): P2; * right twist (abbreviated RT) [*to make RT: K2 tog but do not remove from left-hand needle* (**Fig 1**); *knit first st on left-hand needle again* (**Fig 2**); *then sl both sts off left-hand needle = RT made*], P2; rep from * across.

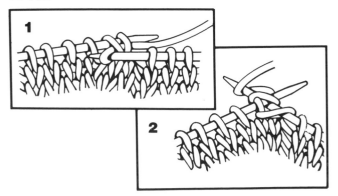

Row 3: Rep Row 1.
Row 4: P2; * K2, P2; rep from * across.
Rep Rows 1 through 4 for patt.

BONNET INSTRUCTIONS
Beg at front edge, with smaller size needles, CO 74 sts. Knit 8 rows for garter st border. **Inc row:** K2; * inc in next st, K5; rep from * across = 86 sts. Change to larger size needles and work Patt St Rows 1 through 4, 9 times; then work Patt St Rows 1 through 3 once more. You should now have 10 RT rows and piece should measure approx 5″ from CO edge. Now work back shaping as follows.
Row 1: P2; * (K2, P2) twice; K2, P2 tog; rep from * 5 times; (K2, P2) 3 times = 80 sts.
Row 2: (K2, P2) 3 times; * K1, P2; (K2, P2) twice; rep from * to last 2 sts, K2.
Row 3: P2; * RT, P2 tog; RT, P2; RT, P1; rep from * across, ending last rep by working P2 instead of P1 = 73 sts.
Row 4: (K2, P2) twice; K1, P2; * K1, P2; K2, P2; K1, P2; rep from * to last 2 sts, K2.
Row 5: P2; * K2, P1; K2, P2 tog; K2, P1; rep from * across, ending last rep by working P2 instead of P1 = 66 sts.
Row 6: K2, P2; * K1, P2; rep from * to last 2 sts, K2.
Row 7: P2; * RT, (P2 tog) twice; (RT, P1) twice; rep from * to last 4 sts; RT, P2 = 56 sts.
Row 8: K2, P2; * (K1, P2) twice; K2, P2; rep from * to last 2 sts, K2.
Row 9: P2, * K2, P2; K2, (P2 tog) twice; rep from * to last 4 sts, K2, P2 = 46 sts.
Row 10: * K2, P2; rep from * to last 2 sts, K2.
Row 11: P2 tog; * RT, P2 tog; rep from * across = 34 sts.
Row 12: * P2 tog; rep from * across = 17 sts. Cut yarn, leaving approx 14″ sewing length.

FINISHING
Thread sewing length into tapestry or yarn needle and draw through all sts. Pull up tightly and fasten securely; then sew back seam (approx 2″). **Neckband:** With right side facing and neck edge across top, use smaller size needles and join yarn in first row at upper right-hand corner; pick up 72 sts (approx one st EOR) across neck edge. Work 4 rows in K1, P1 ribbing. BO all sts loosely in ribbing. Weave in all ends. **Ties:** With crochet hook and 2 strands of yarn, make 2 chains each 12″ long. Sew one tie to each corner of bonnet. **Pompons:** Make 2 pompons (1″ diameter) [see *Pompon* instructions on page 17] and attach one to end of each tie.

BOOTIE INSTRUCTIONS
(Make 2)
Beg at top, with larger size needles, CO 42 sts. Work Patt St Rows 1 through 4, 4 times; then work Patt St Rows 1 through 3 once more (total of 5 RT Rows). **Beading Row:** * P2 tog; YO, K2; rep from * to last 2 sts, P2. Now work Patt St Rows 1 through 3 once. Change to smaller size needles. **Dividing Row:** K8, K2 tog, K4; now sl these 13 sts to first holder; K6, K2 tog, K6, sl rem 14 sts to 2nd holder.

Instep: Continuing on center 13 sts, work in garter st (knit each row) until you have 11 ridges on right side of work, ending by working a wrong-side row. Leave sts on needle; cut yarn, leaving 4 ″ end for weaving in later.

Foot and Sole: With right side facing and smaller size needles, sl 13 sts from first holder to free needle; continuing with same needle, join yarn and pick up 10 sts (approx one st in each ridge) along right side of instep; knit across 13 instep sts; pick up 10 sts along left side of instep; then work across sts on holder as follows: K4, K2 tog, K8 = 59 sts. Work in garter st until you have 6 ridges on right side of work, ending by working a wrong-side row. Now shape heel and toe as follows.

Row 1: K5, K2 tog; K 15, K2 tog; K 11, K2 tog; K 15, K2 tog; K5 = 55 sts.

Row 2: K4, K2 tog; K 15, K2 tog; K9, K2 tog; K 15, K2 tog; K4 = 51 sts.

Row 3: K3, K2 tog; K 15, K2 tog; K7, K2 tog; K 15, K2 tog; K3 = 47 sts.

Row 4: K2, K2 tog; K 15, K2 tog; K5, K2 tog; K 15, K2 tog; K2 = 43 sts.

Row 5: K1, K2 tog; K 15, K2 tog; K3, K2 tog; K 15, K2 tog, K1 = 39 sts.

Row 6: K2 tog, K 15; K2 tog, K1, K2 tog; K 15, K2 tog = 34 sts. BO all sts in knit.

FINISHING

Sew sole and back seam. Weave in all ends. **Ties:** With crochet hook and 2 strands of yarn, make 2 chains each 12″ long. Weave one tie through beading row of each bootie. **Pompons:** Make 4 pompons (1″ diameter) [see *Pompon* instructions on page 17] and attach one pompon to each end of tie.

FORGET ME NOT
Bonnet and Booties
designed by Nancy Dent

SIZE: Written in one size to fit newborn to 3 months (approx 12 pounds).

MATERIALS
Baby weight yarn: 2 oz white;
                    1 oz blue
Size 3, 10″ straight knitting needles (or size required for gauge)
Size 1 steel crochet hook (for ties only)
2 Small stitch holders (for booties only)
Size 20 tapestry needle (for embroidery)

GAUGE: In stock st, 15 sts = 2″; 10 rows = 1″

PATTERN STITCH
Note: Each YO counts as one stitch throughout patt.
Rows 1, 3, 5 and 7 (wrong side): Purl.
Rows 2, 4 and 6: * K4, K2 tog, YO; rep from * to last 5 sts, K5.
Row 8: * K2 tog, YO; rep from * to last st, K1.
Rep Rows 1 through 8 for patt.

BONNET INSTRUCTIONS
Beg at front edge, with white, CO 69 sts.
Rows 1, 3 and 5: Purl.
Rows 2 and 4: Knit.
Row 6 (turning ridge): * K2 tog, YO; rep from * to last st, K1. **Note:** Throughout patt, each YO counts as one st.
Row 7: Purl.
Row 8 (inc row): Inc in first st, K5; * inc in next st, K6; rep from * across = 79 sts.

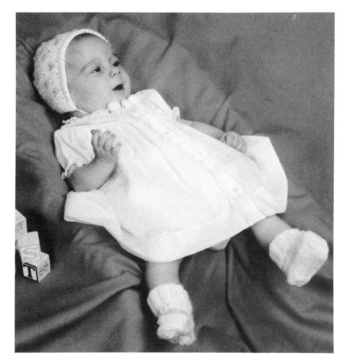

Rows 9, 11 and 13: Purl.
Rows 10 and 12: Knit.
Row 14 (inc row): (K2 tog, YO) 4 times; * K1, YO; (K2 tog, YO) 3 times; rep from * to last st, K1 = 89 sts. This completes front band and hem; continue as follows for crown. Work Patt St Rows 1 through 8, 6 times. **Next Row:** Purl. Now work back shaping as follows.

Row 1: * K9, sl 1, K2 tog, PSSO, YO; rep from * to last 5 sts, K5 = 82 sts.
Rows 2, 4, 6, 8 and 10: Purl.
Row 3: * K8; sl 1, K2 tog, PSSO, YO; rep from * to last 5 sts, K5 = 75 sts.
Row 5: * K7; sl 1, K2 tog, PSSO, YO; rep from * to last 5 sts, K5 = 68 sts.

Row 7: * K6, sl 1, K2 tog, PSSO, YO; rep from * to last 5 sts, K5 = 61 sts.
Row 9: * K5, sl 1, K2 tog, PSSO, YO; rep from * to last 5 sts, K5 = 54 sts.
Row 11: * K2 tog; rep from * across = 27 sts. Cut yarn, leaving approx 12" sewing length. Thread into tapestry needle and draw through all sts. Do not fasten until embroidery has been completed.

EMBROIDERY
Steam bonnet lightly on wrong side. To embroider a flower, refer to instructions and diagrams in **Fig 1.**

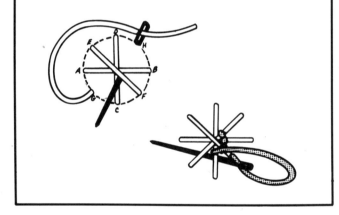

1

Embroidered Flower

Work 4 straight sts, each ⅝" long, across an imaginary circle (dotted lines); bring yarn up at center between 2 of the resulting 8 "spokes." Begin to "whip" each spoke by bringing yarn back over the spoke then **sliding** needle beneath it and the next spoke; 2 or 3 times around the circle will fill the spokes. End yarn by weaving through work on wrong side.

Thread tapestry needle with blue yarn and embroider on alternate patt repeats (see **Fig 2**) a total of 39 flowers.

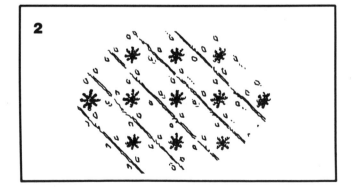

2

FINISHING
Pull yarn up tightly at end of back shaping and fasten securely; then sew back seam to neck edge (approx 1½"). Fold hem to inside at front of bonnet and sew loosely in place. **Neckband:** With right side facing and neck edge across top, join white yarn in first row at upper right-hand corner; pick up 52 sts across neck edge. Work 6 rows in K1, P1 ribbing. BO all sts loosely in ribbing. Weave in all ends. **Ties:** With crochet hook and 2 strands of white, make 2 chains each 12" long. Sew one tie to each corner of bonnet. **Pompons:** Make 2 white pompons (1" diameter) [see *Pompon* instructions on page 17] and attach one to end of each tie.

BOOTIE INSTRUCTIONS
(Make 2)
Beg at cuff, with white, CO 42 sts. **Ribbing Row 1:** * K2, P2; rep from * to last 2 sts, K2. **Ribbing Row 2:** P2; * K2, P2; rep from * across. Rep these 2 rows until ribbing measures 3½" from CO edge, ending by working Ribbing Row 2. Now work as follows.
Row 1 (right side): Knit.
Row 2 (beading row): * P2 tog, YO; rep from * to last 2 sts, P2. **Note:** Each YO counts as one st.
Row 3: Knit.
Row 4: Purl.
Row 5 (dividing row): K 14 and sl these sts to first holder; K 14 for instep; sl rem 14 sts to 2nd holder.

Instep: Continuing on center 14 sts, beg with a purl row and work 15 rows in stock st (ending with a purl row). Leave sts on needle; cut yarn, leaving 4" end for weaving in later.

Foot and Sole: With right side facing, sl 14 sts from first holder to free needle; continuing with same needle, join white yarn and pick up 12 sts along right side of instep; knit across 14 instep sts; pick up 12 sts along left side of instep; then K 14 from 2nd holder = 66 sts. Now work as follows.
Row 1 (wrong side): Knit.
Row 2: Purl.
Row 3: Knit.
Rows 4 through 10: Beg with a knit row and work 7 rows in stock st (ending with a knit row).
Rows 11 through 13: Rep Rows 1 through 3.
Row 14: K4, K2 tog; K 21, K2 tog; K8, K2 tog; K 21, K2 tog; K4 = 62 sts.
Row 15: P3, P2 tog; P 21, P2 tog; P6, P2 tog; P 21, P2 tog; P3 = 58 sts.
Row 16: K2, K2 tog; K 21, K2 tog; K4, K2 tog; K 21, K2 tog; K2 = 54 sts.
Row 17: P1, P2 tog; P 21, P2 tog; P2, P2 tog; P 21, P2 tog; P1 = 50 sts.
Row 18: K2 tog, K 21; (K2 tog) twice; K 21, K2 tog = 46 sts. BO all sts in purl.

FINISHING
Do not block. Thread tapestry needle with blue yarn and embroider 3 flowers as shown in **Fig 1** on instep of each bootie—one in the center and one at each corner toward the toe. Sew sole and back seam. Weave in all ends. **Ties:** With crochet hook and single strand of white yarn, make 2 chains each 14" long; knot and trim each end of tie. Weave one tie through beading row of each bootie.

HELMET and MITTENS for toddlers

designed by Mary Thomas

SIZES: Written for toddler sizes 1-2 with changes for 3-4 in parentheses.

MATERIALS
Worsted weight yarn: 4(5) oz light green
Size 7, 10″ straight knitting needles (or size required for gauge)
Size 9, 10″ straight knitting needles [for mitten size 3-4 only] (or size required for gauge)
2 Stitch markers
2 Small stitch holders

GAUGE: With smaller size needles in Patt St,
5 sts = 1″
With larger size needles in Patt St,
9 sts = 2″

PATTERN STITCH
(double seed stitch)
Rows 1 and 2: * K2, P2; rep from * across.
Rows 3 and 4: * P2, K2; rep from * across.
Rep Rows 1 through 4 for patt.

HELMET INSTRUCTIONS
Beg at bottom ege, with smaller size needles, CO 76(80) sts. Work Patt St Rows 1 through 4, twice; then work Patt St Rows 1 and 2 once. **Dec Row:** * K2 tog, P2 tog; rep from * across = 38(40) sts. Work 6(8) rows in K1, P1 ribbing for neck. **Inc row:** * Knit in front and back of next st; purl in front and back of next st; rep from * across = 76(80) sts. Work Patt St Rows 1 through 4 once.

Dividing Row: (K2, P2) 7 times, K2; BO next 16(20) sts for face opening; P1, (K2, P2) 7 times. **Next Row:** (K2, P2) 7 times, K2; join new yarn and work across other side as follows: (P2; K2) 7 times, P2. Working across each side of face opening with a separate ball of yarn, continue in established Patt St (beg with Row 3) and work until each side measures 2¾(3¼)″ from BO sts for face opening, ending by working Row 2 or Row 4.

Joining Row: Work across first 30 sts in established Patt St; continuing with same yarn (finish off yarn from other side), CO 16(20) sts (see *Casting On, Method 2* on page 12); work in established Patt St across rem sts = 76(80) sts. Continuing in Patt St as established, work until piece measures 2½(3)″ from CO sts above face opening, ending by working Row 2 and Row 4.

Top Shaping: Dec Row 1: * K2 tog, P2 tog; rep from * across = 38(40) sts. Work 5(7) rows in K1, P1 ribbing. **Dec Row 2:** * K2 tog; rep from * across = 19(20) sts. Cut yarn, leaving approx 30″ end.

FINISHING
Thread end into tapestry or yarn needle and draw through all sts twice. Draw up tightly and fasten securely. Then sew back seam. **Pompon:** Make 2″ diameter pompon (see *Pompon* instructions on page 17) and attach securely to top of helmet. Weave in all ends.

MITTEN INSTRUCTIONS
(Make 2)
For sizes 1-2, use smaller size needles; for sizes 3-4, use larger size needles. Beg at cuff, CO 32 sts. Work Patt St Rows 1 through 4, twice; then work Patt St Rows 1 and 2 once more. **Dec Row:** * K1, P1, K2 tog; P1, K1, P2 tog; rep from * across = 24 sts. Work 3 rows in K1, P1 ribbing for wrist. Now work gusset shaping as follows.

Row 1 (right side): Knit in front and back of first st; purl in front and back of next st; (K2, P2) twice, K1; knit in front and back of next st; P2, (K2, P2) twice; knit in front and back of next st; purl in front and back of last st = 29 sts.
Row 2: (K2, P2) 3 times, K1; knit in front and back of next st; P3, (K2, P2) 3 times = 30 sts.

Row 3 (marking row): (P2, K2) 3 times, P2; place marker for thumb sts, inc in each of next 2 sts [*to inc: knit in front and back of st*], place marker; (K2, P2) 3 times, K2 = 32 sts. **Note:** Sl markers on each following row.

Row 4: (P2, K2) 3 times, P2; purl across thumb sts (between markers); (K2, P2) 3 times, K2.

Row 5: (K2, P2) 3 times, K2; inc in next st (st after first marker), knit to within one st of next marker, inc in next st; (P2, K2) 3 times, P2 = 34 sts.

Row 6: (K2, P2) 3 times, K2; purl across thumb sts; (P2, K2) 3 times, P2.

Row 7: (P2, K2) 3 times, P2; inc in next st (st after first marker), knit to within one st of next marker, inc in next st; (K2, P2) 3 times, K2 = 36 sts.

Rows 8 through 10: Rep Rows 4 through 6. You should now have 38 sts.

Dividing Row: (P2, K2) 3 times, P2; sl 14 sts just worked to one holder; knit next 10 sts for thumb; sl rem sts to 2nd holder.

Thumb: Continuing on 10 center sts only, beg with a purl row and work 5 rows in stock st. **Dec Row:** * K2 tog; rep from * across = 5 sts. Cut yarn, leaving approx 12" end. Thread into tapestry or yarn needle and draw through all sts. Draw up tightly and fasten securely. Leave sewing length (do not cut) for thumb seam later.

Hand: With right side facing and continuing with same size needles, sl sts from holder on left side of thumb to needle; join yarn next to thumb and work as follows across these sts: (K2, P2) 3 times, K2. **Next Row:** (P2, K2) 3 times, P2; sl sts from rem holder to free needle; continue with same yarn and work across these sts as follows: (K2,

P2) 3 times, K2 = 28 sts. Continuing in Patt St as established (beg with Row 1), work until piece measures 3½(4)" above ribbing at wrist, ending by working Row 4.

Top Shaping: Row 1: * K2 tog, P2 tog; rep from * across = 14 sts. **Row 2:** * K1, P1; rep from * across. **Row 3:** * K2 tog; rep from * across = 7 sts. Cut yarn, leaving approx 20" end.

FINISHING
Thread end into tapestry or yarn needle and draw through all sts twice. Draw up tightly and fasten securely; then sew side seam. Sew thumb seam. Weave in all ends.

TUBE DOLLS –
Violet, Danny, Polly and Sam

These delightful dolls are adapted from a traditional German technique. The bodies are worked as a tube, in one piece on four double-pointed needles. They are then stuffed, and the sculpturing for arms, legs, etc. is sewn in. We've given you four dolls — your own imagination will let you create dozens of variations of clothes, hairstyles and faces.

SIZE: Approx 11" tall
MATERIALS
Worsted weight yarn: amounts and colors given with each specific doll instructions
Size 8, double pointed needles [dpn] (or size required for gauge)
Size F aluminum crochet hook (for Violet and Polly only)
Size 16 tapestry needle
Polyester filling (for stuffing)
GAUGE: In stock st, 9 sts = 2"; 6 rnds = 1"

GENERAL INSTRUCTIONS
BASIC TUBE PATTERN
[**Note:** Follow this pattern for each doll, changing colors as indicated in individual doll instructions.] Beg at feet, CO 36 sts on one needle; then divide sts evenly on 3 needles (12-12-12). Join, being careful not to twist sts.
First 6 Rnds: Knit.
Dec Rnd for Ankles: * K2 tog; rep from * around = 18 sts.
Inc Rnd: * Knit in front and back of st (inc made); rep from * around = 36 sts.
Knit even until piece measures 7" from CO edge.

Dec Rnd for Neck: * K2 tog; rep from * around = 18 sts.
Inc Rnd: * K1, (inc in next st) 5 times; rep from * around = 33 sts.
Knit 3" even for head; then shape top as follows. **Rnd 1:** * K1, (K2 tog) 5 times; rep from * around = 18 sts. **Rnd 2:** Knit. **Rnd 3:** * K2 tog; rep from * around = 9 sts. **Rnd 4:** Knit.

Cut yarn, leaving approx 12" sewing length. Thread into tapestry needle and draw through rem sts. Pull up tightly and fasten securely on inside. Weave in all loose yarn ends. [**Note:** CO edge is left open for stuffing.]

STUFFING AND SCULPTURE
First, stuff head firmly; roll between hands to achieve desired shape. Thread skin color yarn into tapestry needle and sew running sts around neck decrease rnd; pull up to desired neck size, keeping stuffing from slipping. Fasten securely on inside.

Next, stuff body to ankles (adjust amount of stuffing to give a plumper or thinner doll, as desired). Sew (use matching yarn) running sts around ankle decrease rnd; pull up firmly and fasten securely on inside.

Before stuffing feet, sculpture arms and legs. Use matching yarn doubled and sew running sts through entire body, from front to back through stuffing as shown in **Fig 1.** Pull stitching tightly and fasten securely on inside.

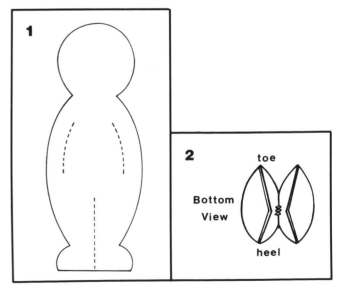

Last, stuff each foot. Shape as shown in **Fig 2** and sew bottom seams with matching yarn.

BALLERINA VIOLET
designed by Carol Wilson Mansfield

Yarn Requirements: 2 oz each pink, violet and medium brown; 1 yd each red and bright green

INSTRUCTIONS

Following General Instructions on page 124, beg with violet and work Basic Tube Pattern, changing colors as follows:

    7 rnds (including Dec Rnd for Ankles): violet
13 rnds: pink
    4 rnds: violet
All following rnds: pink

When tube is completed, stuff and sculpture doll following General Instructions. Then sew one pink horizontal short straight st tightly on front of tube for navel.

Hair: Thread brown into tapestry needle doubled. Work long and short straight sts (see **Fig 3**) from hairline to top of head until crown is covered. For braid, cut 18 strands of brown, each 18" long; divide strands equally and braid, fastening each end with a matching piece of yarn. Coil braid on top of crown, tucking in ends; then sew in place. Tie a small violet yarn bow at side of coil.

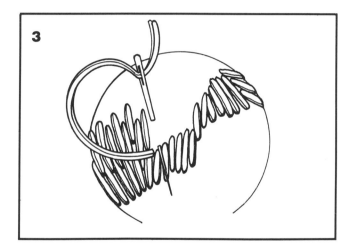

Eyes: Cut 2 pieces of heavy-weight paper for shape of eyes (as shown in photo); glue pieces to face. Use single strand of green and embroider satin sts over paper (**Fig 4**). [**Note:** Paper can be left on doll.].

Mouth: Use single strand of red and work 3 horizontal backstitches (**Fig 5**); then embroider several vertical satin sts over center backstitch.

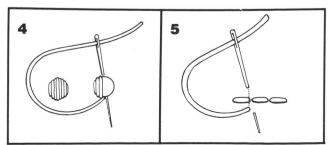

Halter Top: Make 2 pieces (front and back) as follows. With 2 needles and violet, CO 8 sts. Work 5 rows in stock st; then BO. Sew side edges of one piece each to back and front of doll between arms, having BO edge aligned at underarms. **Straps:** With crochet hook and violet, make 2 chains, each 12 sts long. Sew each strap to front and back of halter at top outer edge; then tack at shoulders. Shape front of halter by working several vertical satin sts (use matching yarn) around center front (see photo); pull up tightly and fasten securely to doll.

Tutu: With violet, CO 40 sts on one needle; divide sts on 3 needles (12-12-16). Join, being careful not to twist sts. **Rnd 1:** Knit. **Rnd 2 (beading rnd):** K1, YO; * K2, YO; rep from * to last st, K1 = 60 sts. **Rnds 3 through 5:** Knit. **Rnd 6:** K1, YO twice; * K2, YO twice; rep from * to last st, K1. **Rnd 7:** Knit, dropping each YO = 60 sts. **Rnd 8:** Purl. **Rnd 9:** Rep Rnd 6. BO all sts as to purl, dropping each YO. Weave in yarn ends. **Drawstring:** Cut 36" strand of violet; fold in half and weave through beading rnd. Slip tutu on doll; tie drawstring tightly into a bow at center front. Trim and knot each end of drawstring. With violet, embroider 2 duplicate sts (**Fig 6**) at front crotch area and 3 at rear crotch area to define underpants.

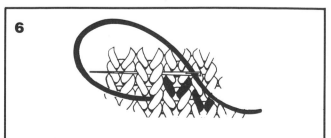

Bobsled DANNY
designed by Carol Wilson Mansfield

Yarn Requirements: 2 oz bright blue;
                         1 oz each pink,
                                 medium brown, white
                                 and
                                 red;
                         5 yds each yellow and
                                 bright green;
                         1 yd light blue

INSTRUCTIONS

Following General Instructions on page 124, beg with red and work Basic Tube Pattern, changing colors as follows:

     11 rnds: red
     Each following rnd to Dec Rnd for Neck: bright blue
     All following rnds: pink

When tube is completed, stuff and sculpture doll following General Instructions.

Hair: Work same as in Ballerina Violet, excluding braid.

Eyes: With light blue, work same as in Ballerina Violet.

Mouth: Use single strand of red and embroider several outline sts as shown in **Fig 7**; then work one short straight st on each side of mouth.

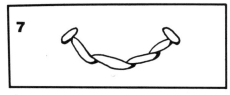

Hat: With red, CO 42 sts on one needle; then divide sts evenly on 3 needles (14-14-14). Join, being careful not to twist sts. Work 4 rnds in K1, P1 ribbing. Cut red; join white. Change to stock st and work the following stripe sequence: 2 rnds each of white, yellow, white, bright blue, white and green. When stripe sequence is completed, shape top (continuing striping) as follows. **Rnd 1:** With white, * K2, K2 tog; rep from * to last 2 sts, K2 = 32 sts. **Rnd 2:** Knit. **Rnds 3 and 4:** With red, knit. **Rnd 5:** With white, * K1, K2 tog; rep from * to last 2 sts, K2 = 22 sts. **Rnd 6:** Knit. **Rnds 7 and 8:** With yellow, knit. **Rnd 9:** With white, * K2 tog; rep from * around = 11 sts. **Rnd 10:** Knit. **Rnds 11 and 12:** With bright blue, knit. **Rnds 13 and 14:** With white, knit. **Rnds 15 and 16:** With green, knit. **Rnd 17:** With white, K1, * K2 tog; rep from * around = 6 sts. Cut yarn, leaving approx 9" sewing length. Thread into tapestry needle and draw through rem sts. Pull up tightly and fasten securely on inside. Weave in all ends. **Pompon:** With equal amounts of each color yarn used in hat, make 1" diameter pompon (see *Pompon* instructions on page 17) and attach securely to top of hat. Sew hat on doll, leaving hair exposed as shown in photo. Bring tip of hat to one side and tack in place.

Scarf: With 2 needles and red, CO 7 sts. **Row 1 (right side):** Knit. **Row 2:** K1, P5, K1. Continuing to rep Rows 1 and 2, work the following stripe sequence: 2 rows each of * white, green, white, bright blue, white, yellow, white and red; rep from * 4 times more. BO all sts; weave in all ends.

Fringe: Cut 14 strands of red, each 4" long. Tie one knot (see *Fringe* instructions on page 16) in each st across each short end of scarf. Trim fringe evenly to 1½". Place scarf around doll's neck (do not knot) as shown in photo and tack in place.

Schoolgirl POLLY
designed by Nannette M. Berkley

Yarn Requirements: 2 oz each light brown,
                                 black and turquoise;
                         1 oz white;
                         3 yds yellow;
                         ½ yd red

INSTRUCTIONS

Following General Instructions on page 124, beg with black and work Basic Tube Pattern, changing colors as follows:

     4 rnds: black
     8 rnds: white
     8 rnds: brown
     11 rnds: turquoise
     Each following rnd to within 3 rnds of Dec Rnd for Neck (6½" from CO edge): white
     All following rnds: brown

When tube is completed, stuff and sculpture doll following General Instructions.

Hair: [**Note:** Hair is formed by working crocheted loops in rows, starting at hairline and working progressively inward toward top of crown.] Beg at center back, 3 rows above Neck Dec Rnd. With black (leave 4" end for weaving in later), * insert hook around knit st, hook yarn and pull loop back around st; YO hook and pull ¼" loop through loop on hook; remove hook, leaving ¼" loop hanging free; sk next st (working from left to right); rep from * until crown is completely covered. Finish off; weave in ends. Tie a small bow (use 2 strands of turquoise) at top of crown; knot and trim ends.

Eyes: With black, work same as in Ballerina Violet.

Mouth: Use single strand of red and embroider 3 backstitches as shown in **Fig 8**.

Pinafore: Beg at bottom, with turquoise, CO 60 sts on one needle; divide sts evenly on 3 needles (20-20-20). Join, being careful not to twist sts. **Rnd 1:** Knit. **Rnd 2:** Purl. **Rnds 3 and 4:** Rep Rnds 1 and 2. **Rnd 5:** Knit. **Rnd 6:** Join yellow; drop turquoise (do not cut); * K1, YB (yarn behind work as to knit), sl 1 as to purl; rep from * around. **Rnd 7:** * K1, P1; rep from * around. Cut yellow; continue with turquoise. **Rnds 8 through 13:** Knit. **Rnd 14:** * K2 tog; rep from * around = 30 sts. **Rnd 15:** Purl. **Rnd 16:** Knit. **Rnd 17:** BO 19 sts in purl; purl rem sts. Continue on rem 11 sts for bib as follows, working with 2 needles only. **Bib: Row 1 (wrong side):** Purl. **Row 2:** P2, K7, P2. **Rows 3 through 6:** Rep Rows 1 and 2, twice. **Row 7:** Purl. **Row 8:** Join yellow; drop turquoise; K1, * YB, sl 1 as to purl, K1 rep from * across. **Row 9:** K2; (P1, K1) 4 times, K1. Cut yellow; continue with turquoise. **Rows 10, 11 and 12:** Knit. **Row 13 (divide for shoulder straps):** K2, sl these 2 sts to sm safety pin; BO next 7 sts as to knit; K1. Continuing on rem 2 sts, knit each row until strap measures 4"; BO, leaving 6" sewing length. Sl 2 sts from safety pin to needle and work same as other strap. Slip pinafore on doll; cross straps across back and sew ends to skirt. Tack straps to doll at shoulders. Weave in all ends.

Shoe Straps: For each strap, thread 18" strand of black into tapestry needle doubled. Weave around ankle by inserting needle from front to back through center of doll and then through one st at back of shoe and one st at front of shoe. Tie into a small bow; trim ends.

Sailor SAM
designed by Nannette M. Berkley

Yarn Requirements: 2 oz each light tan, black, bright blue and white;
½ yd red

INSTRUCTIONS
Following General Instructions on page 124, beg with black and work Basic Tube Pattern, changing colors as follows:

    4 rnds: black
    8 rnds: white
    9 rnds: tan
    11 rnds: blue
    Each following rnd to within 3 rnds of Dec Rnd for Neck
        (6½" from CO edge): white
    All following rnds: tan

When tube is completed, stuff and sculpture doll following General Instructions.

Hair: With black, work same as in Ballerina Violet (excluding braid).

Eyes: With black, work same as in Ballerina Violet.

Mouth: With single strand of red, embroider several horizontal satin sts as shown in photo.

Collar: With 2 needles and blue, CO 10 sts. **Row 1 (right side):** Knit. **Row 2:** K1, P8, K1. Rep Rows 1 and 2 until piece measures 1¼" from CO edge, ending by working Row 2. **Dividing Row for Ties:** K3, sl these sts to sm safety pin; BO next 4 sts; knit rem sts. Continuing on rem 3 sts, work tie as follows. **Row 1:** K1, P2, K1. **Row 2:** Knit. Rep last 2 rows until tie measures 5", ending by working Row 1. K3 tog; cut yarn (leaving 4" end) and pull through last st on needle. Sl sts from safety pin to needle and work same as other tie. Place collar around neck of doll, crossing ties at front. With matching yarn, tack in place at neck edge and then work several horizontal satin sts over

ties at center front (**Fig 9**) to simulate knot, and secure to doll. Use single strand of white and embroider one cross stitch in each corner on back of collar (**Fig 10**).

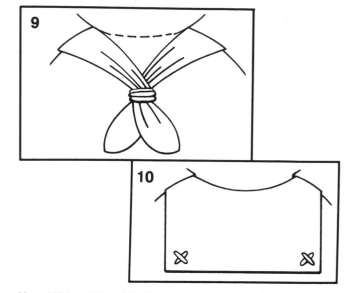

Hat: With white, CO 36 sts on one needle; divide sts evenly on 3 needles (12-12-12). Join, being careful not to twist sts. **Rnds 1 through 4:** Knit. **Rnds 5 through 7:** Purl. **Rnd 8:** * P1, P2 tog; rep from * around = 24 sts. **Rnd 9:** Purl. **Rnds 10 and 11:** * P2 tog; rep from * around. Cut yarn, leaving 6" sewing length. Thread into tapestry needle and draw through rem 6 sts. Pull up tightly and fasten securely on inside. Leaving first 4 rnds free for rim, sew hat to top of head.

Toddler SCARF

designed by Mary Thomas
face designs by Carol Wilson Mansfield

This delightful scarf with cute embroidered faces is worked in a double-knitting pattern — a slip stitch pattern that forms two layers of knitting.

SIZE: Approx 5″ wide x 31″ long (without fringe)

MATERIALS
Sport weight yarn: 2 oz orange; ¼ oz yellow; ½ oz each green and white;

10 yds brown; 2 yds blue; 1 yd each pink and red (for embroidery)
Size 10, 10″ straight knitting needles (or size required for gauge)
Size 16 tapestry needle (for embroidery)

GAUGE: In stock st, 4 sts = 1″

INSTRUCTIONS

With green, CO 40 sts. Mark last CO st (use sm safety pin or piece of contrasting yarn) to identify edge for changing colors later. Now work in patt as follows. **Patt Row:** * K1, bring yarn to front of work; sl 1 as to purl, bring yarn to back of work; rep from * across. Continuing to rep Patt Row, work the following striping sequence. **Note:** Change colors at marked edge only.

Green 2″
Yellow ½″
Orange 2″
White 3″
Orange 16″
White 3″
Orange 2″
Yellow ½″
Green 2″

When striping sequence is completed, scarf should measure approx 31″ long. Now BO as follows: K1; * K2 tog, pass first st over 2nd st on right-hand needle; rep from * to last st; sl last st as to knit, pass first st over sl st on right-hand needle. Finish off; weave in all ends.

FRINGE
Following Fringe Instructions on page 16, make Single Knot Fringe. Cut 10″ strands of green. Use 4 strands for each knot of fringe. Tie 10 knots evenly spaced across each short end of scarf.

EMBROIDERY
Following diagrams in **Fig 1** (for face #1) and **Fig 2** (for face #2), embroider one face on each white section of scarf, using colors and number of strands as indicated below.

FACE #1
    Hair: 12 strands brown (each 12″ long)
    Each hair bow: 2 strands orange (each 6″ long)
    Eyes: 2 strands blue
    Nose: 1 strand pink
    Mouth: 1 strand red
    Collar: 1 strand orange

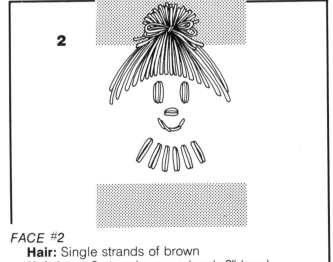

FACE #2
    Hair: Single strands of brown
    Hair bow: 2 strands green (each 6″ long)
    Eyes: 2 strands blue
    Nose: 1 strand pink
    Mouth: 1 strand red
    Collar: 1 strand green

128

GINGERBREAD BOY

designed by Mary Thomas

This appealing fellow is just the right size for small hands to cuddle, and may be used as a pillow for a sleepy head.

SIZE: Approx 19″ tall

MATERIALS
Aunt Lydia's Heavy Rug Yarn in 70-yd skeins: 3 skeins Brown and 1 skein White
Size 10, 10″ straight knitting needles (or size required for gauge)
Small stitch holder
Size 16 tapestry needle (for embroidery)
Polyester filling (for stuffing)

GAUGE: In stock st, 7 sts = 2″; 5 rows = 1″

INSTRUCTIONS
Note: Throughout patt, slip each sl st as to purl.

FRONT
Right Leg: With Brown, CO 6 sts.
Row 1: Knit.
Row 2: * *Purl in front and back of st (inc made)* *; purl to last st, rep from * to * once = 8 sts.
Row 3: * *Knit in front and back of st (inc made)* *; knit to last st, rep from * to * once = 10 sts.
Rows 4 and 5: Rep Rows 2 and 3 = 14 sts.
Row 6: Purl.
Row 7: Knit.
Row 8: Purl.
Row 9: Inc in first st [*to inc: knit in front and back of st*]; knit to last 2 sts, K2 tog = 14 sts.
Rows 10 through 13: Rep Rows 8 and 9, twice.
Row 14: P7, YO twice; P4, YO twice, P3. Cut Brown (leave 4″ end for weaving in later); join White.

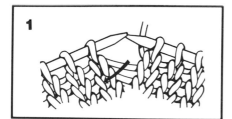

Row 15: Inc in first st, K2; * **drop both wraps (YO's), sl 1, K1; insert right-hand needle into next st two rows below (Fig 1), wrap yarn around needle as to knit and pull this loop through loosely; knit next st, then pass loop over this knit st, K1** *; rep from * to * once; K1, K2 tog = 14 sts.
Row 16: P5; (sl 1, P3) twice, P1.
Row 17: Rep Row 9 = 14 sts.
Row 18: P5, (YO twice, P4) twice; YO twice, P1. Cut White; join Brown.
Row 19: Inc in first st; rep from * to * (in Row 15) 3 times, ending last rep by working K2 tog instead of K1 = 14 sts.
Row 20: (P3, sl 1) 3 times, P2. Cut yarn, leaving 4″ end; sl sts to holder. Set aside.

Left Leg: Work same as Right Leg until Row 7 has been completed. Then work as follows.
Row 8: Purl.
Row 9: K2 tog, knit to last st, inc in last st = 14 sts.
Rows 10 through 13: Rep Rows 8 and 9, twice.
Row 14: (P4, YO twice) twice, P6. Cut Brown; join White.
Row 15: K2 tog, K4; rep from * to * (in Row 15 of Right Leg) twice, ending last rep by working increase in last st instead of K1.
Row 16: P4; (sl 1, P3) twice, P2.
Row 17: Rep Row 9.
Row 18: P2, (YO twice, P4) 3 times. Cut White; join Brown.
Row 19: K2 tog, K2; rep from * to * (in Row 15 of Right Leg) twice; drop both wraps, sl 1, inc in last st.
Row 20: P2, (sl 1, P3) 3 times. Continue with same yarn and work as follows.

Body: Row 1 (joining row): Knit across 14 sts of left leg; CO 2 sts (see *Casting On, Method 2* on page 12); with right side facing, sl sts from right leg holder to free needle; then knit across these 14 sts = 30 sts.
Row 2: Purl.
Row 3: K2 tog, knit to last 2 sts; K2 tog = 28 sts.
Rows 4 and 5: Rep Rows 2 and 3 = 26 sts.
Row 6: Purl.
Row 7: Knit.
Row 8: Purl.
Row 9: Inc in first st, knit to last st; inc in last st = 28 sts.
Row 10: Purl.
Rows 11 and 12: Rep Rows 9 and 10 = 30 sts.
Rows 13 through 25: Work 13 rows even in stock st, ending by working a knit row.
Rows 26 through 29: Rep Rows 2 and 3, twice = 26 sts. Mark first and last st on Row 29 (use sm safety pins or pieces of contrasting yarn) to be used later for arms.

129

Rows 30 through 32: Rep Rows 6 through 8.
Row 33: Rep Row 3 = 24 sts.
Rows 34 through 37: Rep Rows 30 through 33 = 22 sts.
Row 38: Purl.
Row 39: Knit. Continue with same yarn and work as follows.

Collar: Row 1: P5, (YO twice, P4) 4 times, P1. Cut Brown; join White.
Row 2: K2 tog, K3; rep from * to * (in Row 15 of Right Leg) 4 times, ending last rep by working K2 tog instead of K1 = 20 sts.
Row 3: (P3, sl 1) 4 times, P4.
Row 4: Knit.
Row 5: P4, (YO twice, P4) 4 times. Cut White; join Brown.
Row 6: K2 tog, K2; rep from * to * (in Row 15 of Right Leg) 3 times; drop both wraps, sl 1, K1, K2 tog = 18 sts.
Row 7: P2, (sl 1, P3) 4 times. Continue with same yarn and work as follows.

Head: Rows 1 through 4: Beg with a knit row and work 4 rows even in stock st.
Row 5: Inc in first st, knit to last st; inc in last st = 20 sts.
Rows 6 through 8: Beg with a purl row and work 3 rows even in stock st.
Row 9: Rep Row 5 = 22 sts.
Rows 10 through 16: Beg with a purl row and work 7 rows even in stock st.
Continuing in stock st, dec one st at each end EVERY row until 6 sts rem on needle. BO all sts.

Right Arm: Hold work with right side facing and right side edge across top. Beg at last row of Collar; join Brown and pick up 14 sts along edge to marker.
Row 1: Purl.
Row 2: K2 tog, knit rem sts = 13 sts.
Row 3: Purl to last 2 sts, P2 tog = 12 sts.
Rows 4 through 6: Beg with a knit row and work 3 rows even in stock st.
Row 7: Purl to last st, inc in last st = 13 sts.
Row 8: Knit.
Row 9: P5, (YO twice, P4) twice. Cut Brown; join White.
Row 10: K4, rep from * to * (in Row 15 of Right Leg) twice, K1 = 13 sts.
Row 11: P4, (sl 1, P3) twice, P1.
Row 12: Knit.

Row 13: Rep Row 9. Cut White; join Brown.
Row 14: K2 tog, K2; rep from * to * (in Row 15 of Right Leg) twice, ending last rep by working K2 tog instead of K1 = 11 sts.
Row 15: P2 tog, P1; sl 1, P3; sl 1, P1, P2 tog = 9 sts.
Row 16: K2 tog, knit to last 2 sts; K2 tog = 7 sts.
Row 17: P2 tog, purl to last 2 sts; P2 tog = 5 sts. BO all sts.

Left Arm: Hold work with right side facing and left side across top. With Brown, pick up 14 sts along edge to correspond to Right Arm.
Row 1: Purl.
Row 2: Knit to last 2 sts, K2 tog = 13 sts.
Row 3: P2 tog, purl rem sts = 12 sts.
Rows 4 through 6: Beg with a knit row and work 3 rows even in stock st.
Row 7: Inc in first st, purl rem sts = 13 sts.
Rows 8 through 17: Rep Rows 8 through 17 of Right Arm. BO all sts.

BACK
Work same as Front.

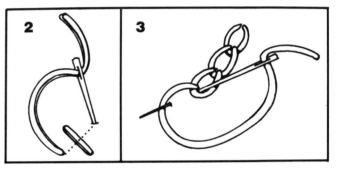

FINISHING
Weave in all ends. Thread White into tapestry needle and embroider facial features on Front piece (see photo for placement) as follows. Use yarn doubled and work one cross st (**Fig 2**) for each eye. Use single strand of yarn and work chain sts (**Fig 3**) for mouth. **Pompons:** Make 2 white pompons (1½" diameter) [see *Pompon* instructions on page 17] and attach to Front piece. Now with right sides tog, sew Front and Back pieces tog, leaving a small opening. Turn right side out and stuff lightly. Then slip st opening closed.

INFANT SEAT HOODED WRAP

designed by Doris England

Here's an entirely new type of garment — one designed to keep baby snug and warm in the popular infant seat.

SIZE: Measures approx 50″ wide (across middle section below hood) and 48″ long (from top of hood to bottom edge).

MATERIALS
Sport weight yarn: 18 oz yellow
Size 13, 29 ″ circular knitting needle (or size required for gauge)
Materials Note: Yarn is used doubled throughtout patt.

**GAUGE: With 2 strands of yarn in Patt St,
10 sts = 3″**

PATTERN STITCH

Row 1 (wrong side): K2 for garter st edge; * woven stitch (abbreviated WS) [*to work WS: P2 tog but do not remove from left-hand needle; YB (yarn to back of work), then knit same 2 sts tog again; now sl both sts off left-hand needle = WS made*]; rep from * to last 2 sts, K2 for garter st edge.

Row 2: Knit.

Row 3: K2, P1; * WS; rep from * to last 3 sts, P1, K2.

Row 4: Knit.
Rep Rows 1 through 4 for patt.

INSTRUCTIONS

[**Note:** Wrap is worked in one piece, using 2 strands of yarn throughout patt.] Beg at top of hood, with 2 strands of yarn, CO 46 sts. Do not join; work back and forth in rows. Knit 4 rows. Now work Patt St Rows 1 through 4, 3 times; then work Patt St Rows 1 through 3 once more. Continue with shaping for back of hood as follows.

Row 1 (right side): K 18, K2 tog; K6, K2 tog; K 18 = 44 sts.

Rows 2 through 4: Rep Patt St Rows 1 through 3.

Row 5: K 18, K2 tog; K4, K2 tog; K 18 = 42 sts.

Rows 6 through 8: Rep Patt St Rows 1 through 3.

Row 9: K 18, K2 tog; K2, K2 tog; K 18 = 40 sts.

Rows 10 through 12: Rep Patt St Rows 1 through 3.

Row 13: K 18, (K2 tog) twice; K 18 = 38 sts.

Rows 14 through 17: Rep Patt St Rows 1 through 4.

Row 18 (beading row): K2; * YO, P2; rep from * to last 2 sts; YO, K2 = 56 sts (counting each YO as one st). This completes hood; continue with middle section as follows.

Row 1: Beg in first st and CO 56 sts as shown in *Casting On, Method 1* **(Figs 8, 9 and 10)** on page 6; now knit across these CO sts and 56 sts of hood = 112 sts.

Row 2: CO 56 sts in same manner as prev row; knit across CO sts; K2, (WS) 26 times; K2, knit rem 56 sts = 168 sts.

Row 3: Knit.

Row 4: K 58, P1; (WS) 25 times; P1, K 58.

Row 5: Knit.
Now rep Patt St Rows 1 through 4 until piece measures approx 17″ from beading row, ending by working Row 4. Then complete middle section as follows.

Row 1 (wrong side): K 58, (WS) 26 times, K 58.

Row 2: Knit.

Row 3: BO 56 sts [one st now on right-hand needle]; knit next st, P1; (WS) 25 times; P1, K 58 = 112 sts.

Row 4: BO 56 sts, knit rem sts = 56 sts. This completes middle section; continue with bottom section.
Rep Patt St Rows 1 through 4 until piece measures approx 47″ from CO edge of hood, ending by working Row 3. Knit last 3 rows. BO all sts in knit.

FINISHING

Fold CO edge of hood in half with right sides tog; then sew edges tog for top of hood. Weave in all ends. **Drawstring:** Using 4 strands of yarn, make a twisted cord (see *Twisted Cord* instructions on page 15) 40″ long; or use crochet hook (size I) and 3 strands of yarn and make a chain to same measurement. Knot and trim each end of drawstring. Weave drawstring through beading row at bottom of hood.

VALENTINE BABY AFGHAN

designed by Jean Leinhauser

SIZE: Approx 44″ wide x 40″ long with edging

MATERIALS
Sport weight yarn: 10 oz red;
3 oz white
Size 8, 29″ circular knitting needle (or size required for gauge)
Size 10, 10″ straight knitting needles (for edging)

GAUGE: With smaller size needle in Patt St,
9 sts = 2″

INSTRUCTIONS

With circular needle and red, CO 182 sts. Do not join; work back and forth in rows as follows.
Pattern Stitch
Rows 1 and 3 (wrong side): Purl.
Row 2: K1; * K3, YO; sl 1 as to knit, K2 tog, PSSO, YO; rep from * to last st, K1. **Note:** Each YO counts as one st throughout patt.
Row 4: K1; * YO, sl 1 as to knit, K2 tog, PSSO; YO, K3; rep from * to last st, K1.
Rep Rows 1 through 4 until piece measures approx 36″ from CO edge, ending by working Row 4. BO all sts in purl.

EDGING

With straight needles and white, CO 8 sts.
Row 1 and all odd-numbered rows: Purl.
Row 2 (right side): Sl 1 as to knit (now and throughout edging), K2 tog; YO, K3 tog; YO, K2 tog = 6 sts. **Note:** Each YO counts as one st throughout edging.

Row 4: Sl 1; (YO, K1) 3 times; YO, K2 tog = 9 sts.
Row 6: Sl 1, K2 tog; YO, K1, YO; K2, YO, K1, YO; K2 tog = 11 sts.
Row 8: Sl 1, K2 tog; (YO, K1) twice, K2 tog; (K1, YO) twice, K2 tog = 12 sts.
Row 10: Sl 1, K2 tog; (YO, K1) twice, K3 tog; (K1, YO) twice, K2 tog = 12 sts.
Row 12: Sl 1, K2 tog; YO, K2, K3 tog; K2, YO; K2 tog = 10 sts.
Row 14: Sl 1, K2 tog; YO, K1, K3 tog; K1, YO, K2 tog = 8 sts.

Rep Rows 1 through 14 until edging measures approx 18″ from CO edge, ending by working Row 2. Then work first corner as follows. [**Note:** Corner is shaped by working short rows; when instructions say "TURN", leave rem st(s) on needle unworked, turn your work and begin next row.]

Corner Shaping: Row 1 (wrong side): P5, TURN. **Row 2:** Sl 1, P2; YO, K2 tog. **Row 3:** P4, TURN. **Row 4:** Sl 1, K1; YO, K2 tog. **Row 5:** P3, TURN. **Row 6:** Sl 1; YO, K2 tog. **Row 7:** Purl = 6 sts. This completes corner shaping.

Now work Rows 4 through 14 of edging once; then rep Rows 1 through 14 of edging until piece measures approx 36″ from prev corner shaping, ending by working Row 2. Work rem corners and edges in same manner, ending last edge approx 18″ from 4th corner by working Row 14. BO all sts in purl.

FINISHING

Weave CO and BO edges of edging tog. Pin edging to afghan piece, having joining seam of edging at side edge of afghan piece. Use white and covercast edges tog. Weave in all ends. Lightly steam press on wrong side.

OWL SWEATER
for toddlers
designed by Mary Thomas

The cables worked into the yoke of this sweater form charming little owls; add small buttons for eyes, or use the sew-on wiggly eyes as we did.

SIZES: Written for toddler sizes 1-2 with changes for 3-4 in parentheses.

MATERIALS
Worsted weight yarn: 5 (6) oz yellow
Sizes 6 and 8, 10″ straight knitting needles (or size required for gauge)
2 Small stitch holders
Cable needle
6 Moving eye buttons (⅜″ diameter)

GAUGE: With larger size needles in stock st,
9 sts = 2″; 6 rows = 1″

INSTRUCTIONS
BACK
With smaller size needles, CO 51(55) sts. **Ribbing Row 1:** * K1, P1; rep from * to last st, K1. **Ribbing Row 2:** P1, * K1, P1; rep from * across. Rep last 2 rows until ribbing measures 1½″ from CO edge, ending by working Ribbing Row 2.

Change to larger size needles and work even in stock st until piece measures 8(9½)″ from CO edge or desired length to underarm, ending by working a purl row.

Shape Armholes: Continuing in stock st, BO 2 sts at beg of next 2 rows = 47(51) sts. Dec one st at each edge EOR twice = 43(47) sts. Now work even until armhole measures 4(4¾)″, ending by working a purl row.

Shape Neck and Shoulders: Row 1: BO 4 sts, knit *next* [do not count st already on needle] 8(9) sts; sl next 17(19) sts to holder for back of neck; join new ball of yarn and knit across rem sts. Continue to work across each side with a separate ball of yarn as follows. **Row 2:** BO 4 sts, purl across sts of left shoulder to within 2 sts of neck edge, P2 tog; P2 tog at neck edge of right shoulder, purl rem sts. **Row 3:** BO 4 sts, knit rem sts. **Row 4:** Rep Row 2. **Row 5:** BO rem 3(4) sts of right shoulder; knit sts of left shoulder. BO rem 3(4) sts.

FRONT
Work same as Back until ribbing is completed, increasing one st at end of last row (Ribbing Row 2) = 52(56) sts. Change to larger size needles and work even in stock st until piece measures 7(8½)″ from CO edge or 1″ (6 rows) less than back length to underarm, ending by working a purl row.

OWL STITCH YOKE

Row 1 (right side): K 19(20), P 14(16), K 19(20).

Row 2: Purl.

Rows 3 and 4: Rep Rows 1 and 2.

Row 5 (cable twist row): K 19(20), P3(4); work cable twist over next 8 sts [to work cable twist: sl next 2 sts onto cable needle and hold at **back** of work; knit next 2 sts, then K2 from cable needle; sl next 2 sts onto cable needle and hold at **front** of work; knit next 2 sts, then K2 from cable needle = cable twist made]; P3(4), K 19(20).

Row 6: P 19(20), K3(4); P8, K3(4); P 19(20).

Row 7: BO 2 sts for underarm [one st now on right-hand needle]; K1, P 18(20), K8, P 18(20), K4 = 50(54) sts.

Row 8: BO 2 sts for underarm [one st now on right-hand needle]; P 16(17) sts, K0(4), P0, K0(4), purl rem sts = 48(52) sts.

Row 9: K2 tog, P 18(20); K8, P 18(20); K2 tog = 46(50) sts.

Row 10: P 16(17), K3(4); P8, K3(4); purl rem sts.

Row 11 (cable twist row): P2 tog, P3; cable twist (same as in Row 5); P6(8), K8; P6(8), cable twist; P3, P2 tog = 44(48) sts.

Row 12: K4, P8; K6(8), P8, K6(8), P8, K4.

Row 13: P4, K8; P6(8), K8, P6(8), K8, P4.

Row 14: Rep Row 12.

Row 15 (cable twist row): P4, K8; P6(8), cable twist; P6(8); K8, P4.

Rows 16 through 20: Rep Rows 12 and 13, twice; then rep Row 12 once more.

Row 21 (cable twist row): P4; * cable twist, P6(8); rep from * once more; cable twist, P4.

Row 22: K4, P8, K 20(24); P8, K4.

Row 23: P4, K8, P 20(24); K8, P4.

Rows 24 through 26: Rep Rows 22 and 23, once; then rep Row 22 once more.

Row 27 (cable twist row): P4, cable twist; P 20(24), cable twist; P4.

Row 28: Knit.

SIZE 3-4 ONLY: (Purl one row, knit one row) twice [4 rows total].

Shape Neck and Shoulders: Row 1: P 14(15), sl next 16(18) sts to holder for front of neck; join new ball of yarn and purl across rem sts. **Row 2:** Knit across sts of right shoulder to within 2 sts of neck edge, K2 tog; K2 tog at left neck edge, knit rem sts of left shoulder. **Row 3:** Purl across sts of each shoulder. **Rows 4 and 5:** Rep Rows 2 and 3. **Row 6:** Rep Row 2. **Row 7:** BO 4 sts, purl rem sts. **Row 8:** BO 4 sts, knit rem sts. **Rows 9 and 10:** Rep Rows 7 and 8. **Row 11:** BO 3(4) sts, purl rem sts. BO rem 3(4) sts.

SLEEVE
(Make 2)

With smaller size needles, CO 29(33) sts. Rep Ribbing Rows 1 and 2 (in Back instructions) until ribbing measures 2½(3)" from CO edge, ending by working Ribbing Row 2.

Change to larger size needles. Work 8 rows even in stock st. Continuing in stock st, inc one st at each edge on next row and each following 8th row, 3 times more = 37(41) sts. Work even until sleeve measures 9½(10½)" from CO edge or desired length to underarm, ending by working a purl row.

Shape Cap: Continuing in stock st, BO 2 sts at beg of next 2 rows = 33(37) sts. Dec one st at each edge EOR 4 times = 25(29) sts. Then dec one st at each edge EVERY row until 9 sts rem. BO all sts.

FINISHING

Sew right shoulder seam. **Neck Ribbing:** With right side facing and smaller size needles, beg at left front neck edge; join yarn and pick up 10 sts along left front neck shaping; sl sts from front holder to free needle and knit these 16(18) sts; pick up 10 sts along right front neck shaping to shoulder seam; pick up 5 sts along right back neck shaping; sl sts from back holder to free needle and knit these 17(19) sts; pick up 5 sts along left back neck shaping = 63(67) sts. Rep Ribbing Rows 1 and 2 (in Back instructions) until ribbing measures ¾". BO all sts loosely in ribbing.

Sew left shoulder seam and weave ends of neck ribbing tog. Sew in sleeves. Then sew side and sleeve seams. Weave in all ends. Sew buttons on "owls" for eyes as shown in photo.

Afghans

Chapter 7

This selection of nine afghans provides a project for every knitter, from the beginner to the advanced.

We've included two variations of what must be the most popular knit afghan design of all time: the ripple or zig-zag. Our variations, *Sunrise* and *Seascape,* show the wide range of color and stitch possibilities offered by ripples.

Another classic is the easy to make *Irish Islands* Fisherman knit made with bulky weight yarn or two strands of worsted weight yarn. As a bonus, we've provided instructions for two pillows to display with the afghan — one using the same Fisherman pattern stitches, the other featuring a Norwegian knit-in design.

A traditional lace pattern combines with mohair yarn to create the soft, airy *Lacy Mohair* afghan. *Summer Skies* features an effective fan pattern, worked in strips of shadings of blue (or any color of your choice).

Shades of brown, orange, and cream are artfully combined in the *Bargello* afghan, and color and texture are both featured in *Pennsylvania Dutch Tiles*. This afghan's floral squares are worked with bobbins following a charted design; the sculptured white squares echo the floral motifs.

Embroidered flowers climb the cable trellises of the *Cable Garden,* a magnificent afghan worked in panels. And for a final fillip, try our colorful *Christmas Snowflakes and Ribbons,* crafted in fascinating textured stitches with red, green and white yarns.

Whichever afghans you choose to make, you're sure to create a family heirloom.

SUNRISE
designed by Mary Thomas

SIZE: Approx 42″ x 58″ before fringing
MATERIALS
Worsted weight yarn: 18 oz white;
⠀⠀⠀⠀⠀⠀⠀⠀⠀⠀⠀⠀⠀⠀⠀5 oz orange ombre;
⠀⠀⠀⠀⠀⠀⠀⠀⠀⠀⠀⠀⠀⠀⠀9 oz orange
Size 11, 29″ circular knitting needle (or size required for gauge)
GAUGE: In stock st, 7 sts = 2″

INSTRUCTIONS

With orange, CO 157 sts. Do not join; work back and forth in rows.

Row 1 (right side): Purl.

Row 2: Knit.

Row 3: Purl. Finish off orange; join white.

Row 4: P2; * P2 tog, P 13; P2 tog through back lps **(Fig 1)**; rep from * across to last 2 sts, P2 = 139 sts.

Row 5: K2; * sl 1 as to knit, K1, PSSO; K 11, K2 tog; rep from * across to last 2 sts, K2 = 121 sts.

Row 6: Knit.

Row 7: K5; * (YO twice, K1) 7 times; YO twice, K6; rep from * across, ending last rep with K5 instead of K6.

Row 8: K5; * (knit first YO, drop next YO, K1) 7 times; knit first YO, drop next YO, K6; rep from * across, ending last rep with K5 instead of K6 = 193 sts.

Row 9: K2; * sl 1 as to knit, K1, PSSO; K 17, K2 tog; rep from * across to last 2 sts, K2 = 175 sts. Finish off white; join orange.

Row 10: P2; * P2 tog, P 15; P2 tog through back lps **(Fig 1)**; rep from * to last 2 sts, P2 = 157 sts.

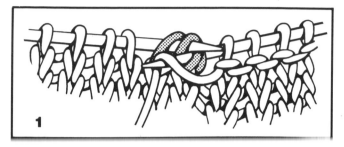

Rows 11 through 19: Rep Rows 1 through 9. Finish off white; join ombre.

Row 20: Rep Row 10.

Row 21: Purl.

Row 22: P4; knit across to last 4 sts, P4.

Rows 23 through 25: Rep Rows 21 and 22 once; then rep Row 21 once more. Finish off ombre; join white.

Rows 26 through 32: Rep Rows 4 through 10.
Rep Rows 1 through 32, 8 times more. Rep Rows 1 through 10 once; then rep Rows 1 and 2 once more. BO all sts *loosely* in purl. Weave in all ends.

FRINGE

Follow *Basic Fringe Instructions* on page 16 and make *Spaghetti Fringe*. Cut 10″ strands of orange. Knot one strand in each st across both short ends of afghan.

SEASCAPE
designed by Jean Leinhauser

SIZE: Approx 52″ x 73″
MATERIALS
Worsted weight yarn: 24 oz light blue;
                       12 oz medium blue;
                        4 oz medium green;
                       9 oz white
Size 9, 36″ circular knitting needle (or size required
   for gauge)
GAUGE: In stock st, 9 sts = 2″; 13 rows = 2″

PATTERN STITCH (multiple of 12 sts + 3)
Row 1: K1; sl 1 as to knit, K1, PSSO; * K9, double dec [*to
work double dec: insert right-hand needle into next 2 sts
as if to knit* **(Fig 1); do not knit,** *but instead sl these 2 sts
tog to right-hand needle* **(Fig 2);** *K1, pass both sl sts tog
over knit st = double dec made*]; rep from * across to last
12 sts; K9, K2 tog, K1.

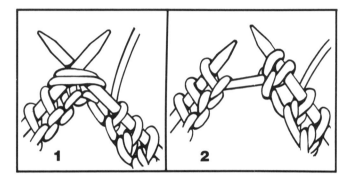

Row 2: P6; * double inc [*to work double inc: purl next st
but leave st on left-hand needle; YO and purl again in
same st* **(Fig 3);** *now sl st off left-hand needle = double
inc made*], P9; rep from * across to last 7 sts; double inc,
P6.

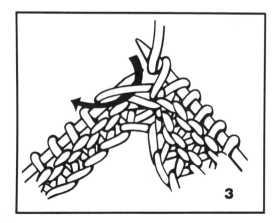

Note: On next row, work each YO as one st.

Rep Rows 1 and 2 for patt.

INSTRUCTIONS
With med blue, CO 303 sts *loosely*. Do not join; work back
and forth in rows. Work in Pattern Stitch using the following 24-row color sequence.
6 rows med blue
6 rows lt blue
2 rows white
2 rows med green
2 rows white
6 rows lt blue

Rep 24-row color sequence, 15 times more; then work 6
more rows with med blue. You should have a total of 390
rows.

BO all sts *loosely*. Weave in all ends. On wrong side,
lightly steam ends and side edges to keep from curling.

137

IRISH ISLANDS
designed by Barbara Retzke

SIZE: Approx 40″ x 56″
MATERIALS
Bulky weight yarn or 2 strands of worsted weight
  yarn: 42 oz ecru
Size 13, 14″ straight knitting needles (or size required
  for gauge)
Cable Needle
GAUGE: In stock st, 3 sts = 1″; 4 rows = 1″

PATTERN STITCHES

SEED STITCH (worked on uneven number of sts)
Row 1: * K1, P1; rep from * across to last st, K1.
Rep Row 1 for patt.

HONEYCOMB (multiple of 8 sts)
Row 1 (cable twist row): * S1 next 2 sts onto cable needle and hold at *back* of work; knit next 2 sts, then K2 from cable needle; sl next 2 sts onto cable needle and hold at *front* of work; knit next 2 sts, then K2 from cable needle; rep from * across.

Row 2: Purl.

Row 3: Knit.

Row 4: Purl.

Row 5 (cable twist row): * S1 next 2 sts onto cable needle and hold at *front* of work; knit next 2 sts, then K2 from cable needle; sl next 2 sts onto cable needle and hold at *back* of work; knit next 2 sts, then K2 from cable needle; rep from * across.

Rows 6, 7 and 8: Rep Rows 2, 3 and 4.
Rep Rows 1 through 8 for patt.

LADDER OF LIFE (multiple of 7 sts)
Row 1 (right side): * P1, K5, P1; rep from * across.

Row 2: * K1, P5, K1; rep from * across.

Row 3: Purl.

Row 4: Rep Row 2.
Rep Rows 1 through 4 for patt.

LOBSTER CLAW (multiple of 9 sts)
Row 1: * P1, K7, P1; rep from * across.

Row 2: * K1, P7, K1; rep from * across.

Row 3 (cable twist row): * P1; sl next 2 sts onto cable needle and hold at *back* of work; knit next st, then K2 from cable needle; K1; sl next st onto cable needle and hold at *front* of work; knit next 2 sts, then K1 from cable needle, P1; rep from * across.

Row 4: Rep Row 2.
Rep Rows 1 through 4 for patt.

INSTRUCTIONS
Note: Use single strand of bulky weight yarn or 2 strands of worsted weight yarn throughout patt.

CENTER PANEL
CO 39 sts *loosely*. Work 7 rows in Seed St Patt. **Inc Row:** * (K1, P1) twice; inc in next st [to inc: knit in front and back of st]; rep from * 6 times more; (K1, P1) twice = 46 sts. Now establish patt as follows.

Row 1: Work in Seed St Patt over first 3 sts; work Honeycomb Patt Row 2 over next 40 sts; work in Seed St Patt over last 3 sts.

Row 2: Work in Seed St Patt over first 3 sts; work Honeycomb Patt Row 2 over next 40 sts work in Seed St Patt over last 3 sts.
Continue in patt as etablished until piece measures approx 54″ from CO edge, ending by working Honeycomb Patt Row 1.

Dec Row: K1; (P1, K1) 3 times; * P2 tog; K1, P1, K1; rep from * 6 times more; (P1, K1) twice = 39 sts. Work 6 more rows in Seed St Patt. BO all sts *loosely* in Seed St.

SIDE PANEL (make 2)
CO 39 sts *loosely*. Work 7 rows in Seed St Patt. **Inc Row:** * (K1, P1) 4 times; inc in next st; rep from * 3 times more, K1, P1, K1 = 43 sts. Now establish patt as follows.

Row 1: Work in Seed St Patt over first 3 sts; work Ladder of Life Patt Row 1 over next 7 sts; P2; work Lobster Claw Patt Row 1 over next 9 sts; K1; work Lobster Claw Patt Row 1 over next 9 sts; P2; work Ladder of Life Patt Row 1 over next 7 sts; work in Seed St Patt over last 3 sts.

Row 2: Work in Seed St Patt over first 3 sts; work Ladder of Life Patt Row 2 over next 7 sts; P2; work Lobster Claw Patt Row 2 over next 9 sts; P1; work Lobster Claw Patt Row 2 over next 9 sts; P2; work Ladder of Life Patt Row 2 over next 7 sts; work in Seed St Patt over last 3 sts.
Continue in patt as established until piece measures approx 2″ less than Center Panel, ending by working Ladder of Life Patt and Lobster Claw Patt Row 1.

Dec Row: * (K1, P1) 3 times; K2 tog, P1; rep from * 3 times more; K1, (P1, K1) 3 times = 39 sts. Work 6 more rows in Seed St Patt. BO all sts *loosely* in Seed St.

FINISHING
Weave in all ends. Weave or sew panels tog, being sure that BO edge of each panel is at same end of afghan.

Fisherman
PILLOW

designed by Barbara Retzke
(photo on page 140)

SIZE: Approx 12″ square

MATERIALS
Worsted weight yarn: 4 oz ecru
Size 7, 10″ straight knitting needles (or size required for gauge)
Cable needle
Pillow form (12″ square, knife edge)

GAUGE: In stock st, 5 sts = 1″; 7 rows = 1″

PATTERN STITCHES
Same as is bulky Fisherman IRISH ISLANDS afghan (see page 138).

INSTRUCTIONS
(MAKE 2 PIECES)
CO 59 sts. Work 6 rows in Seed St Patt. **Inc Row:** (K1, P1) 3 times; * inc in next st [*to inc: knit in front and back of st*]; P1, (K1, P1) twice; rep from * to last 5 sts; K1, (P1, K1) twice = 67 sts. Now establish patt as follows.
Row 1: Work in Seed St Patt over first 5 sts; work Lobster Claw Patt Row 1 over next 18 sts; work Ladder of Life Patt Row 1 over next 21 sts; work Lobster Claw Patt Row 1 over next 18 sts; work in Seed St Patt over last 5 sts.
Row 2: Work in Seed St Patt over first 5 sts; work Lobster Claw Patt Row 2 over next 18 sts; work Ladder of Life Patt Row 2 over next 21 sts; work Lobster Claw Patt Row 2 over next 18 sts work in Seed St Patt over last 5 sts.
Continue in patt as established until piece measures approx 10″ from CO edge, ending by working Lobster Claw Patt and Ladder of Life Patt Row 4.
Dec Row: (K1, P1) 3 times; * K2 tog; P1, (K1, P1) twice; rep from * to last 5 sts; K1, (P1, K1) twice = 59 sts. Work 5 more rows in Seed St Patt. BO all sts in Seed St.

FINISHING
Weave in all ends. With wrong sides of pieces tog and CO edges at same end of pillow, sew 3 edges. Insert pillow form; then sew last edge.

NORWEGIAN PILLOW
designed by Mary Thomas

SIZE: Approx 14″ square
MATERIALS
Worsted weight yarn: 4 oz ecru;
1½ oz rust;
½ oz brown
Size 7, 10″ straight knitting needles (or size required for gauge)
Pillow form (14″ square, knife edge)
GAUGE: In stock st, 5 sts = 1″; 7 rows = 1″

INSTRUCTIONS

FRONT

Note: Before working design from chart, see instructions on page 18 for changing and carrying colors.

With ecru, CO 65 sts. Working in stock st and changing colors as needed, refer to chart in **Fig 1** and work Rows 1 through 40; then work rows in reverse, beg with Row 39 and end with Row 2. On knit rows (odd-numbered rows of chart), * work chart from A to B; rep from * across, ending by working from A to C. On purl rows (even-numbered rows of chart), work chart from C to A once; then * work from B to A; rep from * across.

When all 78 rows of design have been completed, use ecru and BO all sts in knit.

BACK

With ecru, CO 65 sts. Work even in stock st until piece measures same as Front. BO all sts loosely.

FINISHING

Weave in all ends. With wrong sides of pieces tog, sew 3 edges. Insert pillow form; then sew last edge.

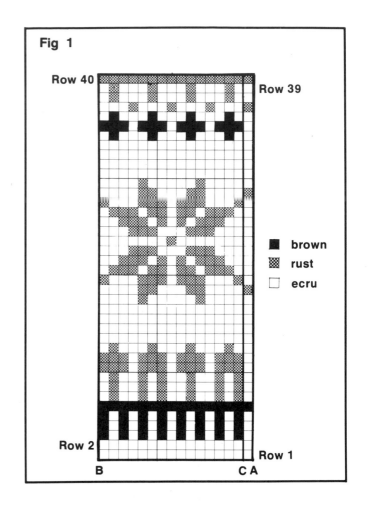

Fig 1

Row 40   Row 39

Row 2   Row 1

B   C A

■ brown
▨ rust
□ ecru

LACY MOHAIR
designed by Jean Leinhauser

SIZE: Approx 45″ x 60″

MATERIALS
Jaeger "Gabrielle" Mohair Yarn in 50 gm (1¾ oz)
   balls: 14 balls Peach
Size 13, 36″ circular knitting needle (or size required
   for gauge)

Materials Note: For yarn source (C. J. Bates & Son), see
page 4.

GAUGE: In garter st, 10 sts = 3½″

INSTRUCTIONS
CO 129 sts *loosely*. Do not join; work back and forth in
rows. Knit first 2 rows; then work in patt as follows.

LACE PATTERN
Rows 1 through 4: Knit.

Rows 5, 7, 9 and 11 (right side): K5; * (K2 tog) twice; (YO,
K1) 3 times; YO; (sl l, K1, PSSO) twice, K1; rep from * to
last 4 sts, K4.

Rows 6, 8, 10 and 12: K4, purl to last 4 sts, K4.
Rep Rows 1 through 12 until work measures approx 59″
from CO edge, ending by working Row 12. Knit 6 more
rows. BO all sts *loosely* in knit. Weave in all ends.

SUMMER SKIES

designed by Mary Thomas

SIZE: Approx 48″ x 62″
MATERIALS
Worsted weight yarn: 4½ oz white;
                            9 oz each of baby, light,
                            medium
                            and dark blue
Size 10½, 10″ straight knitting needles (or size
  required for gauge)
GAUGE: In garter st, 4 sts = 1″

INSTRUCTIONS

STRIP (make 7 total: 1 white and 2 each of baby, lt and med blue)
CO 23 sts *loosely*. Knit first 3 rows; then work in patt as follows.

Row 1 (right side): K1, K2 tog, knit to last 3 sts; dec over next 2 sts [*to dec: sl each of the next 2 sts from the left-hand needle knitwise to right-hand needle; insert tip of left-hand needle from left to right through same 2 sts on right-hand needle (**Fig 1**); now knit both sts tog in this position = dec made*]; K1 = 21 sts.

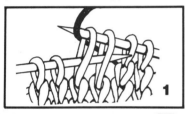

Row 2: K1, K2 tog; purl to last 3 sts, K2 tog, K1 = 19 sts.

Row 3: Rep Row 1 = 17 sts.

Row 4: K2, P1; (YO, P1) 12 times, K2 = 29 sts.

Row 5: Rep Row 1 = 27 sts.

Row 6: Rep Row 2 = 25 sts.

Row 7: Rep Row 1 = 23 sts.

Row 8: Knit.
Rep last 8 rows until strip measures approx 67½″ from CO edge, ending by working Row 8. Knit 2 more rows; then BO all sts in knit.

LEFT EDGE STRIP
With dk blue, CO 25 sts *loosely*. Knit first 3 rows; then work in patt as follows. **Row 1 (right side):** K1, K2 tog; knit to last 5 sts, dec over next 2 sts (see **Fig 1**), K3 = 23 sts. **Row 2:** K3, K2 tog; purl to last 3 sts, K2 tog, K1 = 21 sts. **Row 3:** Rep Row 1 = 19 sts. **Row 4:** K2, P1; (YO, P1) 12 times, K4 = 31 sts. **Row 5:** Rep Row 1 = 29 sts. **Row 6:** Rep Row 2 = 27 sts. **Row 7:** Rep Row 1 = 25 sts. **Row 8:** Knit. Rep last 8 rows until strip measures approx 67½″ from CO edge, ending by working Row 8. Knit 2 more rows; then BO all sts in knit.

RIGHT EDGE STRIP
With dk blue, CO 25 sts *loosely*. Knit first 3 rows; then work in patt as follows. **Row 1 (right side):** K3, K2 tog; knit to last 3 sts, dec over next 2 sts (see **Fig 1**), K1 = 23 sts. **Row 2:** K1, K2 tog; purl to last 5 sts, K2 tog, K3 = 21 sts. **Row 3:** Rep Row 1 = 19 sts. **Row 4:** K4, P1; (YO, P1) 12 times, K2 = 31 sts. **Row 5:** Rep Row 1 = 29 sts. **Row 6:** Rep Row 2 = 27 sts. **Row 7:** Rep Row 1 = 25 sts. **Row 8:** Knit. Rep last 8 rows until strip measures approx 67½″ from CO edge, ending by working Row 8. Knit 2 more rows; then BO all sts in knit.

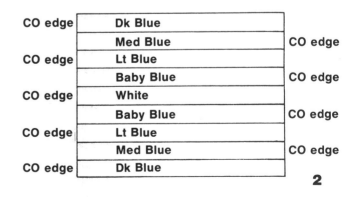

CO edge	Dk Blue	
	Med Blue	CO edge
CO edge	Lt Blue	
	Baby Blue	CO edge
CO edge	White	
	Baby Blue	CO edge
CO edge	Lt Blue	
	Med Blue	CO edge
CO edge	Dk Blue	

2

ASSEMBLING
Refer to diagram in **Fig 2** for arrangement of strips. **Note:** CO and BO edge of strips will be alternating. Sew strips tog.

BARGELLO
designed by Jean Leinhauser

SIZE: Approx 58″ x 70″
MATERIALS
Dawn Sayelle* Knitting Worsted Size Yarn in
   4-oz skeins: 4 skeins Khaki;
            4 skeins Orange;
            4 skeins Honey Beige;
            6 skeins Coffee;
            4 skeins Fisherman
Size 13, 29 circular knitting needle (or size required for gauge)
Materials Note: Yarn is used doubled throughout afghan.
GAUGE: With 2 strands of yarn in Pattern Stitch,
       8 sts = 3″; 16 rows = 4″

INSTRUCTIONS
Note: Use 2 strands of yarn throughout patt.
With 2 strands of Coffee, CO 149 sts. Do not join; work back and forth in rows. Knit first 6 rows for garter st border. Work in patt as follows.

PATTERN STITCH FOUNDATION ROWS
Row 1 (wrong side): K4 (garter st side border); purl across to last 4 sts, K4 (garter st side border).

Row 2: Knit.

Row 3: K4, P3; * wrap yarn twice around needle, P4; rep from * across to last 6 sts; wrap yarn twice around needle, P2, K4. Finish off Coffee; join 2 strands of Honey Beige.

PATTERN STITCH REPEAT ROWS
Row 1: K6, drop both wraps; with yarn at *back* of work, sl 1 as to purl; * K1, insert right-hand needle into next st two rows below **(Fig 1)**, wrap yarn around needle as to knit and pull this loop through *loosely;* knit next st, then pass loop over this knit st; K1, drop both wraps; with yarn at *back* of work, sl 1 as to purl; rep from * to last 6 sts, K6.

Row 2: K4, P2; with yarn at *front* of work, sl 1 as to purl, * P3; with yarn at *front* of work, sl 1 as to purl; rep from * to last 6 sts; P2, K4.

Row 3: Knit.

Row 4: K4; P3 * wrap yarn twice around needle, P4; rep from * to last 6 sts; wrap yarn twice around needle, P2, K4.

Rep last 4 rows in the following color sequence:
    * 4 rows Orange;
      4 rows Khaki;
      4 rows Fisherman;
      4 rows Coffee;
      4 rows Honey Beige;
      rep from * 10 times more; then work as follows.
      4 rows Orange;
      4 rows Khaki;
      4 rows Fisherman;
      3 rows Coffee.

Next Row: Continuing with Coffee, K4; purl to last 4 sts, K4. Knit 6 more rows for garter st border. BO all sts *loosely* in knit. Weave in all ends. Lightly steam edges.

PENNSYLVANIA DUTCH TILES

designed by Anis Duncan

(photo on page 146)

SIZE: Approx 45″ x 54″
MATERIALS
Worsted weight yarn: 26 oz white;
                  4 oz cranberry;
                  1½ oz grass green
Size 7, 10″ straight knitting needles (or size required for gauge)
5 Yarn bobbins
GAUGE: In stock st, 5 sts = 1″; 7 rows = 1″

INSTRUCTIONS

SQUARE A (make 6)
With white, CO 75 sts.

Rows 1 through 5 (seed st border): * K1, P1; rep from * to last st, K1.

Row 6: (K1, P1) twice [side seed st border]; knit across to last 4 sts, (P1, K1) twice [side seed st border].

Row 7: K1, P1, K1; purl across to last 3 sts, K1, P1, K1.

Rows 8 through 17: Rep Rows 6 and 7, five times more.

Next 55 Rows (knit-in design): Keeping 4 sts at each end in seed st and rem sts in stock st, work the next 55 rows from chart in **Fig 1** (refer to page 18 for instructions on working from a chart). Use a separate bobbin for each flower and each leaf; wind 3 bobbins with cranberry and 2 bobbins with green. To join a new color, tie it to the prev color with a knot right up against the needle, leaving approx 4″ end for weaving in later. When changing colors, always bring the color you have just used over and to the left of the color you are going to use, bringing the new color up from underneath. This twists the two colors and prevents a hole in your work (see page 18).

Next 12 Rows: Continuing with white only, keep 4 sts at each end in seed st and rem sts in stock st and work 12 more rows.

Last 5 Rows (seed st border): Rep Rows 1 through 5. BO all sts; weave in all ends.

SQUARE B (make 6)
With white, CO 75 sts. Rep Rows 1 through 17 of Square A. Then work center design (59 rows) from chart in **Fig 2** as follows.

Row 1 of Chart: (K1, P1) twice; K 22, (P1, K1) 12 times; K 21, (P1, K1) twice.

Row 2 of Chart: K1, P1, K1; P22, (K1, P1) 13 times; P 21, K1, P1, K1.
Now refer to chart. You have just completed the first 2 rows; compare your work to the chart. Continue working from chart only; beg with Row 3 and work through Row 59.

Fig 1

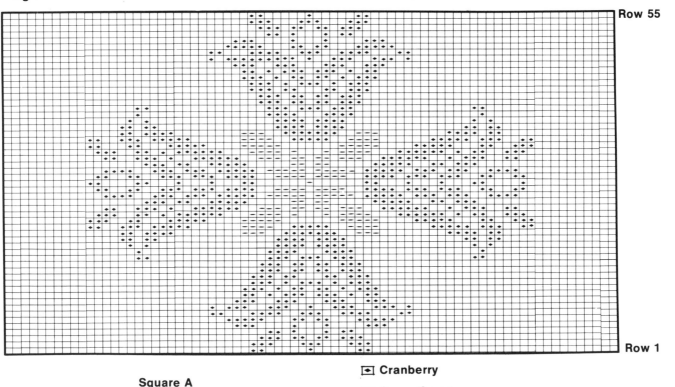

Row 55

Row 1

Square A

⬕ **Cranberry**

⊟ **Grass Green**

☐ **White**

144

Fig 2

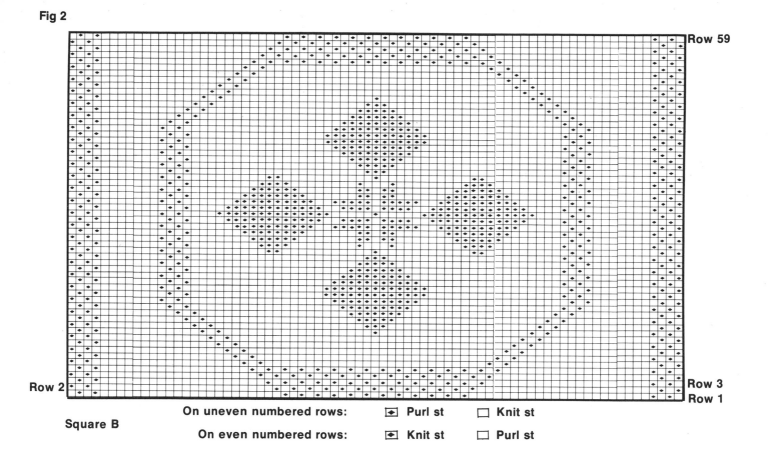

Row 59

Row 2

Row 3
Row 1

Square B

| On uneven numbered rows: | ◆ Purl st | ☐ Knit st |
| On even numbered rows: | ◆ Knit st | ☐ Purl st |

When all rows of chart have been completed, work 12 more rows, keeping 4 sts at each end in seed st and rem sts in stock st.

Last 5 rows (seed st border): Rep Rows 1 through 5 of Square A. BO all sts; weave in all ends.

ASSEMBLING
Arrange squares as shown in **Fig 3.** Use white and sew squares tog. Lightly steam press on wrong side.

Fig 3

A	B	A
B	A	B
B	A	B
A	B	A

145

CABLE GARDEN

designed by Carol Wilson Mansfield

SIZE: Approx 42″ x 56″ before fringing

MATERIALS

Worsted weight yarn: 32 oz ecru

Persian type crewel yarn (3 ply) for embroidery:
   100 yds leaf green;
      30 yds each yellow, gold, orange, rust
         and dark red

Size 10½, 24″ circular knitting needle (or size required for gauge)

Cable needle

Size 16 tapestry needle for embroidery

Materials Note: For cleaning purposes, yarn for embroidery should be of the same fiber content as yarn in afghan.

GAUGE: In stock st, 11 sts = 3″; 11 rows = 2″

PATTERN STITCHES

Cable Pattern A (worked on 12 sts)

Row 1 (wrong side): K2, P8, K2.
Row 2: P2, K8, P2.
Row 3: K2, P8, K2.
Row 4 (cable twist row): P2; sl next 2 sts onto cable needle and hold at *front* of work; knit next 2 sts, then K2 from cable needle; sl next 2 sts onto cable needle and hold at *back* of work; knit next 2 sts, then K2 from cable needle; P2.
Rows 5 through 7: Rep Rows 1 through 3.
Row 8 (cable twist row): P2; sl next 2 sts onto cable needle and hold at *back* of work; knit next 2 sts, then K2 from cable needle; sl next 2 sts onto cable needle and hold at *front* of work; knit next 2 sts, then K2 from cable needle; P2.
Rows 9 through 11: Rep Rows 1 through 3.
Row 12 (cable twist row): Rep Row 8.
Rows 13 through 15: Rep Rows 1 through 3.
Row 16 (cable twist row): Rep Row 4.
Rep Rows 1 through 16 for patt.

Cable Pattern B (worked on 14 sts)

Row 1 (wrong side): K2, P 10, K2.
Row 2: P2, K 10, P2.
Row 3: K2, P 10, K2.
Rows 4 through 7: Rep Rows 2 and 3, twice.
Row 8 (cable twist row): P2; sl next 3 sts onto cable needle and hold at *front* of work; knit next 2 sts, then K3 from cable needle; sl next 2 sts onto cable needle and hold at *back* of work; knit next 3 sts, then K2 from cable needle; P2.
Rows 9 through 11: Rep Rows 1 through 3.
Row 12 (cable twist row): P2, K2; sl next 3 sts onto cable needle and hold at *front* of work; knit next 3 sts, then K3 from cable needle; K2, P2.
Rows 13 through 15: Rep Rows 1 through 3.
Row 16 (cable twist row): Rep Row 12.
Rows 17 through 19: Rep Rows 1 through 3.
Row 20 (cable twist row): P2; sl next 2 sts onto cable needle and hold at *back* of work; knit next 3 sts, then K2 from cable needle; sl next 3 sts onto cable needle and

hold at *front* of work; knit next 2 sts, then K3 from cable needle; P2.
Rows 21 through 24: Rep Rows 1 and 2, twice.
Rep Rows 1 through 24 for patt.

INSTRUCTIONS

CENTER PANEL

CO 90 sts. Do not join; work back and forth in rows. Knit first 2 rows. **Inc Row:** K8, inc in next st [*to inc: knit in front and back of st*]; K2, inc, K 23; (inc, K1) 3 times, K9; (inc, K1) 3 times, K22; (inc, K2) twice; K6 = 100 sts. Now establish patt as follows.

Row 1 (wrong side): K2, P3; * work Row 1 of Cable Patt A over next 12 sts *; P 17; ** work Row 1 of Cable Patt B over next 14 sts **; P4, rep from ** to ** once; P 17, rep from * to * once; P3, K2.

Row 2: P2, K3; * work Row 2 of Cable Patt A over next 12 sts *; K 17; ** work Row 2 of Cable Patt B over next 14 sts **; K4, rep from ** to ** once; K 17, rep from * to * once; K3, P2.

Continue working in patt as established until there are 13 repeats of Cable Pattern B; then work 2 more rows in established patt. You should have a total of 12 large open cables which will be embroidered later with floral design.

Dec Row (wrong side): K8, (K2 tog, K2) twice; K 21, (K2 tog, K1) 3 times; K9, (K2 tog, K1) 3 times; K 22, (K2 tog, K2) twice; K6 = 90 sts. Knit one more row; then BO all sts in knit.

LEFT EDGE PANEL

CO 50 sts. Do not join; work back and forth in rows. Knit first 2 rows. **Inc Row:** K6, (inc, K1) 3 times; K 22, (inc, K2) twice; K 10 = 55 sts. Now establish patt as follows.

Row 1 (wrong side): K6 (for garter st border), P3; work Row 1 of Cable Patt A over next 12 sts; P 12, K2, P3; work Row 1 of Cable Patt B over next 14 sts; P3.

Row 2: K3; work Row 2 of Cable Patt B over next 14 sts; K3, P2, K 12; work Row 2 of Cable Patt A over next 12 sts; K3, K6 (for garter st border).

Continue working in patt as established until there are 13 repeats of Cable Pattern B; then work 2 more rows in established patt. You should have a total of 12 large open cables which will be embroidered later with floral design.

Dec Row (wrong side): K 12, (K2 tog, K2) twice; K 21, (K2 tog, K1) 3 times; K5 = 50 sts. Knit one more row; then BO all sts in knit.

RIGHT EDGE PANEL

CO 50 sts. Do not join; work back and forth in rows. Knit first 2 rows. **Inc Row:** K 12, (inc, K2) twice; K 21, (inc, K1) 3 times; K5 = 55 sts. Now establish patt as follows.

Row 1 (wrong side): P3; work Row 1 of Cable Patt B over next 14 sts; P3, K2, P 12; work Row 1 of Cable Patt A over next 12 sts; P3, K6 (for garter st border).

Row 2: K6 (for garter st border), K3; work Row 2 of Cable Patt A over next 12 sts; K 12, P2, K3; work Row 2 of Cable Patt B over next 14 sts; K3.

Continue working in patt as established until there are 13 repeats of Cable Pattern B; then work 2 more rows in established patt. You should have a total of 12 large open cables which will be embroidered later with floral design.

Dec Row (wrong side): K6, (K2 tog, K1) 3 times; K 22, (K2 tog, K2) twice; K 10 = 50 sts. Knit one more row; then BO all sts in knit.

FINISHING

Sew panels tog, having CO edge of each panel facing same end of afghan. Weave in all loose ends.

Embroidery: (**Note:** Use full 3-ply strand of Persian type yarn throughout.) On each Cable Patt A (2 on center panel and one on each edge panel), work leaf design (see **Fig 1**) with leaf green using lazy daisy sts (**Fig 2**).

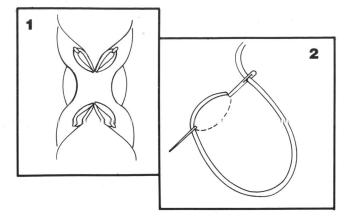

On 12 "open cables" in each Cable Patt B (2 on center panel and one on each edge panel), work floral design (see **Fig 3**) as follows. Begin embroidery at CO edge on

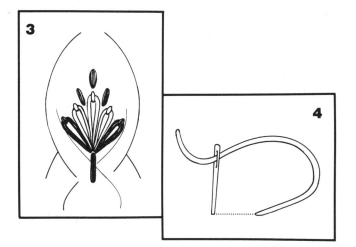

each panel. For all leaf sts (lazy daisy sts) and stems (straight sts — see **Fig 4**), use leaf green. For petals (lazy daisy sts) and stamens (straight sts), use flower sequence in **Fig 5** as follows:

Left Edge Panel: Beg with Flower #1 and work each flower facing BO edge of panel.

Left Cable on Center Panel: Beg with Flower #2 and work each flower facing CO edge of panel.

Right Cable on Center Panel: Beg with Flower #3 and work each flower facing BO edge of panel.

Right Edge Panel: Beg with Flower #4 and work each flower facing CO edge of panel.

Fringe: Following *Basic Fringe Instructions* on page 16, make *Single Knot Fringe*. Cut 12" strands; use 3 strands for each knot of fringe. Tie knots evenly spaced (approx every 3rd st) across each short end of afghan.

5	Petals	Stamens
Flower #1	Yellow	Orange
Flower #2	Gold	Rust
Flower #3	Orange	Dark red
Flower #4	Rust	Yellow
Flower #5	Dark red	Yellow

CHRISTMAS
SNOWFLAKES AND RIBBONS
designed by Jean Leinhauser

SIZE: Approx 54″ x 68″ before fringing
MATERIALS
**Worsted weight yarn: 28 oz white;
12 oz bright red;
8 oz bright green**
Sizes 9 and 13, 36″ circular knitting needles (or sizes required for gauge)
**GAUGE: With smaller size needle in garter st,
7 sts = 2″
With larger size needle in Snowflake Patt St,
7 sts = 2″**

SNOWFLAKE PATTERN STITCH
(multiple of 4 sts + 1)
Note: Use larger size needle.

Row 1 (right side): Knit.
Row 2: * K1; work Snowflake St as follows: P3 tog, leaving the 3 sts on left-hand needle; YO (wrapping yarn around right-hand needle as shown in **(Fig 1)**; purl same 3 sts tog, again, now drop these 3 sts from left-hand needle [Snowflake St made]; rep from * to last st, K1. **Note:** On next row, work each YO as one st [each row of Patt St should have the same number of sts].

Row 3: Knit.
Row 4: K1, P1, K1; * Snowflake St, K1; rep from * to last 2 sts; P1, K1.
Rep Rows 1 through 4 for patt.

INSTRUCTIONS
Note: Afghan is worked lengthwise.

With smaller size needle and red, CO 241 sts. Do not join; work back and forth in rows.

BORDER
Rows 1 through 6: Knit. Cut red, leaving 10″ end; join white. **Note:** Be sure to leave 10″ end when either cutting or joining yarn (ends will be worked in later as part of fringe).
Row 7 (right side): Knit.
Row 8: K1; purl to last st, K1. Drop white, but do *not* cut; join green.

149

Row 9: * K1; keeping yarn at back of work, sl 1 as to purl; rep from * to last st, K1.

Row 10: K2; * P1, K1; rep from * to last st, K1. Cut green; continue with white.

Row 11: Knit.

Row 12: K1; purl to last st, K1. Change to larger size needle.

Rows 13 through 16: Work Snowflake Patt St Rows 1 through 4 once. At end of last row, change to smaller size needle.

Rows 17 through 20: Rep Rows 7 through 10.

Row 21: Knit.

Row 22: K1; purl to last st, K1. Cut white; join red.

Rows 23 through 28: Knit 6 rows. Drop red, but do *not* cut; join green.

Row 29: Knit.

Row 30: K1; purl to last st, K1. Drop green, but do *not* cut; continue with red.

Row 31: * K1; keeping yarn at back of work, sl 1 as to purl; rep from * to last st, K1.

Row 32: K2, * P1, K1; rep from * to last st, K1. Drop red, but do *not* cut; continue with green.

Row 33: Knit.

Row 34: K1; purl to last st, K1. Cut green; continue with red.

Rows 35 through 46: Rep Rows 1 through 12. Change to larger size needle.

SIDE SECTION **(worked in white only):** Following Snowflake Patt St instructions, work Rows 1 through 4, 12 times; then work Rows 1 and 2 once. At end of last row, change to smaller size needle.

CENTER SECTION

Rows 1 through 18: Rep Border Rows 17 through 34.

Rows 19 through 24: Rep Border Rows 1 through 6.

Row 25: Knit.

Row 26: K1, purl to last st, K1.

Rows 27 through 30: Rep Border Rows 7 through 10.

Row 31: Knit.

Row 32: K1; purl to last st, K1. Drop white, but do *not* cut; join red.

Row 33: Rep Border Row 9.

Row 34: K2; * P1, K1; rep from * to last st, K1. Cut red; continue with white.

Rows 35 through 38: Rep Border Rows 7 through 10.

Row 39: Knit.

Row 40: K1; purl to last st, K1.

Rows 41 through 54: Rep Border Rows 21 through 34.

Rows 55 through 66: Rep Border Rows 1 through 12. Change to larger size needle.

SIDE SECTION: Work same as Other Side Section.

BORDER

Rows 1 through 18: Rep Border Rows 17 through 34.

Rows 19 through 40: Rep Border Rows 1 through 22.

Rows 41 through 47: Knit 7 rows. BO all sts in knit.

FRINGE

Following *Basic Fringe Instructions* on page 16, make *Single Knot Fringe.* Cut 16″ strands of each color. Use 5 strands of one color for each knot of fringe. Tie knots (adding matching yarn ends when possible) evenly spaced across each short edge of afghan as follows: 16 white knots at each wide Snowflake section; 2 white knots at each side narrow Snowflake section; 1 green knot at each green/white and red/green stripe; 2 red knots at each side red garter st section; 1 red knot at each rem garter st section and at center red/white stripe. Weave in loose ends.

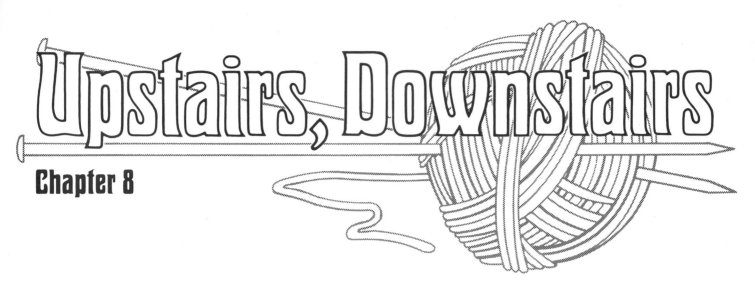

Upstairs, Downstairs

Chapter 8

Here are knitted accessories for your house: an heirloom bedspread; a lace doily for a bit of nostalgia; placemat and table runner; edgings for towels or bed linens; an appealing snug snake to keep drafts away from your doors or windows; and some good bazaar items—a pincushion, potholders and a dishcloth.

HEIRLOOM BEDSPREAD

This pattern is an adaptation of a classic design that has challenged knitters for many years. It is made of up squares, each of which is made with four motifs sewn together.

Although the instructions for each quarter-square (one motif) are lengthy, they are not difficult. Traditionally made with fine cotton thread on steel needles, our version works up much more quickly with sport weight yarn and size 6 needles.

SIZES: Twin size measures approx 64" x 96"; full size measures approx 80" x 96".

MATERIALS

Sport weight yarn: 76 oz for twin size or 96 oz for full size in white or cream color

Size 6, 10" straight knitting needles (or size required for gauge)

Size F aluminum crochet hook (for edging only)

GAUGE: One motif = 8"

INSTRUCTIONS

MOTIF

(Make 96 for twin size or 120 for full size)
Note: Each motif is made in 2 steps: in the First Half, you will increase at end of each row; in the Second Half, you will decrease at end of each row.

First Half

CO one st.

Row 1: Knit in front and back of st (inc made) = 2 sts.

Row 2: K1, inc in next st = 3 sts.

Row 3: K2, inc in last st = 4 sts.

Rows 4 through 22: Knit to last st, inc in last st. At end of Row 22, you should have 23 sts.

Row 23: Purl to last st, inc in last st [*to inc: purl in front and back of st*] = 24 sts.

Note: On next 38 rows (Rows 24 through 61), continue to inc in last st of each row; **this will not be mentioned again in individual row instructions.**

Row 24: K1; (K2 tog, K1, YO) 7 times, K2 = 25 sts.

Row 25: Purl across, working each YO as one st (now and throughout patt).

Rows 26 through 34: Knit.

Row 35: Purl = 36 sts.

Row 36: K1; (K2 tog, K1, YO) 11 times, K2 = 37 sts.

Row 37: Purl.

Rows 38 through 41: Knit. At end of Row 41, you should have 42 sts.

Row 42: K3, YO, K1, YO; (K6, YO, K1, YO) 5 times, K3 = 55 sts.

Row 43: K4, P3; (K6, P3) 5 times, K3.

Row 44: K4, YO, K3, YO; (K6, YO, K3, YO) 5 times, K4 = 69 sts.

Row 45: K5, P5; (K6, P5) 5 times, K4.

Row 46: (K5, YO) twice; (K6, YO, K5, YO) 5 times, K5 = 83 sts.

Row 47: (K6, P7) 6 times, K5.

Row 48: K6; * sl 1, K1, PSSO; K3, K2 tog, K6; rep from * across = 73 sts.

Row 49: K7; * P5, K6; rep from * across = 74 sts.

Row 50: K7; * sl 1, K1, PSSO; K1, K2 tog, K6; rep from * across, ending last rep with K7 instead of K6 = 63 sts.

Row 51: K8; * P3, K6; rep from * across, ending last rep with K7 instead of K6.

Row 52: K8; * K3 tog, K6; rep from * across, ending last rep with K8 instead of K6 = 53 sts.

Rows 53 through 56: Knit.

Row 57: Purl.

Row 58: Knit.

Row 59: Purl.

Rows 60 and 61: Knit. You should now have 62 sts. First Half is now completed; begin Second Half and work decreasing, instead of increasing, at end of each row.

Second Half

Row 1: Knit to last 3 sts, K2 tog, K1 = 61 sts.

Row 2: Purl to last 3 sts, P2 tog, P1 = 60 sts.

Note: On following rows (except Rows 15, 19, 60 and 61—complete instructions will be given for these rows), continue to decrease in this manner at end of each row (work to last 3 sts, dec, work last st); **this will not be mentioned again in individual row instructions.**

Row 3: Knit.

Row 4: Purl.

Rows 5 through 13: Knit. At end of Row 13, you should have 49 sts.

Row 14: Purl.

Row 15: K1; (K2, tog, K1, YO) 15 times, K2 tog = 47 sts.

Row 16: Purl.

Row 17: Knit.

Row 18: Purl.

Row 19: K1; (K2 tog, K1, YO) 13 times; K1, K2 tog, K1 = 43 sts.

Row 20: Purl.

Rows 21 through 29: Knit. At end of Row 29, you should have 33 sts.

Row 30: Purl.

Row 31: Knit.

Rows 32 through 35: Rep Rows 30 and 31, twice.

Row 36: Knit = 26 sts.

Row 37: K 12, YO, K1, YO; knit rem sts = 27 sts.

Row 38: K 12, P3; knit rem sts = 26 sts.

Row 39: K 11, YO, K3, YO; knit rem sts = 27 sts.

Row 40: K 11, P5; knit rem sts = 26 sts.

Row 41: K 10, YO, K5, YO; knit rem sts = 27 sts.

Row 42: K 10, P7; knit rem sts = 26 sts.

Row 43: K9, YO, K7, YO; knit rem sts = 27 sts.

Row 44: K9, P9; knit rem sts = 26 sts.

Row 45: K8, YO, K9, YO; knit rem sts = 27 sts.

Row 46: K8, P 11; knit rem sts = 26 sts.

Row 47: K7; sl 1, K1, PSSO; K7, K2 tog; knit rem sts = 23 sts.

Row 48: K7, P9; knit rem sts = 22 sts.

Row 49: K6; sl 1, K1, PSSO; K5, K2 tog; knit rem sts = 19 sts.

Row 50: K6, P7; knit rem sts = 18 sts.

Row 51: K5; sl 1, K1, PSSO; K3, K2 tog; knit rem sts = 15 sts.

Row 52: K5, P5; knit rem sts = 14 sts.

Row 53: K4; sl 1, K1, PSSO; K1, K2 tog; knit rem sts = 11 sts.

Row 54: K4, P3; knit rem sts = 10 sts.

Row 55: K3, K3 tog; knit rem sts = 7 sts.

Rows 56 through 59: Knit.

Row 60: K2 tog, K1.

Row 61: K2 tog; finish off, leaving approx 20″ sewing length.

ASSEMBLING

Sew four motifs tog (use overcast stitching) as shown in **Fig 1** to make one square. Continue to join motifs into

1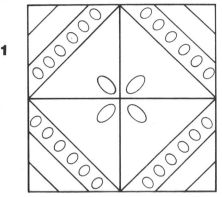

squares in same manner until you have 24 squares for twin size, or 30 squares for full size. Then join squares, having 4 squares wide by 6 squares long for twin size; or 5 squares wide by 6 squares long for full size. Weave in all ends.

EDGING

With right side facing and crochet hook, join yarn with a sl st at center of either short edge of bedspread. **Rnd 1:** Ch 1, work in sc evenly spaced (adjusting sts to keep work flat) across each edge and work 3 sc at each corner around; join with a sl st in beg sc. **Rnd 2:** Do not turn; ch 1, sc in same st as joining; * sc in each st to center st at corner, 3 sc in center st; rep from * 3 times more, sc in each rem st; join with a sl st in beg sc. **Rnd 3:** Rep Rnd 2. Finish off; weave in all ends.

DOILY

Most doilies are crocheted, so we were particularly pleased to find this beautiful old pattern for a striking knitted doily. Even though you are an experienced knitter, you may find working with so few stitches on dpns a bit awkward for the first few rnds, but from then on it is easier to work the pattern.

SIZE: Approx 12″ diameter

MATERIALS
American Thread "Puritan" bedspread weight crochet cotton: 1 ball (250 yds) white
Size 2, five 7″ double pointed needles and 16″ circular knitting needle (or size required for gauge)
Size 3 steel crochet hook (for edging only)
Stitch marker

GAUGE: In stock st, 9 sts = 1″

INSTRUCTIONS

CO 8 sts on 4 needles (2 sts on each needle). Join, being careful not to twist sts.

Rnd 1 and all odd-numbered rnds: Knit. **Note:** Place marker for beg of rnd; sl marker on each following rnd.

Rnd 2: * YO, K1; rep from * around = 16 sts. **Note:** Throughout patt, each YO counts as one st.

Rnd 4: Rep Rnd 2 = 32 sts.

Rnd 6: * YO, K3; YO, K1; rep from * around = 48 sts.

Rnd 8: * YO; sl 1 as to knit (now and throughout patt), K1, PSSO; K1, K2 tog; YO, K1; rep from * around = 48 sts.

Rnd 10: * YO, K1, YO; sl 1, K2 tog, PSSO; (YO, K1) twice = 64 sts.

Rnd 12: Rep Rnd 6 = 96 sts.

Rnd 14: Rep Rnd 8 = 96 sts.

Rnd 16: K1, * YO; sl 1, K2 tog, PSSO; YO, K3; rep from * around, ending last rep by working K2 instead of K3 = 96 sts.

Rnd 18: * YO, sl 1, K1, PSSO; K1, YO; sl 1, K1, PSSO; K1, K2 tog; YO, K1, K2 tog; YO, K1; rep from * around = 96 sts.

Rnd 20: K1, * YO; sl 1, K1, PSSO; K1, YO; sl 1, K2 tog, PSSO; YO, K1, K2 tog; YO, K3; rep from * around, ending last rep by working K2 instead of K3 = 96 sts.

Rnd 22: K2, * YO; sl 1, K1, PSSO; K3, K2 tog; YO, K5; rep from * around, ending last rep by working K3 instead of K5 = 96 sts.

Rnd 24: K3, * YO; sl 1, K1, PSSO; K1, K2 tog; YO, K7; rep from * around, ending last rep by working K4 instead of K7 = 96 sts.

Rnd 26: * K4, YO; sl 1, K2 tog, PSSO; YO, K4; YO, K1, YO; rep from * around = 112 sts. Change to circular needle.

Rnd 28: * Sl 1, K1, PSSO; K3, YO; K1, YO; K3, K2 tog; YO, K3, YO; rep from * around = 128 sts.

Rnd 30: * Sl 1, K1, PSSO; K7, K2 tog; YO, K1, YO; sl 1, K2 tog, PSSO; YO, K1, YO; rep from * around = 128 sts.

Rnd 32: * Sl 1, K1, PSSO; K5, K2 tog; YO, K3; YO, K1, YO; K3, YO; rep from * around = 144 sts.

Rnd 34: * Sl 1, K1, PSSO; K3, K2 tog; YO, K1, YO; sl 1, K2 tog, PSSO; YO, K3, YO; sl 1, K2 tog, PSSO; YO, K1, YO; rep from * around = 144 sts.

Rnd 36: * Sl 1, K1, PSSO; K1, K2 tog; YO, K3; YO, K1, YO; sl 1, K1, PSSO; K1, K2 tog; YO, K1, YO; K3, YO; rep from * around = 160 sts.

Rnd 38: * Sl 1, K2 tog, PSSO; YO, K1, YO; sl 1, K2 tog, PSSO; YO, K3, YO; sl 1, K2 tog, PSSO; YO, K3, YO; sl 1, K2 tog, PSSO; YO, K1, YO; rep from * around = 160 sts.

Rnd 40: * K1, YO, K3; YO, K1, YO; sl 1, K1, PSSO; K1, K2 tog; YO, K1, YO; sl 1, K1, PSSO; K1, K2 tog; YO, K1, YO; K3, YO; rep from * around = 192 sts.

Rnd 42: K2, * YO; sl 1, K2 tog, PSSO; YO, K3; rep from * to last 4 sts; YO, sl 1, K2 tog, PSSO; YO, sl last st to right needle unworked. Remove marker for beg of rnd; sl last st (left unworked) back to left needle. Place marker back on needle for beg of rnd.

Rnd 44: * YO, sl 1, K2 tog, PSSO, YO, K3; rep from * around = 192 sts.

Rnd 46: * K3, YO; sl 1, K2 tog, PSSO, YO; rep from * around = 192 sts.

Rnds 47, 48 and 49: Knit.

Rnd 50: * YO, K2 tog; rep from * around = 192 sts.

Rnds 51, 52 and 53: Knit.

Rnd 54: Rep Rnd 50.

Rnds 55, 56 and 57: Knit. At end of Rnd 57, *do not* bind off; continue with edging.

EDGING RND

With crochet hook, draw up a lp in first st, leaving st on needle. * Ch 8, (insert hook in next st and sl st off needle) 3 times [4 lps now on hook]; YO hook and draw through all 4 lps on hook; rep from * around. Join with a sl st in beg ch; finish off.

FINISHING

Weave in all ends. Place right side down onto flat padded surface. Pin outer edge, using rust-proof pins. Spray with commercial spray starch until wet. Let dry thoroughly before removing pins.

PLACEMAT and TABLE RUNNER
designed by Mary Thomas

SIZES: Placemat measures approx 13″ x 18″; table runner measures approx 13″ x 36″.

MATERIALS
Bedspread weight ecru crochet cotton: 600 yds for placemat or 1200 yds for table runner
Size 5, 10″ straight knitting needles (or size required for gauge)
Materials Note: Thread is used doubled throughout patt.

GAUGE: With 2 strands of crochet cotton in patt st, 11 sts = 2″

INSTRUCTIONS
[**Note:** Placemat and table runner are worked widthwise to desired length.] With 2 strands, CO 73 sts. Knit across to last st, bring thread to front of work, sl last st as to purl.

Note: Throughout patt, sl last st of each row in this manner for a smooth and even edge; **this will not be mentioned again in instructions.** Knit 3 more rows for garter st border. Now work in pattern stitch as follows.

Row 1 (right side): K4; * YO, sl 1, K1, PSSO; K1, K2 tog; YO, K1; rep from * to last 3 sts, K3.

Row 2: K3 for garter st edge; purl across to last 3 sts, working each YO as one st; K3 for garter st edge.

Row 3: K4; * YO, K1; sl 1, K2 tog, PSSO; K1, YO, K1; rep from * to last 3 sts, K3.

Row 4: Rep Row 2.

Row 5: K4; * K2 tog, YO, K1, YO; sl 1, K1, PSSO, K1; rep from * to last 3 sts, K3.

Row 6: Rep Row 2.

Row 7: K3, K2 tog; * K1, (YO, K1) twice; sl 1, K2 tog, PSSO; rep from * to last 8 sts; K1, (YO, K1) twice; sl 1, K1, PSSO; K3.

Row 8: Rep Row 2.

Rep last 8 rows until piece measures (from CO edge) approx 17½″ for placemat, or 35½″ for table runner (or ½″ less than desired length), ending by working Row 7. Knit 4 more rows for garter st border; then BO all sts in knit. Weave in all ends.

LACE EDGINGS

These lovely edgings are adapted from old patterns, and are as charming today as they were many years ago. Use them to trim pillowcases, guest towels, cafe curtains, a little girl's dress.

You can make the edgings with bedspread weight crochet cotton, fingering or baby weight yarn, or sport weight yarn. They can even be made with string! The patterns specify no gauge or yarn/thread yardage requirements as this will vary depending on what yarn/thread and needle sizes you choose.

Here are suggested yarn/thread and needle combinations:

Yarn/Thread	Suggested Needle Size
Bedspread weight crochet cotton	2
Bedspread heavy weight crochet cotton	3
Fingering or baby weight yarn	3
Sport weight yarn	5

EDGING No. 1 (shown on center towel)
CO 9 sts.

Row 1 (wrong side): K1, P6, K2 = 9 sts.

Row 2: Sl 1 as to knit (now and throughout patt), K2; (K2 tog, YO) twice; K1, YO, K1 = 10 sts. **Note:** Each YO counts as one st.

Row 3: Sl 1, P3, K1; P3, K2 = 10 sts.

Row 4: Sl 1, K1; (K2 tog, YO) twice; K3, YO, K1 = 11 sts.

Row 5: K1, P5, K1; P2, K2 = 11 sts.

Row 6: Sl 1, (K2 tog, YO) twice; K5, YO, K1 = 12 sts.

Row 7: K1, P7, K1; P1, K2 = 12 sts.

Row 8: Sl 1, K2; (YO, K2 tog) twice; K1, K2 tog; YO, K2 tog = 11 sts.

Row 9: K1, P5, K1; P2, K2 = 11 sts.

Row 10: Sl 1, K3; YO, K2 tog; YO, K3 tog; YO, K2 tog = 10 sts.

Row 11: K1, P3, K1; P3, K2 = 10 sts.

Row 12: Sl 1, K4; YO, K3 tog; YO, K2 tog = 9 sts.
Rep Rows 1 through 12 until edging is desired length; then rep Row 1 once more. BO all sts in knit.

EDGING No. 2 (shown on towel at right)
CO 15 sts.

Row 1 (right side): K2, YO, K2 tog; K4, YO, K1; YO, K6 = 17 sts. **Note:** Each YO counts as one st.

Row 2: K6, YO; (K3, YO, K2 tog) twice, K1 = 18 sts.

Row 3: K2, YO, K2 tog; K1, K2 tog; YO, K5; YO, K6 = 19 sts.

Row 4: BO 4 sts; K1, YO, K2 tog; K3, K2 tog; (YO, K2 tog, K1) twice = 14 sts.

Row 5: (K2, YO, K2 tog) twice; K1, K2 tog; YO, K2; knit in front and back of last st (increase made) = 15 sts.

Row 6: K5, YO; sl 2, K1, pass both slipped sts over last knit st; YO, K4; YO, K2 tog, K1 = 15 sts.
Rep Rows 1 through 6 until edging is desired length. BO all sts in knit.

EDGING No. 3 (shown on towel at left)
CO 10 sts. Knit one row; then work in patt as follows.

Row 1 (right side): Sl 1 as to knit (now and throughout patt); YO, K9 = 11 sts. **Note:** Each YO counts as one st.

Row 2: Sl 1, K1; YO, K2 tog, K7 = 11 sts.

Row 3: Sl 1, YO, K2; (YO, K2 tog) twice; K4 = 12 sts.

Row 4: Sl 1, K1; YO, K2 tog, K8 = 12 sts.

Row 5: Sl 1, YO, K2; (YO, K2 tog) 3 times; K3 = 13 sts.

Row 6: Sl 1, K1; YO, K2 tog, K9 = 13 sts.

Row 7: BO 3 sts, K9 = 10 sts.

Row 8: Sl 1, K1; YO, K2 tog, K6 = 10 sts.
Rep Rows 1 through 8 until edging is desired length. BO all sts in knit.

SNUG SNAKE
designed by Jean Leinhauser

This friendly reptile, lined and stuffed with sand or kitty litter, snuggles up to the crack under your door or window and keeps the cold drafts out.

SIZE: Approx 40″ long

MATERIALS
Worsted weight yarn: 4 oz lime green;
                                    4 oz forest green;
                                    4 oz bright turquoise
Size 10, 10″ straight knitting needles (or size required for gauge)
Pink felt (⅛″ x 1½″ piece) for tongue
2 Moving eye buttons (⅜″ diameter)
Sturdy fabric (6″ x 41″ piece) for lining
Sand or kitty litter for filling

GAUGE: In patt st, 23 sts = 5″

INSTRUCTIONS

[**Note:** Throughout patt, slip each sl st as to purl.] Beg at tail, with lime green, CO 23 sts. Then work in pattern stitch as follows.
Row 1 (right side): * K3, YB (yarn to back of work), sl 1; rep from * to last 3 sts, K3.
Row 2: * K3, YF (yarn to front of work), sl 1; rep from * to last 3 sts, K3.
Drop lime green (do not cut); continue with forest green.
Note: Colors are carried loosely up side of work.
Row 3: K1; * YB, sl 1, K3; rep from * to last 2 sts; YB, sl 1, K1.
Row 4: K1; * YF, sl 1, K3; rep from * to last 2 sts; YF, sl 1, K1.
Drop forest green; continue with turquoise.
Rows 5 and 6: Rep Rows 1 and 2.
Drop turquoise; continue with lime green.
Rows 7 and 8: Rep Rows 3 and 4.
Drop lime green; continue with forest green.
Rows 9 and 10: Rep Rows 1 and 2.
Drop forest green; continue with turquoise.
Rows 11 and 12: Rep Rows 3 and 4.
Drop turquoise; continue with lime green.
Rep Rows 1 through 12 until piece measures 37″ long, ending by working Row 6 or Row 12.

SHAPE HEAD
[**Note:** Cut forest green, leaving 4″ for weaving in later; continue with lime green and turquoise only.]
Row 1: With lime green, K2 tog, K7; (K2 tog) 3 times; K6, K2 tog = 18 sts.
Row 2: Knit.
Rows 3 and 4: With turquoise, knit.
Row 5: With lime green, K2 tog, K6; (K2 tog) twice; K4, K2 tog = 14 sts.
Row 6: Knit.
Rows 7 and 8: With turquoise, knit.
Row 9: With lime green, K2 tog, K3; (K2 tog) twice; K3, K2 tog = 10 sts.
Row 10: Knit.
Rows 11 and 12: With turquoise, knit.
Row 13: With lime green, K2 tog, K1; (K2 tog) twice; K1, K2 tog = 6 sts.
Row 14: Knit.
Rows 15 and 16: With turquoise, knit. Cut turquoise, leaving 4″ end.
Row 17: With lime green, (K2 tog) 3 times = 3 sts.
Row 18: Knit. Cut yarn, leaving approx 15″ sewing length. Thread into tapestry or yarn needle and weave through rem 3 sts. Pull up tightly and fasten securely. Do not cut yarn (will be used later for sewing head). Weave in all other loose ends.

FINISHING
Turn piece with right sides tog. Thread forest green into tapestry or yarn needle. Leaving head open for inserting filled-lining later, sew seam (use closely placed overcast sts) to within 4″ at end of tail; then sew (using back sts) on an angle to end (see **Fig 1**) to shape tail portion. Turn right side out.

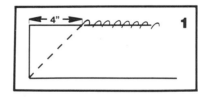

Sew lining piece in same manner (leaving head open) with ½″ seams either by machine or by hand (use backstitching). Turn lining right side out and fill very firmly with sand or kitty litter; turn seam allowance to inside and whipstitch rem portion of head closed. Insert filled-lining into knitted snake; continue with lime green (left on head) and sew rem portion closed. Sew eyes and tongue in place as indicated in photo (seam is bottom of snake). Cut a V-shaped fork in tongue.

PINCUSHION

SIZE: Approx 3½″ diameter x 1″ deep

MATERIALS
Worsted weight yarn scraps in assorted colors of
    your choice
Size 7, 10″ straight knitting needles (or size required
    for gauge)
Thimble

GAUGE: In garter st, 5 sts = 1″

INSTRUCTIONS
Center Ring: With color of your choice, CO 10 sts. Work in garter st (knit every row) until piece measures 2½″ from CO edge. BO all sts in knit. Sew CO and BO edges tog; weave in all ends. Fold in half.

First Outer Ring: Work same as Center Ring until piece measures 4″ from CO edge. BO and finish in same manner as before. Place ring around center ring having folded edges facing up.

2nd Outer Ring: Work same as Center Ring until piece measures 6″ from CO edge. BO and finish in same manner; then place ring around prev ring.

3rd Outer Ring: Work same as Center Ring until piece measures 8″ from CO edge. BO and finish in same manner; then place ring around prev ring. Insert thimble in space at center of rings.

POTHOLDERS
designed by Mary Thomas

SIZES: Each potholder measures approx 8″ square

MATERIALS
Sugar-'n-Cream cotton yarn:
    For Basket Plaid Potholder:
        1 ball each rust, orange and cream
    For Beaded Stripe Potholder:
        1 ball each rust and cream
Size 6, 10″ straight knitting needles (or size required
    for gauge)
Size F aluminum crochet hook (for edging only)
Plastic ring (1″ diameter)

GAUGE: For Basket Plaid Potholder:
                in patt st, 5 sts = 1″
            For Beaded Stripe Potholder:
                in patt st, 9 sts = 2″

BASKET PLAID POTHOLDER INSTRUCTIONS

(Make 2 pieces)
[**Note:** Throughout patt, slip each sl st as to purl.] With rust, CO 39 sts. Then work in pattern stitch as follows.

Pattern Stitch Foundation Rows

Row 1 (right side): Knit.

Row 2: K3; K1 with 3 wraps [*to work K1 with 3 wraps: insert right-hand needle into next st on left-hand needle as if to knit, wrap yarn 3 times around tip of right-hand needle; now knit this st, carrying extra wraps on right-hand needle = K1 with 3 wraps*]; * K7, K1 with 3 wraps; rep from * to last 3 sts, K3. Drop rust (do not cut); join cream. **Note:** Colors are carried loosely along side of work.

Row 3: With cream, K3, YB (yarn to back of work), sl 1 dropping extra wraps off needle; * K7, YB, sl 1 dropping extra wraps; rep from * to last 3 sts, K3.

Row 4: P3, YF (yarn to front of work), sl 1; * P7, YF, sl 1; rep from * to last 3 sts, P3. Drop cream; join orange and work as follows.

Pattern Stitch Repeat Rows

Row 1: With orange, K3, YB, sl 1; * K7, YB, sl 1; rep from * to last 3 sts, K3.

Row 2: * K3, YF, sl 1; K3, K1 with 3 wraps; rep from * to last 7 sts; K3, YF, sl 1, K3. Drop orange; continue with cream.

Row 3: * K3, YB, sl 1; K3, YB, sl 1 dropping extra wraps; rep from * to last 7 sts; K3, YB, sl 1, K3.

Row 4: P3; * YF, sl 1, P3; rep from * across. Drop cream; continue with rust.

Row 5: K7; * YB, sl 1, K7; rep from * across.

Row 6: * K3, K1 with 3 wraps; K3, YF, sl 1; rep from * to last 7 sts; K3, K1 with 3 wraps, K3. Drop rust; continue with cream.

Row 7: * K3, YB, sl 1 dropping extra wraps; K3, YB, sl 1; rep from * to last 7 sts; K3, YB, sl 1 dropping extra wraps, K3.

Row 8: P3; * YF, sl 1, P3; rep from * across. Drop cream; continue with orange.

Rep last 8 rows, 5 times more; then work as follows.

Pattern Stitch Finishing Rows

Row 1: K3, YB, sl 1; * K7, YB, sl 1; rep from * to last 3 sts, K3.

Row 2: K3, YF, sl 1; * K7, YF, sl 1; rep from * to last 3 sts, K3. Cut orange, leaving approx 4" end for weaving in later; continue with cream.

Row 3: K3, YB, sl 1; * K7, YB, sl 1; rep from * to last 3 sts, K3.

Row 4: P3, YF, sl 1; * P7, YF, sl 1; rep from * to last 3 sts, P3. Cut cream, leaving 4" end; continue with rust.

Rows 5, 6 and 7: Knit. BO all sts. Weave in all ends.

EDGING

With crochet hook, join rust with a sl st in ring. Work 16 sc around ring, join with a sl st in beg sc. Continue with edging around both pieces as follows. Hold pieces with wrong sides tog and BO edge of each piece at top. Working through corresponding sts of each piece, sl st at upper right-hand corner; work in sc evenly spaced (approx 3 sc every 4 sts and 2 sc every other row) around all 4 sides, and work 3 sc at each corner. Finish off, leaving approx 6" end. Thread into tapestry or yarn needle and sew base of ring securely to potholder. Weave in ends.

BEADED STRIPE POTHOLDER INSTRUCTIONS

(Make 2 pieces)
[**Note:** Throughout patt, slip each sl st as to purl.] With rust, CO 35 sts. Then work in pattern stitch as follows.

Row 1 (right side): Knit.

Row 2: K1; * P3, K3; rep from * to last 4 sts; P3, K1. Drop rust (do not cut); continue with cream. **Note:** Colors are carried loosely along side of work.

Row 3: K1, YB (yarn to back of work), sl 3; * K3 (carry yarn loosely across back of work), YB, sl 3; rep from * to last st, K1.

Row 4: K1, P1, YF (yarn to front of work), sl 1; * P5, YF, sl 1; rep from * to last 2 sts; P1, K1.

Row 5: Knit.

Row 6: K4; * P3, K3; rep from * to last st, K1. Drop cream; continue with rust.

Row 7: K4; * YB, sl 3, K3; rep from * to last st, K1.

Row 8: K1, P4; * YF, sl 1, P5; rep from * to last 6 sts; YF, sl 1, P4, K1.
Rep Rows 1 through 8, 6 times more; then rep Rows 1 and 2 once. BO all sts. Weave in all ends.

EDGING

Work same as Basket Plaid Potholder.

World's Greatest
DISHCLOTH

Every kitchen should have a few of these! You have no idea how great this cotton dishcloth is until you've tried it; that's why we call it the World's Greatest. Makes a nice gift and bazaar item, too.

SIZE: Approx 8″ square

MATERIALS
Sugar-'n-Cream cotton yarn: ½ ball in color of your
  choice
Size 10, 10″ straight knitting needles (or size
  required for gauge)

GAUGE: In garter st, 4 sts = 1″

INSTRUCTIONS
[**Note:** Throughout patt, each YO counts as one st.] CO 2 sts.

Rows 1, 3 and 5: Knit.
Row 2: K1, YO, K1 = 3 sts.

Row 4: K1, (YO, K1) twice = 5 sts.

Row 6: K1, YO; knit to last st, YO, K1.

Row 7: Knit.
Rep Rows 6 and 7 until you have 43 sts on needle (you will be increasing 2 sts EOR). Now work decreases as follows.

Dec Row 1: K1, YO, K2 tog; knit to last 3 sts, K2 tog, YO, K1.

Dec Row 2: K2, K2 tog; knit to last 4 sts, K2 tog, K2.
Rep last 2 rows until 9 sts rem on needle (you will be decreasing 2 sts every 2 rows). Continue decreasing as follows.

Row 1: K1, YO; (K2 tog) twice, K1; K2 tog, YO, K1 = 8 sts.

Row 2: K2, (K2 tog) twice, K2 = 6 sts.

Row 3: K1, YO; (K2 tog) twice, YO, K1 = 6 sts.

Row 4: K1, (K2 tog) twice, K1 = 4 sts.

Row 5: (K2 tog) twice = 2 sts.

Row 6: K2 tog. Finish off; weave in all ends.